GOD OR GODDESS?

MANFRED HAUKE

God or Goddess?

Feminist Theology:
What Is It? Where Does It Lead?

Translated by
Dr. David Kipp

IGNATIUS PRESS   SAN FRANCISCO

Title of the German original:
Gott oder Göttin?
Feministische Theologie auf dem Prüfstand
© 1993 MM Verlag, Aachen, Germany

Cover by Roxanne Mei Lum

© 1995 Ignatius Press, San Francisco
All rights reserved
ISBN 0-87870-559-2
Library of Congress catalogue number 95-75660
Printed in the United States of America

CONTENTS

5

I. INTRODUCTION

"Once upon a time, a pious man was married to a pious woman. But they were not blessed with children. So they said, 'We are useless before God.' Then they separated from each other. He went off and found a godless wife, who made him godless. She went off and found a godless husband, whom she made upright. Thus we see how everything depends on the woman."

By means of this Jewish midrash on the Book of Genesis, Oda Schneider illustrated, in 1938, the important influence of women in the religious sphere.[1] Oda Schneider—wife (later Carmelite), catechist, and religious writer—was among the female pioneers of the Catholic lay apostolate in the period preceding the Second World War. In her works on the subject of woman, which are enjoying renewed attention at present,[2] she aims to highlight those qualities that constitute the richness of being a woman but require reemphasis in the present-day context. She is convinced that the "power of women" also underpins the Church and needs to be encouraged.

Similarly concerned with the power of women in the sphere of religion is so-called "feminist theology", which has been pursued primarily in the USA since the beginning

---

[1] Oda Schneider, *Die Macht der Frau* [The power of woman] (Salzburg, 1938), 204. Cf. *Der Midrasch Bereschit Rabba,* Bibliotheca rabbinica 1; first translated into German by August Wünsche (Leipzig, 1881; reprint, Hildesheim, 1967), 76 (par. 17, on Gen 2:21).

[2] For example, Teresa Berger, *Liturgie und Frauenseele. Die liturgische Bewegung aus der Sicht der Frauenforschung* [Liturgy and the female soul: The liturgical movement from the perspective of women's studies] (Stuttgart, 1993), passim; Oda Schneider, *Vom Priestertum der Frau* [On women in the priesthood], ed. D. J. Hilla (Abensberg, 1992).

9

of the 1970s and is becoming increasingly influential in German-speaking countries as well. While Oda Schneider—to cite just one example from among countless committed women of past and present—felt quite comfortable within the Church, the comments made by feminists about the ecclesiastical situation are, by contrast, predominantly negative: the Church appears as the stronghold of a destructive "dominion of males" that, with its patriarchal image of God and its predominantly masculine leadership, stifles the effectiveness of women. Naturally, the Catholic Church, which ordains only males as priests, comes under especially severe criticism here: this practice is seen as wrongful discrimination.

Theological feminism has developed its influence most strongly, of course, not in the Catholic but in the Protestant sphere. A broad segment of even the general public knows, for instance, that Maria Jepsen, Lutheran Bishop of Hamburg since 1992, views herself as a "feminist", albeit a "soft" one.[3] At church congresses and academic functions, feminist theology constantly recurs as a topic for discussion. It attracts great sympathy but also arouses strong opposition; and both sorts of reaction occur among women as well as men. Here are just two examples: for the female Protestant theologian Ingeborg Hauschildt, feminist theology is "a new heresy", while the male professor of theology at Tübingen Jürgen Moltmann enthusiastically welcomes theological feminism.[4]

---

[3] "... Das Weib rede in der Gemeinde." Maria Jepsen: Erste lutherische Bischöfin. Dokumente und Stellungnahmen ["... Women should speak in the churches." Maria Jepsen: The first female Lutheran bishop. Documents and critical standpoints] (Gütersloh, 1992).

[4] Ingeborg Hauschildt, " 'Feministische Theologie'—eine neue Irrlehre" ["Feminist theology"—a new heresy], Informationsbrief Nr. 94 der Bekenntnisbewegung "Kein anderes Evangelium" (Gal 1,6) (Lüdenscheid, 1982), 5–13; Die feministische Versuchung und die Antwort der christlichen Frau [The feminist temptation and the response of the Christian woman] (Wuppertal and Zurich, 1989). Jürgen Moltmann, "Der mütterliche Vater. Überwindet trinitarischer Patripassianismus den theologischen Patriarchal-

In the Catholic sphere, feminist theology has generally made its presence felt with rather more restraint. But there, too, the reverberations have been considerable, especially as some of the best-known feminist theologians come from the Catholic Church. Working groups and reading circles have been formed, and feminists like Catharina Halkes have already given quite a few lectures at conferences of the Catholic Women's Association.

The relevant literature is now scarcely surveyable even by specialist scholars; a bibliography from 1988 lists over eighteen hundred titles.[5] Anyone wishing to concentrate professionally on feminist theology alone would have to do nothing else and would still not succeed in completely covering the material. In the past fifteen to twenty years, hardly any other area of theological endeavor has seen the appearance of so many contributions as have been made precisely to the field of feminist theology.

Moreover, feminist theology is but one subarea of study within the literature currently appearing on the theme of "women in the Church". And that broader thematic area, in turn, is just one part of a larger complex of issues being worked through at present in almost all the scholarly and scientific disciplines. Today, the position of women is coming under quite conscious scrutiny. Still determinative here is the situation in the USA, where one speaks of "women's studies", implying, more precisely, "studies on the position

---

ismus?" [The motherly Father: Does trinitarian patripassianism overcome theological patriarchalism?], *Concilium* 17 (1981): 209–13; "Theologie in den Erfahrungen des gelebten Lebens" [Theology in the experiences of lived life], in Herlinde Pissarek-Hudelist and Luise Schottroff, eds., *Mit allen Sinnen glauben: Feministische Theologie Unterwegs. FS E. Moltmann-Wendel* [Believing with all one's senses: Feminist theology under way. Essays in honor of E. Moltmann-Wendel] (Gütersloh, 1991), 151f.

[5] Ursula Vock et al., *Bibliographie zur Feministischen Theologie* (Zurich, 1988); cf. E. M. Blaasvaer, ed., *Bibliography on Feminist Theology* (Geneva, 1986); and also the entries in the *Wörterbuch der Feministischen Theologie* [Dictionary of feminist theology], ed. by Elisabeth Gössmann et al. (Gütersloh, 1991) (abbreviated: Wb).

of women". These "women's studies" are usually pursued by women themselves.[6]

And now along comes this male who sets about writing on a topic concerning women. Isn't that rather odd? Shouldn't this be a job for a woman? Do men have any relevant competence at all?

Three points may be made in this regard. First of all, what is involved in feminism and feminist theology is a matter affecting both sexes. Not only women but also men are addressed by it. The broader conceptual framework that must be covered here could be described as "theological anthropology of the sexes", or rather, more simply, as "man and woman in Christian thought". At issue in "theological anthropology of the sexes" are all the essential factors that affect being a man or a woman and that are also theologically significant. The first reason, then, for my taking up this theme is that it concerns not only women but also men.

The second reason is that the kind of position one takes on feminism has no inherent link to being a man or being a woman. We find "feminism", "nonfeminism", and "antifeminism" among men as well as women. "Dear Sister Gutting"—thus, for example, a German suffragan bishop is referred to, with good-hearted condescension, in the magazine *Emma*.[7] The psychologist Christa Meves, on the other hand, who is active in the pursuit of women's issues and whose paperbacks on vital questions have sold in the millions, makes all feminists "see red". In the end, the sort of position one adopts on a given issue depends on one's

---

[6] H. B. Schöpp-Schilling, "Frauenforschung" [Women's studies], in Anneliese Lissner, Rita Süssmuth, and Karin Walter, eds., *Frauenlexikon* [Lexicon on women] (Freiburg, 1988) (abbreviated: FLex), 334–38; "Women's Studies in den USA", in Claudia Opitz, ed., *Weiblichkeit oder Feminismus?* [Femininity or feminism?] (Weingarten, 1984), 23–42; Anne E. Carr, *Transforming Grace: Christian Tradition and Women's Experience* (San Francisco, 1988), 63–94.

[7] *Emma,* December 1987; cf. *Theol. Revue* 84 (1988): 89 (E. Gössmann).

intellectual outlook, not on one's sex. Otherwise, no communication between men and women would remain possible.

The third reason has a personal cast. After completion of my course of university studies, I expressed a desire to write my research thesis on an ecumenical topic. My professor then suggested that I might deal with the subject of the "priesthood of women". What conclusions I might reach was of little concern to him; the important thing was that the work should be theologically well-founded.

That topic proved to be extraordinarily complex but also highly interesting. Eventually, it was recommended that I should expand my diploma-level research project into a doctoral dissertation. Accepting that recommendation, I went on to earn my Ph.D. (in Munich in 1981) with specialization in the area of "women in the priesthood".[8] In succeeding years, I have been invited again and again to give lectures, lead discussions, or contribute theological papers on the subject of women. At the time of my doctoral work in 1981, feminist theology had just begun to establish itself in the German-speaking world. Since then, I have felt an obligation to observe further developments in the field of theological feminism.

Meanwhile, I have been forced to the realization that feminist theology—even in the case of committed, well-meaning women—increasingly mars relationship to the Church. To me, as both pastor and scholar, this development poses a challenge that the present work is intended to meet. For without the active, cheerful collaboration of women, the Church cannot exist. Here, too, the above-noted wisdom of the midrash holds true: "Thus we see how everything depends on the woman."

To further the opportunities for effective activity by

---

[8] Manfred Hauke, *Women in the Priesthood? A Systematic Analysis in the Light of the Order of Creation and Redemption* (San Francisco, 1988); for a brief author's summary, see: "Das Weihesakrament für Frauen—eine Forderung der Zeit?" [Ordination of women—a demand of our times?], FKTh 3 (1987): 119–34.

women is an important concern of mine as author. On the other hand, the ideas in feminist theology seem fraught with problems. I must frankly admit that I often felt the same as the Protestant historian Lutz von Padberg, who has written a work containing a wealth of material on feminism. In the preface, he speaks of his "unedifying topic".[9] Most of the women and men who dislike feminism quickly reshelve publications about it or avoid even touching them in the first place. According to a recent opinion poll in *Time* magazine in the USA—which is, after all, the favored country for "women's studies"—only 29 percent of the women questioned regard themselves as "feminists", whereas 69 percent reject that classification.[10] That I, too, am no feminist may be openly confessed. But I do find that important concerns and questions raised by feminism are worthy of attention, even if its proffered solutions require critical scrutiny. In any case, I hope to present the feminist positions as objectively as possible and to make them understandable in their historical development, their inner structure, and their detailed subtlety. This expository analysis will constitute the largest portion of this work and will provide a basis for forming one's own balanced opinion. As a second step, critical commentary will then be made on each position in question.

The present volume is an expanded version of a series of special lectures that I gave in the summer semester of 1992 at the University of Augsburg. Integrated into them are some relevant essays from earlier years.[11] The ultimate stimulus to publication of this book was a controversy played out in the Paderborn parish newspaper, *Der Dom:* a female writer quite well-disposed toward feminist theology had described it as an "aid to faith and life".[12] My critical

---

[9] Lutz von Padberg, *Feminismus—eine ideologische und theologische Herausforderung* [Feminism—an ideological and theological challenge], Evangelium und Gesellschaft 5. (Wuppertal, 1985), 8.

[10] FAZ, April 24, 1992, 35.

[11] See the Bibliography, 281–83.

[12] Margarete Niggemeyer, "Feministische Theologie—Hilfe zum Glauben

comments, in the form of a letter to the editor,[13] evoked a veritable flood of responses "pro" and "con", which continued for more than half a year. The need for a source of detailed, clarifying information on feminist theology thus became more than plain. One of the women who intervened in my favor wrote me this:

"I am alarmed at this fanatical intolerance. There is an attempt to 'beat down' anyone who risks openly expressing contrary insights and convictions. . . . Must one fear that your experiences are typical these days of dealings with the trendily 'progressive' committees of our 'democratized', 'sisterly' Church? Are the leading councils dominated by theological dilettantes and ideological fanatics?"

The purpose of the present work is to provide, not a kind of "encyclopedia" on feminist theology, but an introduction and representative survey of central themes that will enable one to form a personal opinion. What would constitute a positive response to the feminist challenge can often only be hinted at. Addressed here are not just specialists in theology but all women and men who desire to inform themselves further about the powerful historical current that is feminist theology.

Before focussing on feminist theology itself, it will be necessary to take account of its most important intellectual precondition, namely, present-day feminism. Next, the development of feminist theology in particular must be outlined. Against that backdrop, the central conceptual aspects of theological feminism will then be introduced individually, ranging from the image of man and the concept of God to eschatology. Each major subsection will be concluded with a critical evaluation: "feminist theology put to the test".

---

und Leben" [Feminist theology—an aid to faith and life"], *Der Dom*, no. 24 (June 14, 1992): 5, 18.

[13] Manfred Hauke, "Feministische Theologie—Hilfe zum Glauben?", *Der Dom*, no. 32 (August 9, 1992): 18.

II. HISTORY AND BASIC CHARACTERISTICS OF MODERN FEMINISM

1. Differentiation from the Women's Movement

The term "women's movement" includes all those particular lines of endeavor along which women organize themselves for the purpose of furthering their own interests.[1] The origin of the women's movement in the nineteenth century was shaped initially by the contemporary economic revolution. The transition from an agrarian culture to an industrial society brought with it immense problems for women in particular: separation from their family and their husband's working-place, their own integration into the industrial labor process, and so on. The idea of the rights of man, which came to the fore after the French Revolution, was also embraced by women, who neverthe-

---

[1] On the women's movement and its history, see: Cordula Koepcke, *Geschichte der deutschen Frauenbewegung. Von den Anfängen bis 1945* [History of the German women's movement: From the beginnings to 1945] (Freiburg, 1981); "Frauenbewegung" [Women's movement], in FLex, 322–33 (bibliog.); Hildegard Bogerts, *Bildung und berufliches Selbstverständnis lehrender Frauen in der Zeit von 1885 bis 1920* [Formation and professional self-image of women teachers in the period 1885 to 1920] (Frankfurt, 1977); Alfred Kall, *Katholische Frauenbewegung in Deutschland. Eine Untersuchung zur Gründung katholischer Frauenvereine im 19. Jahrhundert* [The Catholic women's movement in Germany: A study of the founding of Catholic women's groups in the 19th century] (Paderborn, 1983); Josef Mörsdorf, *Gestaltwandel des Frauenbildes und Frauenberufs in der Neuzeit* [Changes in women's image and women's work in modern times] (Munich, 1958); Herrad Schenk, *Die feministische Herausforderung. 150 Jahre Frauenbewegung in Deutschland* [The feminist challenge: 150th anniversary of the women's movement in Germany], 3d ed. (Munich, 1983).

less saw themselves excluded from participation in politics. For the revolutionaries, the "rights of man" were largely the "rights of males". In 1791, a French woman, Olympe de Gouges, protested against this situation with her *Déclaration des droits de la femme,* or "declaration of the rights of women".[2]

In the course of the Enlightenment, the notion of the "emancipation of women" was conceived. "Emancipation" was originally a concept in Roman law designating the release of a family member from the *"manicipium"*, the power of the father. Anyone who could exercise his own control over possessions and wealth was then "emancipated". Since the eighteenth century, "emancipation" has acquired the general meaning of "reaching maturity" and "freeing oneself from dependencies".[3] "Emancipation" of women thus means freeing oneself from dependency on men and pursuing an autonomously conceived course in life.

The goals of the organized women's movement—which began taking form in Germany mainly after 1848—were first and foremost these: educational opportunities that would enable free self-development, political rights, access to new kinds of careers, and a restructuring of employment conditions that would do justice to the needs of women. Gaining the right of admission to university study, for example, required a lengthy struggle. Just how difficult this was may be concretely illustrated by the following quotation, originating at a conference of rectors and teachers from higher-level schools for girls in 1872:

> It is desirable that women be given access to an educa-
> tion which, in the generality of its approach and interests, is
> intellectually comparable to the education of men, so that
> the German male will not be bored, at the domestic fireside,

---

[2] Hannelore Schröder, ed. *Die Frau ist frei geboren. Texte zur Frauene-manzipation I: 1789–1870* |Woman is born free: Texts on the emancipation of women I: 1789-1870| (Munich, 1979), 36–49.

[3] Magdalena Baus, "Emanzipation", in FLex, 213-15.

by the intellectual myopia and cramped spirit of his wife, and thus impaired in his pursuit of higher sorts of interests.[4]

The possibility of independent intellectual activity by women does not come into the picture here at all; domestic life appears as the only area in which they can apply themselves. Not the least factor behind this difficult situation was the continuing effect of the Reformation. In the sixteenth century, the Reformers had abolished monastic life and, as a consequence, also severely affected the education of women. Celibacy was considered a rare exception for women and was abolished as a recognized way of life, so that women were virtually forced into marriage and motherhood. The restricting of women to the "three C's"— children, cooking, and church—had a decisive point of departure here.[5]

When women were admitted to universities at the beginning of the present century, and won the right to vote after the First World War, definitive demands of the women's movement were attained. Considered in isolation from its Marxist factions, the women's movement did not normally intend that social differentiation between the sexes should be abolished altogether. The Catholic women's movement stressed precisely the independent contribution of women, which should be brought into society and Church.[6] The basic attitude of most committed women was typified by a statement of Helene Lange, a leading figure in the especially influential liberal—or confessionally neutral—women's movement. Lange said:

---

[4] Schenk, 27f.

[5] For a relevant summation without any glossing over, see Mörsdorf, 41-69; cf. Augustin Rösler, *Die Frauenfrage vom Standpunkt der Natur, der Geschichte und der Offenbarung* [The women's question from the standpoint of nature, history, and revelation], 2d ed. (Freiburg, 1907), 334-51; and (from a Protestant viewpoint) Erika Reichle, "Reformation", in FLex, 927-34 (bibliog.).

[6] See Kall, passim; Bogerts, passim.

If women's contribution to the development of culture is to occur only through the exercise of masculine qualities, then that development would far better be left to men. The whole strength of the women's movement lies precisely in its understanding that women, ... down to the very tips of their toes, are anatomically different from men, are psychologically different as well, and can thus serve the cultural development of mankind through other sorts of qualities that have so far been represented only marginally or not at all.[7]

Admittedly, there were (most notably at the turn of the century) radical advocates of women's rights who, among other things, called for free love, demanded legalization of abortion, and tended to view the difference between men and women as rather minor.[8] Only in these extreme circles was the adjective "feminist" accorded a positive reception. Otherwise, up to present times, "feminism" was regarded as a term of abuse in German-speaking countries and was by no means accepted by most advocates of women's rights as aptly self-descriptive.

In countries where French and English are spoken, the situation is somewhat different. There, "feminism" has a stronger general sense connoting active commitment to the cause of equal rights for women.[9] But the term is obviously not devoid of pejorative connotations even in the USA: as mentioned above, only a minority of women there regard themselves as feminists. The word "feminism" was probably coined at the beginning of the nineteenth century by Charles Fourier, an early socialist.[10] In the

---

[7] Helene Lange, "Altes und Neues zur Frauenfrage" [Old and new aspects of the women's question], *Die Frau* 2 (6/1895), h. 9, 538; as cited in Hedwig Meyer-Wilmes, *Rebellion auf der Grenze. Ortsbestimmung feministischer Theologie* [Rebellion on the borders: The present situation in feminist theology] (Freiburg, 1990), 45.

[8] Ute Gerhard, "Feminismus", in FLex, 303f.; Cordula Koepcke, "Frauenbewegung", in FLex, 324f.

[9] L. M. Weber, "Feminismus", LThK, 2d series, 4 (1960): 74f.; Gerhard, in FLex, 301f.

[10] Meyer-Wilmes, 79.

forms of social arrangement advocated by him, a logically consistent equality of the sexes was to prevail.[11] Among followers of another early socialist, Henri de Saint-Simon, many of the objectives of theological feminism were also anticipated. Saint-Amand Bazard and Barthélemy-Prosper Enfantin expected the coming of a female messiah, or, so to speak, a "Jesa Christa". Since this female redemptive figure was not to be found in Europe, some of Saint-Simon's disciples undertook an expedition to the Orient. There, in the Turkish harems, they hoped to find the "free woman", the *femme libre,* the female messiah. In the church of the Saint-Simonists, God was designated as both Father and Mother, as "Mapah". At the beginning of the history of creation, they held, there was a mixed male and female being, a so-called "androgyne": "Evadam".[12]

Influenced by a relevant Platonic myth, the ancient Gnostics, the Jewish Cabbalists, and, following them, the Protestant theosophist Jakob Boehme had already spoken of an androgynous primal human being.[13] The androgyny principle in feminism (about which more will be said later) is thus no new discovery.

The word "feminism", current in Germany at the turn of the century as a term of abuse, did not begin taking on more positive connotations until after 1968. The so-called "new women's movement", which arose at that time in connection with the student revolts, did not content itself with the mere achievement of equal rights but wished to create wholly new social structures. The more recent editions of the *Duden* German dictionary show a very basic

---

[11] On Fourier and his school, cf. Elke Kleinau, *Die freie Frau. Soziale Utopien des frühen 19. Jahrhunderts* [The free women: Social utopias in the early 19th century] (Düsseldorf, 1987), 67–111.

[12] Gottfried Salomon-Delatour, ed., *Die Lehre Saint-Simons* [The teaching of Saint-Simon] (Neuwied, 1962), 22; Kleinau, 29–66.

[13] Bernhard Sill, *Androgynie und Geschlechtsdifferenz nach Franz von Baader. Eine anthropologisch-ethisch Studie* [Androgyny and sexual difference according to Franz von Baader: An anthropologico-ethical study] (Regensburg, 1986).

revision, defining "feminism" as a "direction within the women's movement that strives for a new self-understanding by women and the abolition of the traditional separation of roles".[14] Precisely the latter point is typical of most conceptions put forward in the name of feminism: it is a matter of "abolishing division of labor on sex-specific lines" and "dismantling differentiation in the roles of the sexes".[15]

The same ideal is cited, for instance, by Rita Süssmuth, in Herder's *Frauenlexikon* [Lexicon on women], as the goal of feminist politics: "The division of labor on sex-specific lines is to be abolished."[16] This hypothetical goal finds its most logically consistent practical expression in guidelines aimed at achieving a quota of fifty-fifty in every field of employment. This principle is endorsed, for example, in a resolution passed by the Senate of the Free University of Berlin in 1980 and in a call issued by a working party of female scientists in Nordrhein-Westfalen. According to this, half of all the positions in every area of scientific work are to be filled by women.[17]

There are other sorts of demands made by feminists that will be considered later; the examples cited above, however, seem altogether typical. What we have here is no longer a direct continuation of the established women's movement but something radically new. Looming on the horizon is not only the demand for imposition of employment quotas but also the vision of a totally new society, in which social differentiation between men and women has disappeared. According to Catharina Halkes, "emancipated women" demand, so to speak, only "half of the cake", whereas "feminists" think "that a new cake needs to be baked".[18]

---

[14] *Duden* 1, 20th ed. (Mannheim, 1991), 267.

[15] Schenk, 188.

[16] Rita Süssmuth, "Frauenpolitik" [Politics of woman], in FLex, 372.

[17] Meyer-Wilmes, 61, 240 (n. 35).

[18] Catharina Halkes, "Frau und Mann als Ebenbild Gottes. Aus der Sicht der feministischen Theologie" [Woman and man as God's likeness: From the viewpoint of feminist theology], in H. Erharter and R. Schwarzenberger,

Rather than being a single unified movement, feminism includes some quite varied subcurrents. Their common element consists primarily in agreement about what they do not want. In particular, battle cries are directed again and again at three concepts: patriarchalism, sexism, and androcentrism. All feminists are vigorously opposed to the "patriarchate", to "rule of the father", or, in a more general sense, to the social primacy of males. The word "sexism" was formed on analogy with "racism". It signifies being disadvantaged because of one's sex, and the disadvantage is usually identified with "inequality" or "subjection".[19] More will be said about this later. Occupying a similar semantic gray area is the concept of "discrimination", which means making "distinctions". Objections to "discrimination" can then imply doing away with unjust distinctions but are also used to call into question every sort of social and psychological difference.[20] Another concept central to feminist language is "androcentrism", derived from the Greek word *aner,* "a man". "Androcentrism", or "man-centeredness", thus means placing males (or the masculine) at the center and making them the measure of everything human. Up until now, it is charged, human reality has been regarded wholly from the perspective of men, with the female elements being forgotten.[21]

In the common struggle against patriarchalism, discrimination, sexism, and androcentrism, all feminists are united. And if these concepts are understood in a very general

---

eds., *Frau—Partnerin in der Kirche. Perspektiven einer zeitgemäßen Frauen-Seelsorge* (Vienna, 1985), 91; cf. her "Theologie, feministische", in FLex, 1101. Cf. Jutta Menschik, *Feminismus. Geschichte, Theorie, Praxis* [Feminism: History, theory, practice], Kleine Bibliothek 87 (Cologne, 1977), 42f.; Padberg (1985), 55–58.

[19] Cf., for example, Schenk, 187; Ursula King, "Feminismus", *Evangelisches Kirchenlexikon* 1, 3d ed. (Göttingen, 1986), 1280f.; Sigrid Metz-Göckel, "Sexismus" [Sexism], in FLex, 989–93.

[20] Camilla Krebsbach-Gnath, "Diskriminierung" [Discrimination], in FLex, 160–63.

[21] Ina Praetorius, "Androzentrismus" [Androcentrism], in Wb, 14f.

sense, as the disadvantaging of women on the basis of their sex, then there is certainly a broad consensus in our culture in favor of women's rights. In that sense, even the author of this book could describe himself as a "feminist". Things become more problematic, however, when one attempts to determine the precise meanings of the concepts concerned. What we find then, even within feminism itself, is anything but agreement. To identify some common objective of a positive kind within feminism seems impossible. The decisive source of difference is the view one takes of being a man or being a woman. The majority of feminists regard the difference between men and women — apart from what is strictly biological — as conditioned purely by culture. Thus they demand the aforementioned abolition of all divisions of labor on sex-specific lines. On the other hand, a minority (whose influence seems, however, to be growing) support the view that biology, psychology, and sociology cannot be rigidly separated. There is a distinct female nature, which possesses its own unique value, constitutes the strength of women, and must not be "ironed out" on the board of an abstract equality. These two broad currents within feminism can be termed "equality feminism" and "gynocentric feminism" (from the Greek word *gúne,* "a woman"). Whereas equality feminism tends to demand logically consistent introduction of a fifty-fifty quota arrangement in all areas of employment, "woman-centered" feminists are no longer interested in that.

But before the nature of this so-called "quarrel among sisters" is outlined further, it seems advisable to take a look back over the historical dimension. The "feminism" of the so-called "new women's movement" did not, as it were, descend from heaven like a meteor but is rooted in an extensive intellectual prehistory. Especially notable components of this are Marxism, Simone de Beauvoir's existentialism, and the radicalization of Marxist approaches during the student movement of the 1960s. All these influences are significant not only for feminism in general but also for feminist theology, which is directly and indirectly dependent on the factors to be surveyed here.

2. The Significance of Marxism

Karl Marx is concerned with the creating of a new man who is wholly absorbed in working for the collectivity and who himself experiences comprehensive satisfaction of his needs. Through nationalization of the means of production and the abolition of private property, all social differences are to be dissolved. All "domination of man by man" will be eliminated in the future communist society. Any biological and psychological obstacles on the way to this goal can be overcome, since man is only an "ensemble [totality] of social relationships".[22] Education and environment are the key factors that make men seem moldable to an almost infinite degree.

Marxism was applied to the question of women by August Bebel, in his popular work *Die Frau und der Sozialismus* [Women and socialism] (first published in 1879),[23] and by Friedrich Engels. Both took over from Johann Jakob Bachofen and Lewis Henry Morgan the hypothesis of a prehistoric matriarchate, a "rule of mothers". In all spheres of society, it was not men but women who had assumed decisive leadership responsibility. However, the American, Morgan, refers at the same time to an egalitarian society, free from domination, in the matrilineal period. The primal, maternal form of society was distinguished by liberty, equality, fraternity, sexual promiscuity, and profoundly democratic kinds of behavior.[24] Friedrich Engels, above

---

[22] Karl Marx, "Thesen über Feuerbach" [Theses on Feuerbach], in his *Frühe Schriften* (Stuttgart, 1971), 2:3.

[23] On this, see Mörsdorf, 212–19.

[24] Uwe Wesel, *Der Mythos vom Matriarchat. Über Bachofens Mutterrecht und die Stellung von Frauen in frühen Gesellschaften* [The myth of

all, adopted this view of history. Supposedly, it was only later on that the "patriarchate", the primacy of men, made its appearance. The patriarchate is based on the existence of the family. There, the husband is the bourgeois, and the wife the proletarian whose domestic enslavement must be ended. In opposition to this, Engels posits the ideal of universal equality, under which all domination of man by man is to be eliminated.

As means to this end, Engels cites abolition of the family, uniform integration of men and women into the labor process, and communal raising of children.[25] In the Marxist image of man, there is no predetermined feminine or masculine nature but only irritating biological material that can, however, be reshaped by social influences, to a practically unlimited extent, in the direction of universal equality.

Among those recently promoting the ideas of the early Marxist fathers is the psychologist Ernest Bornemann. With his book *Das Patriarchat* (1975), he intends to perform the same services for the women's movement that Marx once performed, with *Kapital,* [26] for the workers' movement. The goal of the future lies in restoration of the supposedly domination-free matriarchal society, in which the family, monogamy, and private property will have disappeared. The task of bearing children is to be taken over by technology, and even physical dimorphism, or bodily distinctiveness as male or female, is to be largely reduced.[27] Corresponding to the "classless society of the future" is the

---

the matriarchy: On Bachofen's matrilineal hypothesis and the position of women in early societies] (Frankfurt, 1980), 19–25.

[25] Friedrich Engels, *Der Ursprung der Familie, des Privateigentums und des Staates* [The origin of the family, private property, and the state], 17th ed. (Stuttgart, 1919), 62–64.

[26] Ernest Bornemann, *Das Patriarchat. Ursprung und Zukunft unseres Gesellschaftssystems* [Patriarchy: On the origin and future of our social system] (Frankfurt, 1975), 7.

[27] Ibid., 534f.

"sexless future of our species"; "the one is unattainable apart from the other."[28]

The hypothesis of a prehistoric matriarchate was eagerly seized upon in feminist circles, although it was scarcely being advocated any longer even in the orthodox Marxism of recent decades.[29] The main defect of the matriarchate theory lies in its confusing of matrilineal descent (matriliny) and "rule of mothers". Even in matrilineal cultures, the leading functions tended to be looked after by males. The legal historian Uwe Wesel—whose work *Der Mythos vom Matriarchat* [The myth of the matriarchate] led to a change of mind even in many feminist circles—writes: Recent ethnologists "have repeatedly stressed that, despite the formation of kinship groups by succession from the mother, nothing can be seen of a rule by women; on the contrary, if anyone exercised power among them, it was always men, and the corresponding position of women was, at times, even decidedly bad."[30]

Exceptional, to a certain degree, are a few societies, like the Iroquois tribe or Minoan Crete, which might be described as "matrifocal", that is, ones in which the "focus" is on mothers. There, the orientation of the social order toward women resulted from a combination of matrilineal descent and female-based determination of the place of residence. A decisive factor in the genesis of the few known matrifocal societies seems to have been the absence of males from the home environment: the Iroquois were away hunting, and the Cretans at sea, for weeks and months at a time.[31] The eminent sociologist René König knows that he

---

[28] Ibid., 21.

[29] Wesel, 30.

[30] Ibid., 25; cf. Gunter Dux, *Die Spur der Macht im Verhältnis der Geschlechter. Über den Ursprung der Ungleichheit zwischen Mann und Frau* [The position of power in the relationship of the sexes: On the source of the dissimilarity between man and woman] (Frankfurt, 1992), 210–15.

[31] Wesel, passim; cf. Hauke, *Women in the Priesthood?*, 99–103.

can rely on the support of his (female and male) colleagues when he writes that "remnants" of the matriarchate theory are to be found "now only . . . in political journalism and popular Marxism".[32]

Meanwhile, the feminist movement itself seems to be increasingly abandoning the matriarchate hypothesis.[33] Even in Süssmuth's *Frauenlexikon,* one can now read: "The history of women is neither a history of victimization in the context of an over-powerful patriarchate nor a basis for legitimization of matriarchal myths and legends."[34]

This does not, of course, preclude even theologians from continuing to assume that the popular Marxist myth of a matriarchate is an established fact of historical science.[35] More and more feminists, however, no longer base their theories on it. Yet the feminist movement still retains its predominantly socio-cultural perspective, which traces all differences between the sexes essentially back to arbitrarily changeable "roles".

---

[32] René König, *Die Familie der Gegenwart. Ein interkultureller Vergleich* [The family today: An intercultural comparison], 3d ed. (Munich, 1978), 149, n. 43. The theory of a "matriarchate" was also unanimously rejected by the international scholarly colloquium on the "reality of woman"; see Evelyne Sullerot, ed., *Die Wirklichkeit der Frau* [The reality of woman] (Munich, 1979), 484f.

[33] Cf. Marielouise Janssen-Jurreit, *Sexismus. Über die Abtreibung der Frauenfrage* [Sexism: On the miscarriage of the women's question], 2d ed. (Munich and Vienna, 1977), 133; for other critical positions, see Menschik, 130f.; Susanne Heine, *Wiederbelebung der Göttinnen? Zur systematischen Kritik einer feministischen Theologie* [Revival of the goddesses? Toward a systematic critique of feminist theology] (Göttingen, 1987), 86–117; Beate Wagner-Hasel, ed., *Matriarchatstheorien der Altertumswissenschaft* [Theories of a matriarchate in archaeological scholarship] (Darmstadt, 1992). While some contributions to the afore-noted *Frauenlexikon* continue to assume a prehistorical "matriarchate" (e.g., 683, 686, 785, 999, 1093), an author specifically qualified in that area declares this historically untenable: Gisela Bleibtreu-Ehrenberg, "Matriarchat/Patriarchat", in FLex, 710–18; "Eheformen" [Forms of marriage], ibid., 177–81; similarly, Annette Kuhn, "Frauengeschichte" [History of women], ibid., 344.

[34] Kuhn, ibid.

[35] Cf. below, 133.

3. The Influence of Simone de Beauvoir

Decisive impulses to the development of present-day feminism came from Simone de Beauvoir, the life-long companion of the existentialist philosopher Jean-Paul Sartre. In 1949, she published a comprehensive work on women entitled *Le Deuxième sexe,* "the second sex" (or, in its customary German translation, "the other sex"). Feminism and feminist theology were fundamentally marked by this "bible of feminism", as Alice Schwarzer calls the work.[36] Typical of many feminists in this connection is a statement by Rita Süssmuth, who declared in an interview: "Simone de Beauvoir is a great model."[37]

De Beauvoir elaborates the Marxist vision of the future, and enthusiastically embraces the ideals of the Russian revolution,[38] but can probably be associated more closely with the worldview of liberalism. Here, "liberalism" is to be understood, not as a specific party-political program, but rather as making the principle of individual liberty one's all-determining point of departure. Liberal thought is concerned with enabling the autonomous individual, who sets his laws for himself, to have a maximally wide range of options for planning the course of his life.

The idea of freedom that we find in de Beauvoir reflects that of her companion, Sartre. For Sartre, freedom is not the responsible shaping of something independently given in advance, but, rather, sheer choice and pursuit of some self-conceived project: "Man is nothing other than what he makes himself be."[39] In the interest of this freedom, Sartre

---

[36] Alice Schwarzer, *Der Spiegel,* no. 15 (April 5, 1976): 193, as cited in Padberg (1985), 210, n. 112.

[37] *Die Zeit,* no. 37 (September 6, 1985): 8.

[38] Padberg (1985), 89; Simone de Beauvoir, *Das andere Geschlecht. Sitte und Sexus der Frau* (Reinbek, 1968), 141f., 675; English ed.: *The Second Sex* (New York, 1953).

[39] Jean-Paul Sartre, *Ist der Existentialismus ein Humanismus?* [Is existentialism a humanism?] (Zurich, 1947), 14.

postulates atheism. If God exists, then man has been created by him and is responsible to him. If God does not exist, then there is also no specific human essence that could be entrusted to our individual freedom. There is "no human nature because there is no God to conceive it".[40] Or, in Sartre's terminology, "existence", the human projection of being, precedes "essence", or any determinate form of being. "Existentialism" implies here a central emphasis on one's own self-created existence, one's own self-projected plan. The focus is not on a good creation whose continued formation and development has been entrusted to us by God but on one's own decisive action, on self-governing autonomous choice. The human body thus becomes just so much material for use in one's self-projection. Its mode of being, in Sartre's formulation, is that of "one instrument in the midst of other instruments".[41]

Simone de Beauvoir takes her companion's brand of existentialism and applies it with logical consistency to the situation of women. Probably the most frequently quoted lines in her book read: "One does not arrive in the world as a woman, but one becomes a woman. No biological, psychological, or economic fate determines the form that the female human being takes on in the womb of society."[42]

Conceiving oneself as a woman is thus something completely free. Just as there is, for Sartre, no predetermined essence of man, so it is even more true, for de Beauvoir, that there exists no "essence of woman" with specific qualities that must be presupposed when making one's own life choices. Hence, the realization is all the more painful for de Beauvoir that the relations between men and women are not interchangeable but that discourse about women occurs with a view to men, and not vice versa: "She [the

---

[40] Ibid.

[41] Jean-Paul Sartre, *Das Sein und das Nichts* [Being and nothingness] (Hamburg, 1962), 456.

[42] Beauvoir, 265.

woman] is defined and distinguished with regard to the man, but not so he with regard to her; she is the unessential vis-à-vis the essential. He is the subject, he is the absolute; she is the other."[43]

This self-alienation is experienced by a woman not only with respect to society but also with respect to her bodily nature. She is tied to the interests of the species—that is, to the process of gestation, giving birth, and raising children—and is therefore less an independent, autonomous individual than is a man. De Beauvoir writes: "Of all female mammals, woman is the one that is most self-alienated and feels this alienation most passionately; nowhere is the subjugation of the body through the procreative function so pronounced, but nowhere, too, is it suffered with more anguish. . . ." "From puberty to menopause, she is the staging place of a process that goes on inside her without affecting her herself." "If she is compared with a man, the latter appears infinitely advantaged."[44]

Precisely that which is characteristic of the biology of women strikes de Beauvoir as degrading. She therefore appeals to every person (and particularly every woman) "to base one's pride, in disregard of all sexual difference, on the difficult glory of one's free existence".[45]

Her ideal goal, however, is actually not (as she suggests in the just-cited remarks) "being a human" but rather "being a male". For her, even girls aged ten to twelve are "unsuccessful boys, that is, children who are not allowed to be boys". Her account of female puberty is thus a veritable horror story.[46] The same applies to her description of the life of a housewife.[47]

Here, even some feminists acknowledge their dismay about de Beauvoir's image of woman. Marie-Louise Janssen-

---

[43] Ibid., 11.
[44] Ibid., 46, 42, 46.
[45] Ibid., 666.
[46] Ibid., 289, 297ff.
[47] For example, ibid., 428f.

Jurreit, for example, speaks of an existentialist-tinged cult of the male.[48] The basic point of relevant criticism of de Beauvoir is expressed by the philosopher Karen Böhme: "The position advocated by de Beauvoir comes down to saying that a woman can emancipate herself only through emancipation from her femininity, . . . namely, by casting off precisely that which previously constituted her being a woman." "Femininity" stands "as an obstacle to being human . . . , instead of shaping that in a specific direction".[49]

Karl Simpfendörfer strongly emphasizes the biographical background to de Beauvoir's assertions. The form of her own life was prescribed for her by Sartre, who dominated her intellectually, caused her to forego having children, and betrayed her with his philandering. De Beauvoir was unable, inwardly, to cope with this oppression, suffered repeatedly from anxiety attacks, and was obviously anything but a happy woman. What she could not experience in her own life—a faithful husband and children—she disparaged for other women as well. She quite openly boasted about having undergone two abortions.

Her romantic involvement with Sartre grew less and less intense. Despite this, she did not break off with him. Here, certain things that occurred during Sartre's last hours seem to have symptomatic import. Simpfendörfer reports the following:

> Sartre, who was suffering from lung congestion, experienced severe breathing attacks from time to time, the last of which marked the beginning of his slow death. During this final attack, Sartre struggled helplessly with death for hours, until de Beauvoir, arriving for a morning visit, discovered his condition.

---

[48] Janssen-Jurreit, 378.

[49] Karen Böhme, *Zum Selbstverständnis der Frau. Philosophische Aspekte der Frauenemanzipation* [On female self-understanding: Philosophical aspects of the emancipation of women] (Meisenheim am Glan, 1973), 15f.

Sartre was treated for an hour by the emergency doctor before he could be transported to a hospital. Simone de Beauvoir, who had scheduled an appointment for about that time, kept it without waiting to learn what hospital Sartre would be taken to.

When she visited him later on, Sartre—who knew that he was about to die—assured her that he loved her very much and pursed his lips for a kiss. Simone de Beauvoir kissed him, and she would subsequently make the following terse comment on this: "These words, these gestures, unusual for him, signalled his impending death."

As a consequence of failing circulation, Sartre had developed a complaint (gangrene) on his back involving localized tissue-death within the still-living total organism. Thus his illness was an especially unpleasant and painful one.

"When, after some weeks, Sartre had passed away in the company of Arlette, [another woman], de Beauvoir hurried to the side of his corpse" and asked whether she might be left alone with Sartre. She wanted to lie down next to him under the blanket but was restrained by a nurse, who warned: "Take care, the gangrene." De Beauvoir, who had known nothing about that complaint, then lay down on top of the blanket and would later coolly recount how Sartre's corpse was removed not long afterward.

Simpfendörfer comments as follows: "De Beauvoir's indifference toward Sartre in the period before his death was so marked that she was not even interested in her dying friend's condition or the complications of his illness. And yet she felt the urge to be quite close to his decomposing body."[50]

This is not the place to draw up a kind of "psychogram" on Simone de Beauvoir. The above-cited points are intended only to document the enormous personal problems that were bound up with de Beauvoir's version of feminism.

---

[50] Karl Simpfendörfer, *Verlust der Liebe. Mit Simone de Beauvoir in die Abtreibungsgesellschaft* [Loss of love: Toward the abortion society with Simone de Beauvoir] (Stein am Rhein, 1990), 63f.

That its ideas might lead to the liberation of women seems questionable on those grounds alone.

4. The Rise of the "New Women's Movement"[51]

Modern feminism has its most important source in the USA. Parallel developments in other Western countries have been variously stimulated by the "Women's Liberation Movement", albeit without attaining its degree of influence.

The women's movement in the USA was most particularly active from the middle of the nineteenth century. When, however, after the First World War, its main goal was achieved—namely, active and passive voting rights for women—the movement for women's rights grew relatively quiet. During the fifties, therefore, feminism was seen as a concern whose relevance had largely faded. And yet it was not long before a generalized outbreak of uneasiness occurred among American women. Indicative of this, in 1963, was Betty Friedan's best-seller, *The Feminine Mystique,* a work decisively inspired by her reading of de Beauvoir's *The Second Sex.*[52] This American also founded the National Organization of Women (NOW), a women's organization in the USA that has remained supremely influential to this day and includes among its goals total equality of rights. Also included are the rights to abortion and lesbian relationships.[53] "The feminine mystique", Friedan writes, "says that the highest value and only commitment for women is the fulfillment of their own femininity . . . ; the new image this mystique gives

---

[51] Cf. Menschik; Schenk, 82–223; Padberg (1985); King; Gerhard, in FLex, 301–7.

[52] Betty Friedan, *It Changed My Life: Writings on the Women's Movement* (New York, 1963, 1976), 304.

[53] Menschik, 81–83; Cornelia Ferreira, "The Emerging Feminist Religion", HPR 89 (1989): 2f.

to American women is the old image: 'Occupation: house-wife'."[54]

Behind this complaint is, of course, a genuine concern: given that there are fewer children per family than in past centuries, while household work has been reduced by modern technology, many housewives and mothers do not feel fully occupied. That they should be at least partially integrated into the work force makes sense from that perspective, but certain obstacles stand in the way.

Friedan heaps the highest praise on participation by women in the work force, while, at the same time, denigrating life as a housewife. She demands an equivalency of roles for men and women and holds that: "The only way for a woman, as for a man, to find herself, to know herself as a person, is by creative work of her own."[55] Child-raising and housework should be shared equally by husband and wife, so that women are not hindered from undertaking employment and do not thereby incur twice the male workload.[56]

The activities of Betty Friedan and her National Organization of Women were only one example of the so-called "new women's movement", usually seen as having begun in 1968. It is here that we find the decisive point of origin of present-day feminism. So-called "Women's Lib", short for "Women's Liberation Movement", arose in conjunction with the anti-Vietnam demonstrations and the waves of student unrest. Neo-Marxist tendencies coincided with a widespread discontent about "society".[57] According to Kate Millett, the best-known champion of Women's Lib, the most entrenched oppressive structure in human society is not capitalistic class rule but the social primacy of males. Capitalism is a manifestation of patriarchalism, and

[54] Betty Friedan, *The Feminine Mystique* (New York, 1963), 43.
[55] Ibid., 344.
[56] Ibid., 350.
[57] Menschik, 83ff.

not vice versa. In order to enable the free self-development of women, Millett, following Friedrich Engels, calls for the abolition of the family, since that is the "fundamental instrument and the foundation unit of patriarchal society and its roles are prototypical".[58]

The kind of feminism described here is a radicalized version of Marxism, from which it differs through its emphasis on the relationship between men and women. For orthodox Marxists, private property is the source of all oppression, and the family results from that; while for radical feminism, the family structure is fundamental to all other forms of domination.

The thesis that sexual differences are disadvantageous to women is taken still further by Shulamith Firestone. In *The Dialectic of Sex* (1970)—probably the most radical book among the "classics" of American feminism—she calls for the elimination of even the primary sexual characteristics. For linked to these differences, even in the animal world, is a certain subordination of the female sex. The "propagation of the species"[59] enslaves women; "pregnancy", Firestone claims, "is the temporary deformation of the body of the individual for the sake of the species."[60] Firestone looks to biology to provide the possibility of realizing her utopia: "Choice of sex of the fetus, test-tube fertilization . . . are just around the corner."[61]

In certain marginal groupings within Women's Lib, the struggle for "equality" was linked to a radical hatred of men. Valerie Solanas, for instance, complains that men alone are responsible for wars and the ravages of modern civilization. In a "Manifesto of the Society for Cutting Up

---

[58] Kate Millett, *Sexual Politics* (Garden City, N.Y., 1969), 33.

[59] Shulamith Firestone, *Frauenbefreiung und sexuelle Revolution* [Women's liberation and sexual revolution] (Frankfurt, 1975), 19; English ed.: *The Dialectic of Sex: The Case for Feminist Revolution* (New York, 1970).

[60] Ibid., 185.

[61] Ibid., 184.

Men", she describes being a man as "a deficiency disease" and a human deformation. Destruction, murder, and sabotage are the means by which annihilation of men is to be effected. One of her comrades in arms, Betsy Warrior, nevertheless recommends that one might allow a few men to remain alive so that they could be put on display in zoological gardens.[62]

These last-mentioned demands are not, of course, typical of feminism as a whole. They do show, however, how far astray one can go in trying to apply the theoretical apparatus of the class war to the relations between the sexes.

5. Equality Feminism and Gynocentric Feminism

As has been stressed here already, feminism is not a single unified movement; it has its more moderate and more radical variations.[63] Applying the Marxist notion of oppression to the relations between the sexes is, however, an approach they all share.[64] The common enemy is usually taken to be the tying of the female parent more closely to the children but is most certainly the linking of males with the more clearly defined responsibility for leadership tasks.

Within the shared framework—a radicalization of Marxism—significant differences can be found. Above all, two major directions have plainly emerged. The one, which is by and large the more influential, pursues the ideal of equalizing the so-called "roles" of men and women. The feminist historian Herrad Schenk even identifies this goal as the common denominator of feminism per se: "breaking

---

[62] Valerie Solanas, *Manifest der Gesellschaft zur Vernichtung der Männer* [Manifesto of the Society for Cutting Up Men (SCUM), 1968], 5th ed. (Berlin, 1982); Betsy Warrior, *"Man as an Obsolete Life Form": Women's Liberation: Blueprint for the Future* (New York, 1970), 45–47, as cited in Padberg (1985), 219–21; cf. also Menschik, 52–55.

[63] Schenk, 83–103; Padberg (1985), 7f.

[64] Schenk, 139–41; Padberg (1985), 63, 99–102.

down the differentiation in sex roles".[65] Correspondingly,
Hedwig Meyer-Wilmes speaks of an "equality feminism".[66]
Within this broad direction, a distinction is usually drawn
between a liberal and a socialist wing.[67]

Alongside this "equality feminism", however, particularly in recent years, there has been an increasingly evident
second tendency to emphasize typical feminine qualities
that are to be more clearly developed in women than in
men.[68] Here, the female nature is being rediscovered,
even if this is often linked to a devaluation of the male. In
the relevant literature, this direction is sometimes called
"radical feminism".[69] A more accurate term would seem
to be "gynocentric feminism":[70] its guiding ideal is not
androgyny but the conscious shaping of the female nature.
An exemplary study of recent literature on what could be
termed this "woman-centered" feminism (as distinct from
androgynous orientations) is provided by Christa Mulack's
work *Natürlich weiblich* [Naturally feminine] (1990).

Typical of the "quarrel among sisters" that prevails
between these two currents in feminism is the following
debate, as recounted by Christa Mulack:

Taking part in the televised discussion were the journal-
ist Marie-Louise Jannsen-Jurreit; a parliamentary member
from the Green Party, Waltraut Schoppe; and the Hamburg
anthropologist Rainer Knußmann, author of a book entitled *Der Mann—ein Fehlgriff der Natur* [The male—A
blunder of nature].[71]

---

[65] Schenk, 188–204.

[66] Meyer-Wilmes, 82, 114f.

[67] Cf., for example, King, 1282; Meyer-Wilmes, 82.

[68] As already in Betty Friedan, *The Second Stage* (New York, 1981).
Combining the same preference with a description of the present stage of
theorizing in the two basic feminist schools is: Cornelia Giese, *Gleichheit
und Differenz. Vom dualistischen Denken zur polaren Weltsicht* [Similarity
and difference: From dualistic thinking to a polar worldview] (Munich,
1990), 33–96.

[69] Meyer-Wilmes, 82, 85–90.

[70] Ibid., 86f. The adjective "gynocentric" seems to have been coined by
Mary Daly: see below, 84.

[71] Hamburg, 1984.

In this debate, Mulack identifies with Knußmann, who began the discussion by remarking: "Women are more peaceable." To this the "Green" woman responded: "I'm not peaceable." Knußmann replied that this tendency to peaceableness was an average characteristic, not applicable to every individual: there are certainly some women who are more aggressive than men, but women, on the whole, are more peaceable. Schoppe and Janssen-Jurreit, however, resisted the idea that there was any inherent difference in aggressivity between men and women, even though Janssen-Jurreit had herself conceded that point in one of her publications. Christa Mulack observes here:

> For thousands of years, wars have been almost exclusively planned and carried out by men; but even in everyday life, it is they who are noticeably more often involved in aggressive acts. In the Federal Republic of Germany, about 95 percent of all murders are attributable to them, and the high number of women's refuges speaks for itself. To be unable to admit that women are more peaceable would require a gross degree of ideological blindness.[72]

Christa Mulack is critical of the "massive phobias... about contact with any notions of femininity" that she perceives among most feminists of socialist or Marxist persuasion.[73] Their defensive attitude toward biology implies a misunderstanding of the close connection between materiality and culture. No spiritual phenomenon could last for long if it were not underpinned by biological facts.[74] She detects an internal contradiction in the approach of socialist-oriented feminists: on the one hand, they claim to endorse materialism, but, on the other, they categorically

---

[72] Christa Mulack, *Natürlich weiblich. Die Heimatlosigkeit der Frau im Patriarchat* [Naturally feminine: The homelessness of woman in the patriarchate] (Stuttgart, 1990), 85.

[73] Ibid., 15.

[74] Ibid., 89.

deny the relevance of the natural plane of reality.[75] Regarding feminist calls to abolish the differences between the sexes and to replace natural with technological gestation, Mulack observes: "The hostility toward females and the male-centeredness of these statements is beyond description."[76]

Precisely the potentialities of modern genetic technology have led, in some feminist quarters, to a rethinking of the feminine nature and a higher estimation of inherent natural attributes in general. Barbara Sichtermann thinks:

> Only since the danger has arisen that manipulation of, and through, our genetic make-up might actually occur have we once again accepted that our genetic make-up *exists*. Inscribed in it is the quality of having a sex. Does this inscription not, after all, mean more to an individual than privileges or discrimination? It is about time that this "more" were defined—even in the context of the emancipation of women—in such a way as to disclose an opportunity even if remaining a limitation."[77]

Again, Christa Mulack: "To deny man's biological dimension" in order to avoid the possible danger of biologism "would be equivalent to cutting off heads in order to cure headaches."[78]

Mulack cites a whole series of aspects in which women are superior to men: On the biological level, women alone are capable of bearing and nourishing children. Along with a superior sexual capacity, they have a higher life-expectancy and a greater resistance to disease. On the psychological level, women are more sensitive and more intuitive and, on the social level, more considerate and more cooperative. On the intellectual level, women are capable of a more comprehensive kind of perception and are

---

[75] Ibid., 87.

[76] Ibid., 33.

[77] Barbara Sichtermann, *Wer ist wie? Über den Unterschied der Geschlechter* [Who is what? On the difference between the sexes] (Berlin, 1987), 16.

[78] Mulack, 35.

less inclined to break reality up into separate fragments.[79]

From this position, Mulack objects to the notions of the equality, the equal rights, and even the equal worth of the sexes. Men and women are not of equal value, because women, when freed from constraints on independent action, are far superior to men.[80] Under an egalitarian education system, as in coeducation, girls are disadvantaged, since the more aggressive boys in the class attract the teacher's attention much more readily than do the more reserved girls.[81] It also makes sense that work be divided on sex-specific lines, for there has never been a unisex culture in the history of mankind.[82] Quotas for participation in kinds of work more suited to males are not worth striving for. Self-confident women, according to Mulack, "couldn't care less about these proffered sharings in patriarchal power, about the right to enjoy sexual freedom and promiscuity, to read and watch pornography, . . . to haul bricks for buildings or to pollute the environment. . . . As well, they decline the prospect of being admitted, from now on, to active defense of the fatherland."[83]

The rediscovery of the female nature in "gynocentric feminism", while praiseworthy in itself, is often linked to a devaluation of the masculine. Mulack regards the male as a divergence from the basic, female sex. This claim rests mainly on possible kinds of defects in the development of embryos: if production, in male embryos, of the specific sex hormones is inhibited, then female sex organs develop. Mulack claims support from the American anthropologist Ashley Montagu, who, in the late 1960s, had already spoken of a natural superiority of women. Montagu traced the stronger average resistance to disease shown by women to the fact that the two X-chromosomes are more inclusive

---

[79] Ibid., 50.
[80] Ibid., 13, 19–55.
[81] Ibid., 201–25.
[82] Ibid., 40.
[83] Ibid., 51.

than the XY-chromosome combination in males. Whereas 20 to 50 percent more boys are conceived than girls, the higher death rate among male children results in roughly balanced numbers of survivors.[84] The priority of woman, according to Mulack, is also indicated, for instance, by the female egg cell, which is 200,000 times larger than the male sperm cell.[85] At least 70 percent of all political positions should be filled by women, since they have to represent children as well as themselves.[86]

The preference shown for lesbianism over marriage[87] —which is unfortunately found not just in Mulack—is also highly problematic. Primarily in gynocentric feminism, but also in androgynous currents, this standpoint, while not simply representative of the whole, is nonetheless very widespread. "From the beginning, lesbians have played a central role in the women's movement; they were usually its sustaining and driving forces."[88] They have attracted many adherents, especially in the USA, where feminism has been particularly strong in demanding full equivalence of "sex roles", even in the sexual sphere. Lesbian women often see themselves as the very spearhead of the feminist movement. According to a well-known slogan of American lesbianism, "feminism [is] the theory, and lesbianism the practice."[89] Even if the majority of feminists cannot be identified with this, lesbianism nevertheless enjoys at least a well-disposed tolerance among them.[90]

The "quarrel among sisters" about the significance of

---

[84] Ashley Montagu, *The Natural Superiority of Women,* 2d ed. (New York and London, 1968), 70–84; cf. Sullerot, 87, 383ff.

[85] Mulack, 91.

[86] Ibid., 29f.

[87] Ibid., 239 passim.

[88] Monika Barz, Herta Leistner, and Ute Wild, eds., *Hättest du gedacht, daß wir so viele sind? Lesbische Frauen in der Kirche* [Would you ever have thought there were so many of us? Lesbian women in the Church] (Zurich, 1987), 80.

[89] Menschik, 55.

[90] Schenk, 127f.; Barz, 78–81.

the feminine is related to the debate about the concept of "androgyny", or of "man-womanliness". The suggestion here is that the traits constituting psychological and social differences between the sexes should no longer be evident in contrasts between men and women but should all be uniformly integrated into each individual person. Elisabeth Badinter, a French feminist, even flirts with the possibility of men undergoing pregnancy.[91] In child-raising, housework, and employment, there must no longer be any differences between boys and girls, between men and women. "The tension between the . . . poles of 'masculine' and 'feminine' attributes would henceforth exist only in the individual person and no longer between groups."[92] Everyone is to realize within himself—and as far as possible to an equal degree—the attributes that had previously been regarded as masculine or feminine. The androgynous ideal remains characteristic of the mainstream of present-day feminism.[93]

The term "androgyny" is nevertheless avoided by some feminists. Rosemary Ruether, for instance, sees it as still suggesting the existence of masculine and feminine qualities, which she disputes. It would be better, she thinks, to speak of "psychic integration" or "wholeness".[94]

Other feminists dissociate themselves from the notion of "androgyny" because they give preference to the "feminine" qualities and regard the autonomous female being as their ideal:[95] "gynocentric feminism". Even when this

[91] Elisabeth Badinter, *Ich bin Du. Die neue Beziehung zwischen Mann und Frau oder Die androgyne Revolution* [I am you: The new relationship between man and woman, or the androgynous revolution] (Munich, 1987), 267-69.

[92] Schenk, 205.

[93] Cf. Menschik, 60-66; Schenk, 204f.; Padberg (1985), 82, 104; Meyer-Wilmes, 93; Mulack, 12f., 19f., 31f.

[94] R. R. Ruether, *Sexism and God-talk: Toward a Feminist Theology* (Boston, 1983, 1993), 110-13. Cf. Catharina Halkes, *Suchen, was verlorenging. Beiträge zur feministischen Theologie* [Seeking what was lost: Contributions to feminist theology] (Gütersloh, 1985), 19-21.

[95] Cf. Menschik, 60; Mary Daly, *Gyn/Ecology: The Metaethics of Radical Feminism* (Boston, 1978), 1ff.

does not expressly occur, so-called "feminine" values are brought to the fore as guides for shaping the future and are accentuated in contrast to negatively treated "masculine" ones. For example, the neo-Marxist and "Frankfurt School" theorist Herbert Marcuse (whom feminists are fond of quoting) plays the "feminine" "pleasure principle" off against the "masculine" "achievement principle" and identifies as especially positive the qualities of "receptivity, sensitivity, nonviolence, tenderness".[96] Herrad Schenck speaks of the universal goal of "feminizing the systems of norms and values of society as a whole".[97]

Sharply rejected, in any case, is the notion that men and women should complement each other. Any complementarity or polarity, any differentiation between people, men and women, is inevitably seen as implying a reinforcement of the patriarchate.[98] Christa Mulack's statements, which, with those of some other female writers, tend in a different direction, are not (at least so far) typical. The new insistence on a specific femininity seems to have emerged less clearly in the Anglo-Saxon and German-speaking areas than in France—Luce Irigaray may be noted as just one example here—and in Italy.[99] In France, a certain role in this has been played by a scientific colloquium on the "Reality of Woman" (*Le fait féminin*), which was organized by Evelyne Sullerot and whose conclusions were published in 1978. In her recapitulatory introduction, Sullerot, a professor of the sociology of women (and not classifiable as a feminist), stresses the great importance of genetically based differences, which also have an influence on social life. This by no means implies, however, that one sex is superior to the other.[100]

---

[96] Herbert Marcuse, "Marxismus und Feminismus", *Jahrbuch Politik* 6 (Berlin, 1974): 91f.; Padbert (1985), 84f.

[97] Schenk, 204.

[98] Ibid., 188f.; Padberg (1985), 100.

[99] On Irigaray (briefly): Wb, 66, 82, 197f.; on Italy: Mulack, 80; Wb, 293.

[100] Sullerot, 17–30.

6. Connections with the "New Age"

In the beginning, the thing that bound all feminists together was the struggle for legalization of abortion. Historians of feminism see this as the "real melting-pot" in which the new women's movement was produced.[101]

After this initial phase, and pursuant to the American example, so-called self-experience groups became the focus of much interest. "In a logical progression from having laid claim to one's own abdomen, one's own feelings were now at the forefront."[102] As a third, and currently dominant, phase, we see the development of a full-blown feminist subculture, with "women's projects" of all kinds, from health centers and women's refuges to magazines and "autonomous bookstores".[103]

That there is an affinity between feminism and the political party of the "Greens" is generally known. A close association has also come about with the so-called "New Age" movement, whose primary origin can be found in the California of the 1970s.[104] Fritjof Capra, one of the main protagonists of the "New Age", praises the "feminist movement" as providing a most profound impetus to the "new age".[105]

---

[101] Schenk, 87; cf. Padberg (1985), 71.

[102] Padberg (1985), 71.

[103] Ibid., 72-74.

[104] H.-J. Ruppert, *New Age. Endzeit oder Wendezeit?* [New Age: Concluding phase or transitional period?] (Wiesbaden, 1985); Lutz von Padberg, *New Age und Feminismus* [New Age and feminism] (Asslar, 1987); Josef Sudbrack, *Neue Religiosität—Herausforderung für Christen* [The new religiosity: A challenge for Christians] (Mainz, 1987); Martie Dieperink, *New Age en christelijk geloof. Over de invloed van New Age op de Kerk,* 3d ed. (1990), 83-94; B. Haneke and K. Huttner, *Spirituelle Aufbrüche: New Age und "Neue Religiosität" als Herausforderung an Kirche und Gesellschaft* [Spiritual departures: New Age and "New Religiosity" as challenge to Church and society] (Regensburg, 1991). For a syncretistic perspective, see Susanne Schaup, *Wandel des Weiblichen. Der Aufbruch der Frau ins New Age* [Evolving of the feminine: Women's journey into the New Age] (Freiburg, 1988).

[105] Fritjof Capra, *Wendezeit. Bausteine für ein neues Weltbild* [Pivotal

Talk of the "new age" was originally based on astrology. After the so-called Platonic year, the sun requires 25,200 years in order—as seen by us—to pass through the entire zodiac. For every sign of the zodiac, a period of 2,100 years is assumed. The sign of the Fish (Pisces), which still rules at present, corresponds to Christianity. It is to be succeeded, however, by the sign of the Water Bearer (Aquarius), which will usher in a new world unity. Other names for the age of the Water Bearer are the "Aquarian" and the "ecological" age. Estimations of its starting point vary: for example, the beginning of 1950 (Alfons Rosenberg), or 1997 or 2143 (C. G. Jung).[106]

Presupposed in this astrological interpretation is an untenable determinism—that is, the notion that socio-cultural development is governed by the influence of the stars. Human freedom does not enter the picture here. One need test nothing more in this conception than its internal consistency to see that the astrological linkage of intellectual culture and star signs is sheer nonsense. Its very astronomical foundations are defective, for, as a result of the precession of equinoxes, the signs of the zodiac no longer coincide with their appropriate constellations.[107]

Talk of the "New Age" and the "Age of Aquarius" had its origin in the esoteric doctrines of the spiritualist medium Alice Ann Bailey, who died in 1949.[108] Bailey, whose first marriage was to a Protestant minister, claimed to derive her inspirations from the dictations of spirit beings. In 1922, she founded a society called the Lucifer Publishing

---

times: Building blocks for a new cosmology], 10th ed. (Bern, 1985), 24f. 469-72.

[106] Ruppert, 12f.

[107] Ibid., 12.

[108] On what follows here, cf. ibid., 29-33; 98-103; Constance Cumbey, *Die sanfte Verschwörung. Hintergrund und Gefahren der New-Age-Bewegung* [The gentle conspiracy: Background and dangers of the New Age movement], 5th ed. (Asslar, 1987), passim.

Company, changed in 1923 to the Lucifer Trust. In her writings, she glorifies the devil, proclaims the self-redemption of man, and heralds the new religion of world unity. To Alice Bailey, the multihued rainbow, the most important emblem of the New Age movement, signifies the bridge between the Spiritual Hierarchy and men, or, in biblical terms, the giving of oneself over to demons. She claims allegiance to Christ yet calls, at the same time, for the destruction of the Catholic Church; to counter her influence, she regards even the use of atom bombs as appropriate.[109] The far-spread "Great Invocation", the "Great Appeal", which is to usher in the humanism of "One World", is understood, not as a prayer, but more as a conjuring up of magical forces.[110]

Also consignable to this milieu of spiritualism and occultism is the "witches movement", which is widespread in the radical wing of feminism. Referring to oneself as a "witch" can be simply an oblique way of protesting against patriarchalism. But it can also signify a practicing of magical rites based on an energistic notion of the world: the world as a field of forces that one can influence by magical practices.[111]

The New Age movement is not a uniform trend but a conglomerate of quite different ideas and practices. Relevant writings are often shelved in bookstores under the heading "Esotericism". Since the notions involved here are often of a broadly religious kind, reference is also made to a "New Religiosity". Common to the New Age intellectual

---

[109] Cumbey, 75f.

[110] Cf. Ruppert, 50f.

[111] On the present-day witches' movement, cf. H.-J. Ruppert, *Die Hexen kommen: Magie und Hexenglauben heute* [The witches are coming: Magic and belief in witches today] (Wiesbaden, 1987). Concise historical information is given in Gerhard Schormann, "Hexen" [Witches], TRE 15 (1986): 297–304. Seemingly more realistic than Ruppert's assessment, in which occultism is presented as a purely inner-psychic phenomenon, is the evaluation (based on painful first-hand experience) by Dieperink, 95–100.

outlook is a tendency to monism and pantheism—that is, there is no difference, at the ontological level, between God and man.[112] The world did not come about through a creative act originating in God's free love but is identical with God. Typical of this mentality is the so-called "First National Conference for Women's Spirituality", held in Boston in 1976. There, women danced bare-breasted in the church, chanting "The goddess lives!" and "Being a woman is divine." One recommendation by this conference was that women should set up altars with mirrors in their homes so as to be constantly reminded that they are the goddess.[113]

In this philosophy, inner communion with God is not a gift that comes from God's personal love and was reinstated, after the fall, by Christ but is a constantly existent matter of course. Immersion in one's own ego is the decisive path to self-redemption.

The basic ideas of this "New Religiosity" are by no means new. Much in them is nothing but a revival of ancient paganism, which is why the "New Age" has been called "old age philosophy".[114] Numerous aspects of it are reminiscent of the ancient Gnostic movement. The Gnostics hoped to achieve release from the prison of the material world through "knowledge" (Greek: *gnosis*), or, as it would be expressed today, through "expanded consciousness". Ontologically, God and man are not distinguished. In the Gnostics, we already find the androgyne ideal and the practice of referring to God in terms of both masculine and feminine attributes.[115] There is thus nothing surprising in the fact that ancient Gnosticism has been rediscovered and commemorated in hymns of highest praise in feminist circles. (More will be said about this later.) Many observers therefore characterize the New Age movement as a

---

[112] Ruppert, *New Age,* 19, passim; Sudbrack, 21f.

[113] Naomi Goldenberg, *Changing of the Gods: Feminism and the End of Traditional Religions* (Boston, 1979), 92, 94, as cited in Ferreira (1989), 8.

[114] Ruppert, *New Age,* 21.

[115] Hauke, *Women in the Priesthood?,* 158–65.

"neo-Gnosticism" centered on the idea of self-redemption.[116] Man no longer wants to be beholden to God for his existence but worships himself as the supreme being. From the Christian viewpoint, this way of thinking has come under the sway of Satan, who, according to Genesis, seduced the first humans with the enticement "You will be like God" (Gen 3:5).

Christianity, too, promises the man who heeds God that he will gain participation in divine life. From God's side, however, this participation is a gift. Man can open himself to this grace and play a cooperative role through what he is granted—but he cannot attain salvation by his own autonomous efforts.

Prior to this God-given redemption is creation, an aspect of which is creation as man or woman. For Christians, this sexual attribute is no blind accident of evolution but the good creation of a God who loves us. Faith in creation is a decisive criterion for assessing modern feminism from a Christian perspective. Tendencies to suppress and surmount being a man or a woman are incompatible with being a Christian. But more will be said about that later.

---

[116] For example, Ruppert, *New Age,* 18; Sudbrack, 130; 155f.

III. DEVELOPMENT AND DISTINCTIVENESS OF FEMINIST THEOLOGY

1. The Basic Concern

Feminism is opposed to the conventional association of males with positions of leadership in society, which it brands as "patriarchalism" and "sexism". Feminist theology goes on to apply the basic form of this feminist critique to the sphere of religion. Regarded as the deepest foundation and expression of the hegemony of males is the image of God, which must be freed of one-sidedly masculine symbols like "Father", "Lord", and "King". Only then will the "male Church" disappear. Alongside the "our Father", some then place an "our Mother"; "Jesus Christ" is supplemented by "Jesa Christa"; while the third Divine Person appears as the "Holy Spiritess".[1]

2. The Relationship to Marxism

The intellectual origin of modern feminism lies (as was explained earlier) in a radicalization of Marxism. A definitive role in this was played by the student movement at the end of the 1960s. The close alliance between neo-Marxism and feminism, which was promoted, for example, by Herbert Marcuse,[2] persists within feminist theology. As leading feminist theologians stress, they have been strongly influenced by the Marxist system and pursue political links with

---

[1] Cf. below, 144.
[2] Cf. above, 43.

socialism. Among them, however, the Marxist contrast
between oppressor and oppressed is given more radical
form than in Marxism itself: all forms of rule by man over
man, says Catharina Halkes, are "manifestations of that
one dualism . . . which is the most profound of all: the
elevation of the male sex over the female".[3]

To cite a first example: from the very start, one of the
most important writers in the area of feminist theology has
been the Catholic theologian Rosemary Radford Ruether,
since 1976 a professor at a Protestant theological college in
the USA.[4] Despite the widespread interest in feminism,
this professorship represents the sole chair in feminist theology in the United States.[5] In 1975, Ruether described
the relevant book by Friedrich Engels, written in the nineteenth century, as *the* fundamental text for consistent
feminists, sympathized with the developments immediately
following the Russian revolution, and praised the China
of Mao Tse-Tung. Her aim is a "democratic" or "com-
munitarian" "socialism".[6] What is meant by this is not,
to be sure, practical socialism, whose bankruptcy has meanwhile become obvious, but a utopian scheme that Ruether,
in 1983, wanted to see combined with liberal and gynocentric elements.[7] "True" socialism was something still to
come.

---

[3] Catharina Halkes, *Gott hat nicht nur starke Söhne. Grundzüge
einer feministischen Theologie* |God has not only strong sons: Basic
elements of a feminist theology|, 4th ed. (Gütersloh, 1985), 30.

[4] R. R. Ruether, *Sexism,* cover text; *Concilium* 27 (1991): 460;
autobiography: R. R. Ruether, *Disputed Questions: On Being a Christian*
(Nashville, Tenn., 1982; New York, 1989).

[5] At least according to Meyer-Wilmes, 232, n. 14; according to
Concilium 27 (1991): 460, it is a chair in "applied theology".

[6] R. R. Ruether, *New Woman—New Earth: Sexist Ideologies and
Human Liberation* (New York, 1975), 162, 173ff., 204ff.

[7] Ruether, *Sexism,* 227f., 232ff.; on Ruether's Marxist stamp, cf. Elke
Axmacher, "Feministisch von Gott reden? Eine Auseinandersetzung mit
Rosemary Radford Ruethers Buch 'Sexismus und die Rede von Gott' "
|Feminist talk with God? A quarrel with Rosemary Radford Ruether's

A further example of flirtation with Marxist ideas is provided by Catharina Halkes, a Dutch woman. Prior to receiving emeritus status in 1986, she held a chair in Issues in Feminist Theology at the Catholic University of Nijmegen. Feminism and socialism—as she repeatedly stressed with a well-disposed glance toward Herbert Marcuse—belong together, even if feminism is the more fundamental of the two.[8] Hedwig Meyer-Wilmes, an assistant professor who succeeded Halkes, devotes a recent work to attempting to reduce the difference between two well-known feminist theologians to the following formula: the one (Elisabeth Schüssler Fiorenza) is "critical-Marxist", and the other (Rosemary Radford Ruether), "orthodox-Marxist".[9]

A certain turn away from the Marxist image of man and its sociological constrictions suggests itself, however, in feminist-theological currents influenced by gynocentric feminism, an example of which, in the German-speaking sphere, is the Protestant theologian Christa Mulack.[10] Other authors vacillate in their standpoint, as, for instance, Meyer-Wilmes: on the one hand, she regards the difference between man and woman as an ontological, metaphysical reality;[11] but, on the other, she inveighs against any talk of an "essence of woman".[12] At any rate, things have developed to the point that the international journal *Concilium,* which has promoted feminist theology since the mid-1970s, published a special issue in 1991 under the heading "An Essence of Woman?" In a philosophical sense, this question about an essence concerns "what makes a

---

book *Sexism and God-talk*], *Zeitschrift für Evangelische Ethik* 35 (1991): 15, n. 21.

[8] Halkes, *Söhne,* 27–30; 89; 117.

[9] Meyer-Wilmes, 218f. Whether this distinction will gain currency is an open question.

[10] Mulack, *Natürlich weiblich.*

[11] Meyer-Wilmes, 91–93.

[12] Ibid., 79, 141, passim.

thing what it is": Are there certain qualities, remaining constant throughout all cultures, that constitute being a woman? Implied in any purely sociological approach is a negative answer to this question, which corresponds to the fact that most of the authors in the above-noted issue of *Concilium* energetically reject any talk of an "essence" of woman.[13] Still, it is remarkable that this question should be posed at all in one of the most influential media-organs of a theology that describes itself as "progressive"—and not the least pertinent explanation for this is the twilight of the gods into which Marxism has been increasingly vanishing. The Marxist inspiration nevertheless remains determinative, even if not at first glance recognizable to "unschooled" observers.

3. Historical Development

The first gathering of feminist theologians took place in the 1970s in the USA.[14] If one wishes to establish an approximate date of birth for feminist theology, that would be best set as coinciding with the appearance of Mary Daly's book *Beyond God the Father* in 1973.[15] This publication continues to be regarded in feminist circles as "the classic from the initial years";[16] Daly herself is rightly described as the "foster-mother" of feminist

---

[13] *Concilium* 27 (6/1991).

[14] Herlinde Pissarek-Hudelist, "Feministische Theologie—eine Herausforderung?" [Feminist theology—a challenge?], ZKTh 103 (1981): 300; "Feministische Theologie—eine Herausforderung an Kirche und Theologie?" [Feminist theology—a challenge for the Church and theology?], in Wolfgang Beinert, ed., *Frauenbefreiung und Kirche. Darstellung—Analyse—Dokumentation* [Women's liberation and the Church: Survey—analysis—documentation] (Regensburg, 1987), 19.

[15] Mary Daly, *Beyond God the Father: Toward a Philosophy of Women's Liberation* (Boston, 1973).

[16] Halkes, *Söhne*, 36.

theology.[17] "Within the feminist-theological debate", according to Meyer-Wilmes, "her position carries so much weight that all those participating in it refer, and must refer, to it."[18] The development of Mary Daly's ideas will therefore be examined separately following this more general survey of feminist theology.

Feminist theology, as it emerged in the USA of the 1970s, was able to link up with ideas from the early stages of the American women's movement. Repeatedly mentioned here, in particular, is *The Women's Bible,* edited by Elizabeth Cady Stanton in 1895 and 1898. Stanton, head of a committee of twenty participants in the movement for voting rights (suffragettes), denies the revelatory quality of the Bible, which she regards as a product of males, and she suspects it (not wholly without reason in the America of that day) of being a weapon against the emancipation of women. People concerned themselves with the Bible because they saw religion as a main basis for the oppression of women. The two-volume *Women's Bible* brings together scriptural texts on women, presented in new translation, and also provides a critical commentary. Some of the Bible's fundamental religious statements are, to be sure, good—for example, the commandment to love. But Scripture as a whole suffers from a male-centeredness.[19]

By no means the least of factors behind the emergence of feminist theology in the Catholic sphere was commitment to the cause of women in the priesthood. A Swiss

---

[17] Ingeborg Hauschildt, "Die Verunsicherung der Gemeinden durch die Feministische Theologie" [The creation of uncertainty in the churches by feminist theology], in Peter Beyerhaus, ed., *Frauen im theologischen Aufstand. Eine Orientierungshilfe zur "Feministischen Theologie"* [Women in theological revolt: A guidebook to "feminist theology"], Wort und Wissen 14 (Neuhausen and Stuttgart, 1983), 22.

[18] Meyer-Wilmes, 143.

[19] Elisabeth Schüssler Fiorenza, *In Memory of Her: A Feminist Theological Reconstruction of Christian Origins* (New York, 1983), 7–14.

jurist who published a petition for Vatican II in support of the ordination of women claims that her act marked the "beginning" of feminist theology.[20] This piece of self-appraisal can probably be regarded as exaggerated.[21] Its allusion to the significance of the issue of ordination to the priesthood is, however, correct. Above all in the USA, the movement for women priests is still an important catalyst that has affected the nature of feminist theology.[22] Of course, many feminists do not at all wish to hold an office which, as such, bolsters oppressive structures. Others want to force their way into the "patriarchal structure" in order to change it from within.[23] Characteristic of the USA is the large number of radical nuns who have often served as forerunners even of secular feminism.[24] That the members of women's religious orders in Germany normally reject feminism has been noted with great regret by feminist theologians.[25]

In the mid-1970s, feminist theology also gained a foothold in Europe. A not insignificant role was played here by the organizational structure of the World Council of Churches, whose "Department for the Collaboration of Men and Women" held a conference in 1974, in Berlin, on "sexism". At that conference, Pauline Webb, a member

---

[20] Gertrud Heinzelmann, *Die geheiligte Diskriminierung. Beiträge zum kirchlichen Feminismus* [Sanctified discrimination: Contributions to Church-oriented feminism] (Bonstetten, 1986), 90.

[21] Meyer-Wilmes, 34f.

[22] Pissarek-Hudelist (1981), 301; Hauke, *Women in the Priesthood?,* 62f.; Ida Raming, *Frauenbewegung und Kirche. Bilanz eines 25jährigen Kampfes für Gleichberechtigung und Befreiung der Frau seit dem Zweiten Vatikanischen Konzil* [The women's movement and the Church: Assessing the 25-year struggle for equal rights and the liberation of women since the Second Vatican Council] (Weinheim, 1989); Carr, 59–79.

[23] Halkes, *Söhne,* 45; Raming, 88–92; see also 183.

[24] Barbara Haber, *Women in America: A Guide to Books, 1963-1975* (Boston, 1978), 155; Regine Hauch, "Neue Nonnen. Es gärt in Amerikas Frauenorden" [New nuns: It is seething in America's convents], *Neue Ordnung* 41 (1987): 374–81.

[25] Raming, 99–102.

of the central committee of the Ecumenical Council of Churches, gave a semiofficial definition of the concept of "sexism": "By sexism we understand any sort of subordination or devaluation of a person or a group solely on the basis of sex."[26] Another participant in the sexism conference, the general secretary of the World Council of Churches, Philipp Potter, branded the according of any sort of social precedence to men as "demonic".[27]

The function of the husband as the "head" in marriage, which is spoken of in the Pauline letters as part of the order of creation, will be discussed in detail later. To be stressed already here, however, is the fact that feminism views this role allocation as equivalent to a degrading of the wife and "demonizes" it in the truest sense of the word.

---

[26] Pauline Webb, "Address at the Public Meeting", in *Sexism in the 1970s: Discrimination against Women. A Report of a World Council of Churches Consultation, West Berlin, 1974* (Geneva, 1975), 10.

[27] Philipp Potter, "Address at the Public Meeting", *Sexism,* 31. Indicative of currently held opinion is the so-called "Sheffield Report": C. F. Parvey, ed., *Die Gemeinschaft von Frauen und Männern in der Kirche* [The community of women and men in the Church] (Neukirchen and Vluyn, 1985). On the World Council of Churches, cf. also Meyer-Wilmes, 20–24; Veronika Prüller, *Wir Frauen sind Kirche—worauf warten wir noch? Feministische Kirchenträume. Anregungen für das Leben in christlichen Gemeinden* [We women are the Church—What are we waiting for? Feminist dreams of the Church: Suggestions for life in Christian communions] (Freiburg, 1992), 43–61; Janet Crawford, "The Community of Women and Men in the Church: Where Are We Now?", *Ecumenical Review* 40 (1988): 37–47; Mercy Oduyoye, "Frauendekade 1988–1998" [Women's decade 1988–1998], *Ökumenische Rundschau* 37 (1988): 257–70; the appearance of a Korean feminist (Chung Hyung Kyung) who invoked the ancestral spirits as "icons of Holy Ruach" at the seventh General Assembly of the World Council of Churches in Canberra, and the reactions to this, are discussed in several essays in *Una Sancta* 46 (2/1991). A decided feminist, Marga Bührig, was a member of the executive committee of the World Council of Churches in 1983. Cf. Marga Bührig, *Die unsichtbar Frau und der Gott der Väter. Eine Einführung in die feministische Theologie* [The invisible woman and the God of the Fathers: An introduction to feminist theology] (Stuttgart, 1987); and her *Spät habe ich gelernt, gerne Frau zu sein. Eine feministische Autobiographie* [Late have I learned to like being a woman: A feminist autobiography], 3d ed. (Stuttgart, 1988).

In the accepted definitions of "sexism", "devaluation of women" and marital subordination are one and the same thing.[28]

A precondition for feminism's penetration of the World Council of Churches was the World Conference of Churches in Uppsala in 1968, at which "liberation theology" gained prominence and subsequently exerted a high degree of influence on the further work of ecumenism in Geneva.[29] Feminist theologians emphasize again and again their closeness to "liberation theology".[30] Feminist theology and liberation theology are seen as "genitive theologies" (theologies *of* women, *of* the oppressed). Both select for themselves one partial area of theological reflection and make it their all-determining central point. Just as liberation theology is to be pursued by the oppressed and for the oppressed, so feminist theology is to be pursued by women and for women. Like liberation theology, theological feminism understands itself as "contextual theology", that is, theology that is to be developed in relation to a quite specific kind of social context. Liberation theologians claim the right to the "partiality" of adopting the standpoint of the "poor", who are usually understood in the sense of the Marxist proletariat;[31] feminist theologians make the femi-

---

[28] Cf. also, for example, Angela Bauer, "Sexismus" [Sexism], in Wb, 367-70.

[29] Cf. Gottfried Hoffman, *Der Ökumenismus heute. Geschichte— Kritik—Wegweisung* [Ecumenism today: History—criticism—future directions] (Stein am Rhein, 1978), 63ff.; Hanfried Krüger, "Werden und Wachsen des Ökumenischen Rates der Kirchen" [Development and growth of the Ecumenical Council of Churches], in H. J. Urban and H. Wagner, eds., *Handbuch der Ökumenik* 2 (Paderborn, 1986), 59-61.

[30] Renate Rieger, "Befreiungstheologie" [Liberation theology], in Wb, 39-44.

[31] Anton Rauscher, *Kirche in der Welt. Beiträge zur christlichen Gesellschaftsverantwortung* 1 [Church in the world: Essays on Christian social responsibility] (Würzburg, 1988), 397-476. The significance of Marxism as a so-called "social-scientific method" is still emphasized even

nine slant on life, or so-called female "experience", the standard for theologizing. The experience of women, we read in the *Wörterbuch der Feministischen Theologie* [Dictionary of feminist theology], is both the "source" of and "criterion" for theological judgments.[32]

Halkes formulates this perspectival aspect even more clearly: "You, rebellious women, are the theme and subjects of this theology, and you make your relationship with God and the divine the central object of your theology."[33]

Even so, the term "theology", in the feminist view, needs to be used with a certain caution. According to Hedwig Meyer-Wilmes, feminist theology operates on the borderline between scholarship and political activism. "Border crossings" are virtually constitutive of it, which poses an obstacle to its being seriously classified as a science.[34] According to Catharina Halkes, theological feminism is characterized by "a less straightforward and logically consistent kind of thought" than in the "old theology", which is accused of an extreme, distorting intellectualism. To be desired instead is "an inventive, improvised kind of activity, less objectivity and more ambiguity".[35] The place of "theo-logy" (reasoned discourse about God), according to the wish of many authors, is to be taken by "theo-fantasy" or "theo-poesy".[36] The

---

today by Raúl Fernet-Betancourt, "Marxismus", in Horst Goldstein, ed., *Kleines Lexikon zur Theologie der Befreiung* [Concise lexicon of liberation theology] (Düsseldorf, 1991), 146–50.

[32] Christine Schaumberger, "Erfahrung" [Experience], in Wb, 73–78; cf. below, 118–34.

[33] Halkes, *Söhne,* 32.

[34] Meyer-Wilmes, 7, 76, 145f.

[35] Halkes, *Söhne,* 36, 73.

[36] Elisabeth Moltmann-Wendel, *Ein eigener Mensch werden. Frauen um Jesus* [Becoming one's own person: Women around Jesus], 4th ed. (Gütersloh, 1984), 17f.; Ruth Habermann and Dorothee Sölle, "Phantasie" [Imagination], in Wb, 326f.

feminists who worship a "goddess" speak also of "thealogy" and "theasophy".[37]

Since 1976, feminist theology has been promoted in widely circulated periodicals from the "progressive camp" of the Catholic Church. Here, the start was made, at the worldwide level, by the aforementioned journal *Concilium*. In 1977, Halkes was appointed to a special chair in "feminism and Christianity" at the Catholic University of Nijmegen. In 1980, her paperback *Gott hat nicht nur starke Söhne* [God has not only strong sons] appeared and subsequently became a best-seller.[38] The current spreading of feminist theology in Germany can probably be traced back mainly to this initial source. Along with Halkes—whose book was issued by a Protestant publisher—the Protestant Elisabeth Moltmann-Wendel is probably the most influential feminist theologian in Central Europe. Moltmann-Wendel is the wife of the Tübingen professor of systematic theology Jürgen Moltmann, one of the leading spokesmen of so-called "political theology", which is closely related to liberation theology. The annual meetings of the Evangelical Academy of Bad Boll, which were inaugurated by Mrs. Moltmann-Wendel, have become especially effective in promoting relevant ideas.[39]

At the University of Nijmegen, feminist theology is regarded as a major course of study, enrollment in which is mandatory for all students of theology.[40] The relevant teaching position is currently held by the already-mentioned Münster theologian Hedwig Meyer-Wilmes, who assumed those duties before completing her doctoral studies. There is also a professorial chair in this subject, to which new appointments are regularly made on a rotational basis. The quite special conditions existing at Nijmegen account

---

[37] Catharina Halkes, "Theologie, feministische", in FLex, 1102.

[38] Halkes, *Söhne*.

[39] Pissarek-Hudelist (1981), 289, n. 3.

[40] On the situation in Nijmegen, cf. Meyer-Wilmes, 68–75.

for the fact that, while the responsible high chancellor of the university (Cardinal Simonis) did not approve the academic appointments of the feminists, the Faculty of Theology nevertheless acted in disregard of this canonical obstacle.[41]

In German-speaking countries, feminist theology is sometimes introduced into theological faculties as a research topic or lecture subject.[42] The Faculty of Catholic Theology in Bonn has plans for a chair in women's studies, which would, one can hardly doubt, have a feminist orientation if actually instituted. The Faculty of Catholic Theology at the University of Münster even advertised a position directly described as a "Chair in Feminist Theology", to be filled from the autumn of 1992.[43] To my knowledge, no public protest, especially against the latter of these positions, has so far been made (by, for example, the responsible bishop).

In the Protestant sphere, by contrast, the move by the Evangelical Church in Germany to set up a "Center for Women's Studies and Culture" in Gelnhausen (near Fulda) was met with strenuous resistance. The reason for this? Two well-known feminists had been appointed as the center's directors.[44] The public protest made by eight female Protestant professors of theology also merits consideration by those in the Catholic sphere:

> With the appointment of two confirmed representatives of feminism and feminist theology to these positions, the ear-

---

[41] J. P. M. van der Ploeg, "Die theologische Fakultät der katholischen Universität Nijmegen" [The theological faculty of the Catholic University of Nijmegen], *Theologisches* 22 (1992): 504.

[42] Meyer-Wilmes, 63–67, 232, n. 14.

[43] According to circulars sent to the deans of the Catholic theological faculties in Germany.

[44] The Frankfurt minister Renate Jost and the educator from Bad Boll Herta Leistner who, among other things, has been an energetic campaigner for lesbian partnerships: Barz, Leistner, and Wild; hotly debated: *EKD–Frauenzentrum, idea-Dokumentation,* 10/93 (Wetzlar, 1993).

lier commitment that the center would be there to serve the interests of all women, "independently of theological orientation" and "style of piety", has fallen by the wayside. The female theologians object that the council's decision to establish the study center also amounted to a step toward the "institutionalization of feminist theology". In the past, such a step has been consistently rejected by the Protestant theological faculties. The proper locus for the posing of questions by women, as well as women's engagement in theology, is the system of teaching and research that includes both men and women.[45]

Since the 1980s, various feminist-theological periodicals have appeared on the scene—in the German-speaking sphere, two at once (*Schlangenbrut* [Brood of vipers] in Münster, since 1983, and *Fama* in Basel, since 1985)—along with a whole series of so-called "networks" aimed at putting feminist theology into practice.[46]

4. Divergent Directions

Feminist theology is not a unified phenomenon. In particu-

---

[45] *EKD–Frauenzentrum,* 18; some renowned male professors of theology (who are not to be classed in the evangelical spectrum), such as F. W. Graf, M. Hengel, W. Pannenberg, T. Rendtorff, and R. Schröder, have protested in the meantime: *FAZ,* July 19, 1993, 4; *EKD–Frauenzentrum,* passim. According to Martin Hengel, the well-known Tübingen New Testament scholar, the EKD is "at a crossroads: it can take this incident as an occasion to reflect on whether it still today wishes to be the evangelical [Protestant] church. A now obligatory union in faith and ethics with the cultivation of any pious sentiment whatsoever, of sexual 'self-realization', and of fashionable utopias does not deserve the name 'evangelical' or 'church' any more" (ibid., 27).

[46] Christine Schaumberger and Monika Maassen, eds., *Handbuch Feministische Theologie* [Handbook of feminist theology] (Münster, 1986), 116-211; Prüller, 33-42, 212. In the USA, the *Journal of Feminist Studies in Religion* has existed since 1985, and in Great Britain, the journal *Feminist Theology* since 1992.

lar, a distinction is drawn between female theologians who desire, in principle, to remain within the existing framework of Christianity and those who have forsaken the Christian faith as "irretrievably patriarchal".[47] The first main direction, according to Rosemary Ruether, "consists in critically reviewing given historical traditions like Christianity or Judaism. The second attempts to recover a matriarchal, goddess-centered religion believed to have existed at an ancient, prepatriarchal stage of human culture."[48] "Goddess feminism" is the religious offshoot of gynocentric feminism, while its main (and in comparison "moderate") feminist alternative usually embraces the androgyne model.

The boundaries between these two currents, between "moderates" and "radicals", are, of course, fluid.[49] Typical, for example, is the statement by Ursa Krattiger, the translator of the abovementioned book by Halkes: "Whoever has once become a feminist no longer has any choice, in the world as it exists, but . . . to live . . . on the border, where it is no longer so very important whether I am 'still just inside' or 'already just outside'." She approvingly cites Mary Daly, who no longer measures time in terms of "Anno Domini" ["in the year of the Lord"] but introduces a new chronological formula: "Anno Feminarum" ("in the year of women").[50]

The process of breaking through to new perspectives is also stressed by calling attention to one's own "wayfaring" state and shying away from the formation of closed theo-

---

[47] Halkes, *Söhne,* 34–36; Elisabeth Gössmann, *Die streitbaren Schwestern. Was will die Feministische Theologie?* [The quarrelsome sisters: What does feminist theology want?] (Freiburg, 1981), 39.

[48] R. R. Ruether, "Weibliche Symbole und ihr gesellschaftlicher Kontext" [Feminine symbols and their social context], *Reformatio* 36 (1987): 178.

[49] Halkes, *Söhne,* 35f.

[50] Ursa Krattiger, *Die perlmutterne Mönchin. Reise in eine weibliche Spiritualität* [The mother-of-pearl female monk: Journey to a feminine spirituality] (Hamburg, 1987; orig. Zurich, 1983), 83.

logical systems.[51] As Krattiger says, where the path might lead she does not know.[52]

Beyond these two basic groupings within feminist theology—that is, still inside Christianity or already outside it—more precise analytical classification is difficult. Application of various categorical grids produces quite varying results.[53] Classifications are possible, for example, by: (1) area of theological work, (2) type of method employed, or (3) relationship to established feminist principles:

1. Classification by area of theological work.

Among relevant areas of endeavor, feminist theologians show a certain preference for exegesis. Regarding the Old Testament, a special effort is made to highlight the "feminine" symbols of God's nature; while, regarding the New Testament, a history of decline is constructed: at the beginning of the Jesus movement, there was total equality of the sexes; but later on, through formation of a hierarchical system of office and adaptation to the patriarchal family structure, the Church fell away from her egalitarian origins. The best-known advocate of this theory of decline is the German exegete Elisabeth Schüssler Fiorenza, who holds a professorship in New Testament studies in the USA.[54]

Regarding the further history of the Church, an attempt is made to research the deeds and sufferings of women

---

[51] Halkes, *Söhne,* 36; Catharina Halkes and Hedwig Meyer-Wilmes, "Feministische Theologie/Feminismus/Frauenbewegung. I. Im westlichen Kontext" [Feminist theology/feminism/women's movement. I. In the Western context], in Wb, 105.

[52] Krattiger, 96; cf. Halkes, "Theologie, feministische", 1105.

[53] The most comprehensive classificatory analysis to date appears in Meyer-Wilmes, 109–13; cf. also the classification by Elisabeth Schneider-Böcklen and Dorothea Vorländer, *Feminismus und Glaube* [Feminism and belief] (Mainz and Stuttgart, 1991), 45–106.

[54] Cf. below, 207.

more adequately and to foster wider awareness of them.[55] Here, exceptional repute is enjoyed (in academic circles) by the medievalist Elisabeth Gössmann, who—particularly regarding her area of specialization, the Middle Ages—warns against disdain for scholarly method and the blanket denunciation of entire Church-historical epochs as "hostile to women". But Gössmann, too, wants to see feminist theology made (on the model of ecumenical theology) a fundamental branch of theology as such.[56] Beyond exegesis and Church history, there are attempts to interpret ethics and various areas of dogmatics from a feminist viewpoint. Within practical theology, much interest is shown especially for liturgy-related endeavors.

2. Classification by type of method employed.

With respect to intellectual methodology, two general directions can be distinguished in feminist theology, one inspired more by liberation theology and the other proceeding more on psychoanalytic lines. The orientation of the first is more sociological, and that of the second, more psychological. Aligned with liberation theology are the main representatives of so-called "moderate" feminist theology: Rosemary Ruether, Elisabeth Schüssler Fiorenza, Catharina Halkes, and Elisabeth Moltmann-Wendel. The psychoanalytic direction, on the other hand, is definitively inspired by C. G. Jung, the creator of the doctrine of archetypes. Every person, according to C. G. Jung, carries in his soul the psychological archetypes of both his own and the opposite sex—a theory that tends to favor the ideal goal of "androgyny" but has also evoked strong criticism from

---

[55] Gössmann, *Schwestern,* 67–98; Ulrich Köpf, "Bemerkungen zur feministischen Auffassung der Kirchengeschichte" [Remarks on the feminist view of the history of the Church], *Theologische Beiträge* 22 (1991): 139–41.

[56] Gössmann, *Schwestern,* 19–25.

feminists, mainly because of its insistence on the existence of "masculine" and "feminine" qualities.[57]

Strongly oriented toward psychoanalysis are the representatives of "goddess feminism", for example, mainly (in the German-speaking sphere) the Protestants Christa Mulack, Hildegunde Wöller, Jutta Voss, and Elga Sorge. Following C. G. Jung and his student Erich Neumann, this psychoanalytic grouping considers the maternal principle, or the transpersonal unconscious, to be primary. Individual consciousness, according to Neumann, arises only secondarily from the collective unconscious. In the life of the individual as of mankind, primal psychological unity with the mother ("matriarchy") precedes individual consciousness, which brings with it a distancing from that unity ("patriarchy"). Here, Neumann extrapolates from the development of the individual person to that of human history. Ernst Haeckel had similarly maintained, a century ago, that children developing in the womb pass through stages paralleling those of the evolution of the human race—a theory that has since been refuted by modern embryology.[58] In the Jungian school, the "masculine" tends to be associated with the conscious side of the soul, and the "feminine" with the unconscious.[59] On the basis of this priority of the feminine, the hypothesis is made that human history began with an original matriarchy—something which, at the same time, feminists descry on the horizon as a hope for the future. Corresponding to the matriarchy on the religious plane, then, is worship of the goddess.

From the viewpoint of matriarchal religion, the Old Testament takes on a nightmarish aspect. The prophets,

---

[57] D. S. Wehr, *Jung and Feminism* (Boston, 1987); Doris Brockmann, *Ganze Menschen—Ganze Götter. C. G. Jung in der feministischen Theologie* [Whole humans—whole gods: C. G. Jung in feminist theology], with a foreword by Peter Eicher (Paderborn, 1990).

[58] Erich Blechschmidt, *Wie beginnt das menschliche Leben?* [How does human life begin?], 2d ed. (Stein am Rhein, 1984).

[59] Cf. Hauke, *Women in the Priesthood?*, 128-33.

who set themselves against polytheism, and thus also against the cult of the "Great Goddess", appear in many feminist works as virtual incarnations of evil, whereas Canaanite paganism is glorified. A particularly crass form of this approach is found in the book by Gerda Weiler, *Das Matriarchat im Alten Testament.*[60] Since the "matriarchal" intellectual heritage contains some furious attacks on Judaism ("murder of the goddess", and so on), an intense debate has arisen over "anti-Judaism" in feminist theology.[61] Owing in no small part to Jewish protests, female theologians who do not adhere to the "goddess" school are once again inclined to take a more positive view of the Old Testament and Judaism.[62]

Psychoanalytically or matriarchally oriented representatives of "goddess feminism" often possess particularly active imaginations. The more bizarre the theories, the more attention they attract in many circles. To cite one comparatively innocuous example: the Protestant hospital pastor Jutta Voss argues for the existence of an original matriarchy on the basis of a psychoanalytic interpretation of the folk tale about the brave little tailor. The fight with the wild sow in this tale illustrates how the male Church imprisons women (as, in the tale, the sow in the chapel) and has curbed their independence. Women, once powerful wild sows, have been domesticated into pink little house-pigs

---

[60] Gerda Weiler, *Das Matriarchat im Alten Testament* [The matriarchate in the Old Testament] (Berlin, 1989); also on this, Schneider-Böcklen and Vorländer, 83–95. A further example: Helgard Balz-Colchois, "Gomer oder die Macht der Astarte. Versuch einer feministischen Interpretation von Hos 1–4" [Gomer, or the power of Astarte: An attempted feminist interpretation of Hos 1–4], EvTh 42 (1982): 37–65; and, in critical response: H.-J. Hermisson, "Der Rückschritt oder: Wie Jahwe mit Astarte versöhnt werden soll" [The regress, or how Yahweh is to be reconciled with Astarte], EvTh 42 (1982): 290–94.

[61] Leonore Siegele-Wenschkewitz, ed., *Verdrängte Vergangenheit, die uns bedrängt* [The repressed past that troubles us] (Munich, 1988); "Antijudaismus" [Anti-judaism], in Wb, 22–24.

[62] Cf. the treatment of the topic "Antijudaismus" (Reg.) in the Wb.

with as many piglets (that is, children) as possible and have themselves embraced this degraded status.[63]

3. Classification by relationship to established feminist principles.

The tension between "equality feminism" and "gynocentric feminism" carries over to the theological sphere. In the "goddess feminism" of Mary Daly, Carol Christ, Elga Sorge, Christa Mulack, and others, the relevant social ideal is transferred to the world of religious symbolism, which is to be rearranged so as to give priority to the feminine. "God" is to be replaced by "Goddess". Inwardly, and very often outwardly as well, the advocates of "goddess feminism" have detached themselves from the Christian communions.

Within "Christian feminism", it is not the promoters of the "goddess" but the (female and male) adherents of the androgyne ideal who set the tone. According to their ideas, briefly put, the "our Father" is to be combined with an equally important "our Mother".

5. Feminist Theology as Reflected in Criticism[64]

In Germany, intense debates about feminist theology are to be found primarily within Protestantism. A large portion

---

[63] Jutta Voss, *Das Schwarzmondtabu. Die kultische Bedeutung des weiblichen Zyklus* [The black-moon taboo: The cultic significance of the female cycle] (Stuttgart, 1988); cf. Schneider-Böcklen and Vorländer, 103.

[64] The following survey is concentrated on the development in German-speaking countries and in the neighboring Netherlands. A critical insight into the American situation can be gained from (among other sources) the articles by Cornelia Ferreira listed in the Bibliography. Indicative of the divided reactions to feminist theology among the US episcopate is the controversy surrounding the various drafts of the "women's" pastoral letter, which was finally abandoned after the fourth attempt; on this see *30 Tage* 2 (12/1992): 21–23, 23–25 (G. Cardinale); *Herder Korrespondenz* 42 (1988): 267f.; 44 (1990): 207–9; 47 (1993): 7, 87–92 (K. Nientiedt). The

of the educational activities of the Protestant state churches is devoted to the propagation of theological feminism, but this has been, since the beginning of the 1980s, meeting with resistance.[65] As early as 1983, the Theological Convention of Confessing Communions [*Theologische Konvent bekennender Gemeinschaften*] published an instructive paperback providing relevant information and guidance, which was edited by Peter Beyerhaus, the Tübingen professor of missionary and religious studies.[66] A collaborator in this project was Ingeborg Hauschildt, who has also commented publicly via two further books and a series of essays.[67] In the Netherlands, Martie Dieperink—once herself inspired by feminism and engaged in the New Age movement—experienced a radical reversal of views and now aligns herself with the biblical image of woman, energetically opposing feminist theology.[68] Another well-known

---

American translation of the *Catechism of the Catholic Church* was considerably delayed by questionable consideration paid to feminism and the process of correcting it: cf. *30 Tage* 3 (3/1993): 27f. (G. Cardinale). Especially typical for the USA are controversies about liturgical language; cf. below, 218–19.

[65] Along with the works by Ingeborg Hauschildt (n. 67), cf. Georg Huntemann, *Die Zerstörung der Person—Umsturz der Werte—Gotteshaß der Vaterlosen—Feminismus* [Destruction of the person—overthrow of values—hatred of God by the fatherless—feminism] (Bad Liebenzell, 1981), 65ff.; Werner Neuer, *Mann und Frau in christlicher Sicht* [Man and woman from the Christian viewpoint], 5th ed. (Gießen, 1993; orig. 1981).

[66] Beyerhaus, *Aufstand.*

[67] Ingeborg Hauschildt, "Feministische Theologie. Eine fragwürdige neue Welle" [Feminist theology: A questionable new trend], *idea-Dokumentation* no. 40 (Wetzlar, 1981); " 'Feministische Theologie'—eine neue Irrlehre", 5–13; "Die Verunsicherung der Gemeinden durch die Feministische Theologie" [The creation of uncertainty in the churches by feminist theology], in Beyerhaus, *Aufstand,* 11–22; *Gott eine Frau? Weg und Irrweg der feministischen Theologie* [God a woman? The direction and aberration of feminist theology] (Wuppertal, 1983); *Die feministische Versuchung und die Antwort der christlichen Frau* [The feminist temptation and the response of the Christian woman] (Wuppertal and Zurich, 1989); see also: "Feministische Theologie", in ELTG 1 (1992): 604f.

[68] Martie Dieperink, *Vrouwen op zoek naar God. Wat is er gaande in de feministische theologie?,* 2d ed. (The Hague, 1988); *God roept de vrouw. Over de plaats en taak van de christenvrouw* (Kampen, 1990).

critic of feminist theology is Elisabeth Motschmann.[69] Her husband—the Bremen minister Jens Motschmann—provides a comprehensive assessment of liberal tendencies in Protestantism in his book *So nicht, Herr Pfarrer! Was wird aus der evangelischen Kirche?* [Not like that, Mr. Pastor! What is happening to the Protestant church?] (1991); included in this brilliantly written polemical jeremiad is a chapter on feminist theology.[70] The feminist image of Mary is critically illumined by the Augsburg theologian Wolfhart Schlichting.[71]

The conservative circles that have become active here are sometimes referred to as "evangelical Christians". Within German Protestantism as a whole, they are admittedly only a minority, albeit an intellectually and spiritually active, as well as a self-confident, one. In their writings, the evangelicals characterize feminist theology as a "heresy" that cannot be reconciled with biblically oriented Christianity.[72]

More representative of German state Protestantism is a position taken (in 1985) on feminist theology by the Lutheran bishops of the Northern Elbe region. It is, to be sure, predominantly critical, stating that central aspects of theological feminism lie outside the bounds of legitimate theology. Since, however, the positive concerns in feminism are to be valued, feminist theology is granted what is termed "broad scope".[73] The extent to which this "broad scope"

---

[69] Elisabeth Motschmann, "Religiöse Selbstversorgerinnen. Die Feministische Theologie" [Religious self-providers: Feminist theology], *Die neue Ordnung* 39 (1985): 289–96.

[70] Jens Motschmann, *So nicht, Herr Pfarrer! Was wird aus der evangelischen Kirche* [Not like that, Mr. Pastor! What is happening to the Protestant Church] (Berlin and Frankfurt, 1991), 110–28.

[71] Wolfhart Schlichting, *Maria. Die Mutter Jesu in Bibel, Tradition und Feminismus* [Mary: The Mother of Jesus in the Bible, tradition, and feminism] (Wuppertal and Zurich, 1989).

[72] Cf., for example, Hauschildt (1982); Padberg (1985), 183; Jens Motschmann (1991), 128.

[73] Dokumentation "Jenseits der Grenzen legitimer Theologie. Stel-

has, in the meantime, become part of the general defining image of German Protestantism is shown not least by the appointment, in the Northern Elbe state church, of a "bishopess" who actively supports so-called "soft feminism".[74] Similar in import is the position taken by the council of the German Protestant church on the protests about the feminist directorship of the earlier-mentioned women's center: it was stressed that syncretistic revival of the "goddess" and nonacceptance of the Cross would be allowed no place in the center's work; on the question of whether homosexuality is sinful—one of the two female directors is a committed lesbian—it was thought best to express no view at all, and the controversial staffing decision would not be revoked.[75]

Meanwhile, nevertheless, in one particularly extreme case, things have reached the point of a withdrawal of authority to teach. Early in 1987, Elga Sorge, a teacher of religion at the Kassel Polytechnic Institute, appeared on a television show in which she presented her transformation of the "Ten Commandments" into the "Ten Permissions". These permissions sanctioned, among other things, adultery and unfaithfulness. The personal background: the lady had entered into a "one-day marriage" with a professional schoolteacher named Sorge but curtailed the wedding festivities by returning home to spend a few nights with a former male friend and soon filed for divorce. As a result of this television program, Elga Sorge was given notice of dismissal by the Protestant church (effected con-

---

lungnahme der nordelbischen Bischöfe zum Thema Feministische Theologie" (1.7.85) [Beyond the bounds of legitimate theology: Statement by the bishops of the northern Elb region on the subject of feminist theology (July 1, 1985)], *Materialdienst der EZW* 50 (1987): 104f.

[74] Cf. *idea-Dokumentation,* no. 8 (1992): *Die erste Frau im Bischofsamt. Reaktionen auf die Wahl von Maria Jepsen zur Bischöfin von Hamburg* (Wetzlar, 1992); Jepsen.

[75] *EKD-Frauenzentrum,* 76f. (communiqué of June 26, 1993).

siderably more quickly than comparable proceedings in
the Catholic sphere). Also taken into account was the fact
that Sorge customarily referred to herself as a "goddess".
"But staffing arrangements in our church", as the regional
bishop phrased it, "provide no positions for gods and
goddesses."[76] Nevertheless, at the Protestant Church Congress in 1991, Elga Sorge received enthusiastic applause
when, in the course of giving an official address, she characterized God as "Head-eunuch".[77]

Disciplinary proceedings for doctrinal offenses were
initiated against the previously mentioned hospital pastor,
Jutta Voss, who, among other things, plays female menstrual blood off against the "male homicidal blood" of
Jesus and also views a pagan swine-goddess as exemplify-
ing the highest form of consciousness. In place of the
Christian Trinity, she puts the sacred "goddess Physis", or
matter.[78]

In the German-speaking sphere, a widely noted critique
of particularly audacious theories in feminist theology has
been provided by Susanne Heine, a Protestant theologian
who, to be sure, shares many of the concerns of feminism.
Heine criticizes, for example, the preservation of the out-
dated matriarchy thesis, accuses feminist literature of an
ongoing "murder of method", and calls for greater scholarly exactitude.[79] Regarding the situation in the Protestant church, Susanne Heine writes:

---

[76] *Deutsche Tagespost,* December 10, 1987, 2; January 16, 1988, 5 (the
latter from *idea*); cf. also *Der Spiegel,* no. 28 (1989), 50f.; Elga Sorge,
Religion und Frau. Weibliche Spiritualität im Christentum [Religion and
woman: Feminine spirituality in Christianity], 2d ed. (Stuttgart, 1987).

[77] *Idea spektrum* 24 (1991): 27.

[78] Cf. FAZ, October 20, 1992, 10; January 22, 1993, 3; *Publik-Forum,*
January 29, 1993, 22f.; see also Schneider-Böklen and Vorländer, 100–106.

[79] Susanne Heine, *Frauen der frühen Christenheit. Zur historischen
Kritik einer feministischen Theologie* [Women of early Christianity: Toward
a historical critique of feminist theology] (Göttingen, 1986); *Wiederbelebung der Göttinnen? Zur systematischen Kritik einer feministischen
Theologie* [Revival of the goddesses? Toward a systematic critique of

Meanwhile, in a certain way, feminism and feminist theology have acquired a standing somewhere between acceptance and recognition.... Today, female theologians can conduct religious services using words and concepts purged of everything male: God becomes the Goddess, Jesus Christ becomes Jesa Christa, the Holy Spirit becomes the Holy Spiritess. [It would seem] that this sort of religious service is no longer particularly disturbing to anyone.... Then there are those "progressive" circles eager to seize upon everything that is "modern" and slightly offensive or upsetting: the second-hand avant-garde. A certain measure of recognition (not too much and not too little) first encourages the grasping of an iron that proves, precisely in the grasping, to be already growing cold. Meanwhile, there are enough theologians, men, who trickle feminist ideas down from their pulpits, and enough teachers of religion who, moved to tears, unfold to little ones of both sexes the horrible story of the patriarchy.[80]

Apparently intended as an inner-feminist critique is a work by two female theologians closely associated with the Protestant Center for General Philosophical Issues [*Evangelische Zentrale für Weltanschauungsfragen*]: Elisabeth Schneider-Böklen and Dorothea Vorländer, *Feminismus und Glaube* [Feminism and faith] (1991). However, important aspects of the criticisms put forward there bear on the substance of the feminist approach, inasmuch as the significance of biblical revelation is stressed.

Also in 1991, Ulrich Schmidhäuser published a vehement critique of feminist theology, sparked by biblical translations presented at the previous Protestant Church Congress in 1989 in Berlin. In the official program, a so-called "woman-true" rendering of biblical texts was

---

feminist theology] (Göttingen, 1987); "Feministische Theologie — Zur Unterscheidung der Geister" [Feminist theology — Toward a differentiation of positions], in Paulus Gordan, ed., *Gott schuf den Menschen als Mann und Frau* [God created mankind as male and female]. Salzburger Hochschulwochen 1988 (Graz, Vienna, and Cologne, 1989), 155–84.

[80] Heine, *Göttinnen,* 9f.

proposed. Accordingly, any masculine terms and grammatical forms applying to "God" were eliminated. Above all, the title "Lord" had to disappear. Schmidhäuser compares feminist theology, whose source and criterion is so-called "female experience", with the "German Christians" of the Nazi era. Then, Protestant theologians who were particularly well aligned with the spirit of the times had censored the Bible and wanted to introduce a Christianity appropriate to the Aryan race. In place of race, according to Schmidhäuser, feminists put sex. The categories "woman-true" [*frauengerecht*] and "species-suitable" [*artgemäß*] are on the same sort of level.[81]

Public statements of position from academic theological quarters have so far been relatively restrained but are increasing in number and intensity of commitment. In 1989, the Marburg professor of systematic theology Carl Heinz Ratschow described feminist theology as an "alien, anti-Christian religion" (with express reference to Jutta Voss and Dorothee Sölle).[82] Elke Axmacher, a theology professor in Berlin, made the criticism in 1990 that feminist theology had given too little scrutiny to its inner consistency and its presuppositions. She closes her study of Rosemary Ruether's theology with the conclusion, "A feminist approach to language about God has as much chance of success as an atheist approach to belief in God."[83] Further critical voices were raised within academic theology in 1993, when two feminists were appointed to directorship of the new women's cultural center being set up by the Lutheran church in Germany.[84]

---

[81] Ulrich Schmidhäuser, *Soll "Gott" nicht mehr "Herr" genannt werden? Zum gegenwärtigen Feminismus in Gesellschaft und Kirche* [Should "God" no longer be called "Lord"? On present-day feminism in society and the Church] (Stuttgart, 1991), 124.

[82] *Idea,* no. 58 (June 22, 1989), 6.

[83] Axmacher, 17.

[84] Cf. above, 59–60.

In October 1990, members of the Protestant Theological Faculty in Tübingen published a detailed statement of position on feminist theology. This was done at the request of the Württemberg regional synod, just as action by synod members had led, at the beginning of the 1950s, to a report by relevant experts on Rudolf Bultmann's theology.[85] The Tübingen statement, whose participant authors included one female and five male theologians, recognizes warranted concerns in feminist theology but takes a predominantly critical stance.[86] Accordingly, most public reactions to it have been enraged.[87]

In the Catholic sphere, feminist theology has so far made fewer inroads than in the Protestant, but its influence is constantly increasing even here. Strong criticisms of feminist theology are expressed by persons like Barbara Albrecht, who has years of experience in the training of female parish counselors; the theologian and educator Jutta Burggraf; and the psychologist Christa Meves.[88] Eva

---

[85] The parallel here to the Bultmann report is pointed out by Heike Schmoll, "Ist Gott-Vater für Frauen unerträglich? Feministische Theologie und christlicher Glaube" [Is God as Father unbearable to women? Feminist theology and Christian belief], FAZ, March 12, 1992, 14.

[86] "Tübinger Stellungnahme zu Fragen der Feministischen Theologie" [The Tübingen position on questions of feminist theology], *Theologische Beiträge* 22 (3/1991): 118–53; Elisabeth Moltmann-Wendel and Günter Kegel, eds., *Feministische Theologie im Kreuzfeuer. Der Streit um das "Tübinger Gutachten". Dokumente—Analysen—Kritiken* [Feminist theology under fire: The controversy over the "Tübingen Report". Documents—analyses—critiques] (Gütersloh, 1992), 13–69.

[87] Moltmann-Wendel and Kegel.

[88] Barbara Albrecht, *Vom Dienst der Frau in der Kirche* [On women's service in the Church] (Vallendar and Schönstatt, 1980); *Jesus—Frau—Kirche* [Jesus—woman—Church] (Vallendar and Schönstatt, 1983), 52–57; Jutta Burggraf, "Die Mutter der Kirche und die Frau in der Kirche. Korrektur der Irrwege feministischer Theologie" [The Mother of the Church and women in the Church: Correcting the aberrations of feminist theology], *Offerten-Zeitung ("Theologisches")* 38 (1985): 6445–53, 6507–13; *Die Mutter der Kirche und die Frau in der Kirche. Ein kritischer Beitrag zum Thema "feministische Theologie"* [The Mother of the Church and women in the Church: A critical essay on "feminist theology"], Kleine

Schmetterer, the author of a doctoral dissertation on feminist theology, obviously embarked on her studies of theological feminism with great interest but had to confess at the end: "The more I . . . progress in my knowledge of the literature, the more I find myself, as a woman and as a theologian, disappointed by this theology."[89]

However, so-called "published opinion"—which, in accordance with the law of "the spiral of silence",[90] exerts an ever-greater influence on actually held opinions—exhibits a predominantly positive attitude to theological feminism. Only goddess feminism is almost universally rejected.[91] Particularly in the upper leadership circles of the German Catholic Women's Association [*Katholische Frauengemeinschaft Deutschlands,* or KFD], there are

---

Schriften des Internationalen Mariologischen Arbeitskreises (Kevelaer, 1986); numerous press articles by Christa Meves, e.g.: "Verführerisch erklingt das alte Lied der Schlange" [The serpent's old song makes itself temptingly heard], *Deutsche Tagespost,* August 14, 1987, 3; "Gemeinsam am Reich Gottes wirken. Warum es in der Kirche unterschiedliche Dienste von Frauen und Männern gibt" [Working together for God's Kingdom: Why there are differing roles for women and men in the Church], *Deutsche Tagespost,* April 9, 1991, 5; "Die Krise der Katholischen Kirche in Deutschland" [The crisis in the Catholic Church in Germany], *Theologisches* 22 (3/1992): 106–14; "Feministische Theologie ante portas" [Feminist theology ante portas], *Theologisches* 22 (9/1992): 370f; cf. also the works by Courth; Emmerich; Hauke; Moll; Schuhmacher; Seifert; and Sudbrack listed in the Bibliography.

[89] Eva Schmetterer, *"Was ist die Frau, daß du ihrer gedenkst". Eine systematisch-dogmatische Untersuchung zum hermeneutischen Ansatz Feministischer Theologie* ["What is woman that you are mindful of her": A systematic-dogmatic inquiry into the hermeneutic approach of feminist theology] (Frankfurt, 1989), 9; cf. also her "Trägt Feministische Theologie zur Befreiung von Frauen bei? Einige kritische Gedanken zu fragwürdigen Tendenzen in der feministischen Theologie" [Does feminist theology contribute to the liberation of women? Some critical thoughts on questionable tendencies in feminist theology], *Wissenschaft und Glaube* 2 (1989): 137–49.

[90] Elisabeth Noelle-Neumann, *Die Schweigespirale* [The spiral of silence] (Frankfurt, 1982); English ed.: *The Spiral of Silence: Public Opinion, Our Social Skin,* 2d ed. (Chicago, 1993).

[91] Cf., for example, Marie-Theres Wacker, "Die Göttin kehrt zurück. Kritische Sichtung neuerer Entwürfe", in her *Der Gott der Männer und die Frauen* [Men's God and women] (Düsseldorf, 1987), 11–37.

extensive sympathies for feminist theology, which finding increasingly clear expression[92] in that association's educational activities and in its magazine, *Frau und mutter.*[93]

So far, direct statements of position by bishops have been rare. The most significant example is an article by Cardinal Simonis. He makes reference to the situation in the Netherlands, where, in the meantime, feminist theology has probably gained more influence than in any other country in the world. According to the Cardinal, furthering the activity of women and elaborating a theology of being a woman are important tasks for the Church. But feminist theology is unsuited to those tasks. It denies fundamental truths of the faith, repudiates revelation, distorts the image of God, diminishes the Person of Christ, misuses the Holy Spirit, and presents a false image of Mary. Obsessed with the specter of sexism, feminists lure people away from God

---

[92] Cf., for example, the contributions by its long-time secretary-general, Anneliese Lissner, *Erneuert euch in eurem Denken. Eine Auswahl von Referaten, Ansprachen, geistlichen Worten* [Renew yourselves in your thinking: A selection of scholarly papers, addresses, spiritual sayings] (Düsseldorf, 1989), 143–95; *Seid nicht so geduldig! Warum der Kirche widersprochen werden muß* [Don't be so patient! Why the Church must be contradicted], with a foreword by Rita Süssmuth (Zurich, 1993); or the work of the editor-in-chief of *Frau und mutter* from 1974–1986, Ruth Ahl, *Eure Töchter werden Prophetinnen sein: Kleine Einführung in die Feministische Theologie* [Your daughters will be prophets: A short introduction to feminist theology] (Freiburg, 1990); for a review of this, see Manfred Hauke, *Katholische Bildung* 91 (1990): 382f. The same feminist-friendly direction is represented by the main spiritual protector of the KFD, suffragan bishop Ernst Gutting, "Kinder, Küche, Kirche?—Und was dann?" [Children, cooking, Church—and what then?], *Neue Stadt* 30 (10/1987): 4–7; KNA, June 4 and July 2, 1987 (lecture in June 1987 at the University of Münster on his *Offensive gegen den Patriarchalismus;* acknowledgment of the "many valuable approaches in feminist theology"); *Offensive gegen den Patriarchalismus. Für eine menschlichere Welt* [Offensive against patriarchalism: For a more human world], 4th ed. (Freiburg, 1988).

[93] The word "mother" in the title of the journal is deliberately not capitalized, a practice the association's officials have defended against the protests of women: cf. *Deutsche Tagespost,* September 6, 1988; September 9, 1988, 9.

and the Church. It is extraordinarily sad that precisely women should have struck at the Church in this way, even deserting her and taking their husbands and children with them. He admits that women have not always been accorded their appropriate place in the Church, but feminist theology is constructing a new church that no longer has anything to do with divine revelation, to which men are also subject.[94] In indignation over this manifestation of so-called "discrimination of women", feminists initiated two legal actions against Cardinal Simonis, which they lost however.[95]

Cardinal Ratzinger, in *The Ratzinger Report,* criticizes radical feminism as the fruit of male ideologies that, although pretending to want to liberate women, in fact uproot them most profoundly. Such an ideology is irreconcilable with Christianity.[96] The statements on feminist theology by Bishop Lehmann tend to be critical, as do, even more clearly, those by Archbishop Degenhardt.[97] Above all, however, an indirect response to feminism is contained in John Paul II's apostolic letter on the dignity and calling of women, *Mulieris dignitatem,* which appeared in 1988. Here, in the form of a biblical meditation, the Pope delineates the positive foundations of the Catholic image of woman.[98]

---

[94] A. J. Simonis, "Einige beschouwingen rond de feministische theologie", *Communio* (Flemish ed.) 11 (6/1986): 464–84; cf. "Maria und der Feminismus. Zur Wirkung der Gottesmutter in der Freiheitsgeschichte der Menschheit" [Mary and feminism: On the influence of the Mother of God in the history of human freedom], *L'Osservatore Romano* (German ed.) 17, no. 27 (July 3, 1987): 8.

[95] C. A. Tukker, "Der Prozeß gegen Kardinal Simonis" [The case against Cardinal Simonis], in Remigius Bäumer and Alma von Stockhausen, eds., *Luther und die Folgen für die Geistesgeschichte,* FS Theobald Beer (Weilheim-Bierbronnen, 1992), 195–203.

[96] Joseph Ratzinger, *The Ratzinger Report* (San Francisco, 1985), 93–99.

[97] Karl Lehmann, "Das Bild der Frau. Versuch einer anthropologisch-theologischen Standortbestimmung" [The image of woman: An attempt at anthropologico-theological assessment of the current situation], *Herder Korrespondenz* 41 (1987): 484f.; J. J. Degenhardt, *Marienfrömmigkeit* [Marian piety] (Paderborn, 1987), 50–60.

[98] Cf. below, 108–9, 192, 200, 248, 259.

In 1993, on the occasion of an ad-limina visit of United States bishops, the Pope condemned an extreme feminism, which undermines the Christian faith.[99]

This historical survey of the development of feminist theology attests to the radicalness of that theology and the problems implicit in it. Before, however, particular themes in theological feminism are presented in greater detail, one quite central figure still needs to be considered separately here.

---

[99] The "role of woman in the Church's life" merits "careful attention". The question about women can certainly "not be resolved by a compromise with feminism, which has itself split into rigid ideological views irreconcilable among themselves. In its extreme form, it is Christian faith itself which risks being destroyed. Sometimes various forms of nature religions, and the exaltation of myths and symbols replace the worship of the God who has revealed himself in Jesus Christ. Unfortunately, certain groups in this church support this kind of feminism, including some women religious whose opinions, positions and behavior are no longer in harmony with the teaching of the Gospel and the Church." Pastors have the obligation to resist these ideas and to engage in "honest and open dialogue" with those who have been influenced by them.

IV. MARY DALY AS "FOSTER MOTHER" OF FEMINIST THEOLOGY

The best-known and most distinguished feminist theologian is the earlier-mentioned Mary Daly, a former nun. Daly is the first American[1] woman to have earned (in 1963 at Fribourg) a doctorate in Catholic theology.[2] Her name can be found in almost all the relevant publications. In the index of persons in the new *Wörterbuch der Feministischen Theologie* [Dictionary of feminist theology], Daly is the second-most-frequently cited name, just after "Jesus". Again and again, Mary Daly's decisive role is emphasized by her colleagues,[3] even if they shy away from some of the implications of her thought. Catharina Halkes, for instance, speaks of a "streak of lightning" that has "cast everything in a new light" and "brought clarity" to her.[4] It is appropriate, then, to outline Daly's intellectual history before moving on to a systematic review of specific theses in feminist theology.

Daly's first long publication appeared in the turbulent years following the Second Vatican Council: *The Church and the Second Sex.*[5] Not just its title is reminiscent of

---

[1] Meyer-Wilmes, 34.

[2] For biographical details, see Michel Dion, "Mary Daly, théologienne et philosophe féministe", in *Études théologiques et religieuses* 61 (1987): 516–18.

[3] For example, Halkes, *Söhne,* 10, 36; Elisabeth Moltmann-Wendel, *Das Land, wo Milch und Honig fließt. Perspektiven einer feministischen Theologie* [The land flowing with milk and honey: Prospects for a feminist theology], 2d ed. (Gütersloh, 1987), 42; Ruether, *Sexism,* 187; Gössmann, *Schwestern,* 44; Wb, Personenregister [index of persons].

[4] Halkes, *Söhne,* 10.

[5] Mary Daly, *The Church and the Second Sex* (New York, 1968);

Simone de Beauvoir; the book's content is also strongly influenced by the French existentialist's views, which Daly all but wholly makes her own.[6] For Daly, too, one does not arrive in the world as a woman but becomes one.[7] She endorses the idea that we must "abandon the notion of a fixed and static human nature in favor of an evolutionary vision of man in the world".[8] Not the least of the sources influencing her here are the writings of Teilhard de Chardin, whose stress on feminine characteristics[9] she nevertheless dismisses as an inconsistency.[10] There is no essential form of being a man or being a woman that was established by divine creation. Where the course of evolution might yet lead remains an open question.[11]

She makes a particularly sharp attack on Gertrud von le Fort's writing *Die ewige Frau* [The eternal woman], a work which, since its appearance in 1934, has influenced a whole generation of Catholic women and is being rediscovered today.[12] In *Die ewige Frau,* this well-known German writer outlines the essential attributes of the feminine nature that transcend any particular culture and whose symbolic significance is concentrated in the figure of Mary. According to Daly, Le Fort has confused the symbolic significance of woman with the "concrete, historical reality". There is no such thing as an enduring symbolic significance, because the underlying facts—including those of biology—exist in

---

Boston, 1985); German ed.: *Kirche, Frau und Sexus* (Olten, 1970).

[6] Daly, *Church,* 56, 69-73.

[7] Ibid., 71-72.

[8] Ibid., 55; cf. 71.

[9] Cf. esp. Pierre Teilhard de Chardin, *Hymne an das Ewig Weibliche* [Hymn to the Eternal Feminine], with a commentary by H. de Lubac (Einsiedeln, 1968).

[10] Daly, *Church,* 151-53.

[11] Ibid., 220.

[12] Munich, 1968 (orig. 1934). Gutting, *Offensive,* 109; Jutta Burggraf, "Maria als Vorbild für die Frau. Das Marienbild bei Gertrud von Le Fort" [Mary as a model for women: The image of Mary in Gertrud von Le Fort], in Pontificia Academia Mariana Internationalis, *De cultu mariano saeculis XIX-XX* 7 (Rome, 1991), 125-45.

time and are always "changing".[13] All talk of an essential form of woman is just speculation by "androcentric society".[14] It is woman as an independent person, who strives creatively for "self-realization", that is decisive.[15] The "eternal woman", by contrast, is a "demon" to be expelled.[16] For this, Daly coins the notion of an "exorcism".[17]

The "evolutionary vision" is also applied to the Church: her teachings and practices are subject to constant change.[18] Daly welcomes the encyclical by John XXIII *Pacem in terris* and the statements by Vatican II, which she interprets as implying the elimination of all inequalities between men and women. Statements by the Council that run counter to this, that accentuate not only an equality of worth but also a difference in nature, she either assiduously ignores or softens in tone.[19] The Council is seen, so to speak, as taking three steps forward; then Pope Paul VI, unfortunately, took a step back again.[20]

Just as the Council is played off against tradition, so is one text from Holy Scripture against another. The first account of creation is set against the second,[21] Jesus against Paul,[22] and one quotation from Paul against another.[23] An undervaluing and silencing of women—which undoubtedly did occur—is generalized into a feature of the entire history of the Church. The Church Fathers, in particular, become the whipping boys here.[24] Veneration

---

[13] Daly, *Church,* 148.
[14] Ibid., 149.
[15] Ibid.
[16] Ibid., 171, 176.
[17] Ibid., 176–78.
[18] Ibid., 73.
[19] Ibid., 119–21; on Vatican II, cf. Hauke, *Women in the Priesthood?,* 55–60.
[20] Daly, *Church,* 122.
[21] Ibid., 77.
[22] Ibid., 79–80.
[23] Ibid., 81, 198.
[24] Ibid., 85–90.

of Mary is presented in a gloomy light by Daly, because an unattainable ideal is thereby insinuated that humiliates all real women.[25]

The image of God also comes in for extensive criticism. Following the "God is dead" theologian Leslie Dewart, she protests against an omnipotent and immutable God who establishes an unchangeable order of things.[26] The Incarnation, according to Daly, is perpetuated in human progress,[27] which should mount "toward a higher order of consciousness and being, in which the alienating projections will have been defeated and wholeness, psychic integrity, achieved" for women and men.[28]

This first work of Daly's was already enough to "cause the spark of feminist dialogue to jump across to the Catholic and ecumenical side".[29] The actual breakthrough to feminist theology, however, did not occur until 1973, with *Beyond God the Father.*[30] In that work, she announces a radical departure from Christianity. The Christian language of religious symbolism is no more capable of being reformed than is a triangle capable of being constructed with four corners.[31] "If God in 'his' heaven is a Father ruling 'his' people, then it is in the 'nature' of things . . . that society be male-dominated."[32] The irredeemable sexism of Christianity is manifest above all in the figure of Christ himself, who, as a male symbol, excludes women.[33] This "Christolatry"[34] is bolstered further by the veneration of Mary, since Mary, the woman, is subordinate to the man, Jesus.

---

[25] Ibid., 61, 88.
[26] Ibid., 182.
[27] Ibid., 185.
[28] Ibid., 223.
[29] Pissarek-Hudelist (1981), 299.
[30] Daly, *Father.*
[31] Ibid., German ed. forword, 5.
[32] Ibid., 13.
[33] Ibid., 80.
[34] Ibid., 96.

With all this, Christianity has "enchained" the ancient "Mother Goddess" of primeval times.[35]

The patriarchal system is life-threatening today, because it views rape of the earth as a task integral to creation[36] and promotes a high degree of military preparedness.[37] Christianity pursues "rape" as a "way of life".[38] Daly thus calls for all feminists to undertake "a castrating of the language and images" that reflect and perpetuate suppression of women.[39] It is necessary "to castrate . . . *the system* that castrates—that great 'God-Father' of us all".[40] Daly characterizes this project equally as an "exorcism of demons" and a "form of deicide".[41]

Daly no longer believes in a personal God. Following primarily the American philosopher A. N. Whitehead, who advocates a so-called "process philosophy", she aligns herself with a pantheistic, or panentheistic, view of "God" that assumes an identity between God and the world.[42] Since "God" has no inherent personal status, the word "God" is to be seen, not as a noun, but as a verb. "Transcendence" is the verb, the being, in which we participate.[43] Here, the theological source is primarily the Protestant Paul Tillich, who is much read in the USA. Tillich speaks of God as the "ground of being". What is emphasized is solely God's immanence, his presence in this world, while his superiority to the world, his transcendence, is left out of the picture. God is, therefore, no longer a personally acting Being who could exert an efficacious influence on this

---

[35] Ibid., 83.
[36] Ibid., 177–78.
[37] Ibid., 120f.
[38] Ibid., 116f.
[39] Ibid., 9.
[40] Ibid., 10.
[41] Ibid., 10, 12.
[42] Ibid., 37, 188–89.
[43] Ibid., 34.

world but, rather, is identical with the totality of this world.[44]

Attributes that are otherwise only predicated of God are now predicated, by Mary Daly, of man. "In a moment of illumination, a radical feminist" had once exclaimed: "We are the final cause!" On this, Daly comments: "I believe that she was right."[45]

Now that the image of God has been destroyed, she calls for "the becoming of psychologically androgynous human beings, since the basic crippling complementarity has been the false masculine/feminine polarity" of traditional sexual stereotypes.[46] Daly thus radically rejects the idea that the natures of man and woman are mutually supplementary, that there is any complementarity or polarity. This rejection is the decisive point at which there is a parting of ways between supporters and opponents of feminism. An added catalyst for rejecting the idea that the sexes are mutually complementary is probably Daly's lesbianism, a practice which she passionately advocates.[47]

For Daly, the pivotal means to attaining the androgynous future is the "sisterhood" of feminists as the "Antichurch".[48] After the destruction of the matriarchy, Daly intends to prepare the way for the "*Second Coming of woman*", which is synonymous with the coming of the Antichrist.[49] "In its depth, because it contains a dynamic that drives beyond Christolatry, the women's movement *does* point to, seek, and constitute the primordial, always present, and future Antichrist." It does this by "breaking the Great Silence" and "raising up female pride".[50]

---

[44] Ibid., 6, 20-21, 28-29, 103 passim. On Tillich, cf. Leo Scheffczyk, *Gott-loser Gottesglaube?* [God-less belief in God?] (Regensburg, 1974), 128-52; Hauke, *Women in the Priesthood?*, 70, 126, 271, 311.

[45] Daly, *Father*, 180.

[46] Ibid., 26.

[47] Ibid., 9 (German ed.), 124-27 (English ed.); cf. later Daly, *Gyn/Ecology*, for example, 376, 382-84.

[48] Daly, *Father*, 138.

[49] Ibid., 96.

[50] Ibid.

The next stop on Daly's feminist "journey of exorcism and ecstasy"[51] is the book *Gyn/Ecology* (1978), a testimony to the close association between feminism and the ecology movement: "eco-feminism". From now on, Daly wishes to avoid the term "God", "because *God* represents the necrophilia of patriarchy, whereas *Goddess* affirms the life-loving be-ing of women and nature".[52] An outright hatred of everything male runs through the entire book, which consists largely of a muddled obsession with hideous things that women have actually or allegedly experienced at the hands of men. Daly now avoids the adjective "androgynous"—which, after all, still includes something "masculine"—and replaces it with "gynocentric" or "woman-identified".[53] Masculine or neuter personal pronouns are replaced by feminine ones.[54] Her so-called "Courage to Blaspheme"[55] manifests itself in various ways, including repeated mockery of the Cross as an instrument of torture, which she contrasts with the "feminine" tree of life.[56] As opposed to the Crucified, the feminist stands "stably on the earth, self-assuring and self-centering".[57]

Daly sees herself as a "witch" who is rediscovering an "esoteric knowledge" of earlier matriarchal culture.[58] Her most prominent symbol, appearing in constantly mutated forms, is that of "weaving": the "spinsters", the feminists, are to weave their web around the entire world[59] and move, at the same time, continually closer "to the agitated midpoint", "the Eye of the cosmic cyclone, the 'I' who says

---

[51] Ibid., German ed. foreword, 5.

[52] Daly, *Gyn/Ecology*, xi.

[53] Ibid., xii.

[54] Foreword to the German translation: *Gyn/Ökologie—eine Meta-Ethik des radikalen Feminismus* (Munich, 1980), 10.

[55] Daly, *Gyn/Ecology*, 264.

[56] Ibid., 79–80.

[57] Ibid., 388.

[58] Ibid., 221.

[59] Ibid., 3, 424.

I am ".[60] The place of prayer—a key word absent from this very thick book—is taken by a "theology of weaving", the self-centered "inward Journey".[61]

In Daly's next work, *Pure Lust* (1984),[62] the conscious anti-Christian quality is intensified still further. The cover of the original American edition is resplendent with the image of a serpent, interpreted by Daly as satanic secret knowledge and extolled in lofty tones as "Dragon-identified" life.[63] She refers to herself proudly as a "Nag-Gnostic",[64] who takes the (supposed) "Deadly Sin of lust" as the departure point for her reflections.[65] In continually varied ways, she appeals to the "Elemental spirits", the demonic powers, which she wants to call forth from her own "depths", from her feminine "Self".[66] The symbol of "heaven" is derogated so that full attention can be given to the "earth".[67] By her own testimony, Daly is proud of the unpredictability and willfulness of her expostulations.[68] She takes untiring delight in a language "woven" by herself, in which, according to the foreword by her German translator, "alliteration [is] more important than 'logical' coherence in the patriarchal sense."[69] The goal of all endeavors is "lust" as "abundance of being", complete empowerment.[70]

Mary Daly's most recent work is a feminist dictionary that introduces a completely new vocabulary, thereby taking the social separatism of radical feminism to the ultimate extreme. The title of this book also concretely

---

[60] Ibid., 405.

[61] Ibid., 403.

[62] Mary Daly, *Pure Lust: Elemental Feminist Philosophy* (Boston, 1984); German ed.: *Reine Lust. Elemental-feministische Philosophie* (Munich, 1986).

[63] Daly, *Pure Lust,* 390–92.

[64] Ibid., 12, 411.

[65] Ibid., 2.

[66] Ibid., 4–5, 7–19, 260.

[67] Ibid., 8–9.

[68] Ibid., x.

[69] Daly, *Reine Lust,* German translator's foreword, xii.

[70] Daly, *Pure Lust,* 3, 19–20.

expresses the sense of "weaving" that Daly herself likes to use to describe her activities; it reads: *Websters' First New Intergalactic Wickedary of the English Language* (1987).[71]

Perhaps one more small item to conclude this chapter: after all this, Mary Daly remained a professor at the Jesuit college in Boston. Since her position is tenured, she continues to teach "Catholic theology".[72]

---

[71] Mary Daly and Jane Caputi, *Websters' First New Intergalactic Wickedary of the English Language* (Boston, 1987).

[72] Heinzelmann, *Diskriminierung*, 224, n. 90. This information was confirmed to me in May 1990 by an American familiar with the situation. After the appearance of *The Church and the Second Sex* (1968), there were apparently efforts to block her being appointed on a permanent basis. However, the authorities at Boston College were ultimately persuaded by student demonstrations to permit Daly to stay on (Heinzelmann, ibid.). On American theological colleges, cf. Heinzelmann, 212-15.

V. THE IMAGE OF MAN AS FUNDAMENTAL POINT OF DEPARTURE

1. On the Methodology of the Following Inquiries

The foregoing observations on feminism, the development of feminist theology, and its main inspirer, Mary Daly, suffice to complete the preliminary historical survey here. Against the backdrop of this historical sketch, an attempt at systematic review of the contents of feminist theology may now be made. While all the themes addressed in it will be central, the aim is not to achieve exhaustive coverage (which would be impossible anyway because of the subject's continuing development). In each case, presentation of the relevant ideas and positions will be followed by critical commentary on them. It seems best to begin by focussing on anthropology, which plays a key role in relation to the other main topics.

Despite the fact that feminist theology is still in the process of development (Elisabeth Moltmann-Wendel speaks of "workshop tests")[1] and includes quite varied currents, certain basic principles that recur in almost all contexts have, in the course of twenty years, become increasingly evident. The following sketch is based primarily on three widely read, representative authors who—in contrast to Mary Daly—wish to remain within the framework of Christianity: Catharina Halkes, Elisabeth Moltmann-Wendel,[2] and Rosemary Radford Ruether, who was a decisive influ-

---

[1] Elisabeth Moltmann-Wendel, "Werkstatt ohne Angst. Zur 'Feministischen Theologie'" [Workshop without fear: On "feminist theology"], *forum religion* (3/1987): 34.

[2] Cf. above, 58.

ence (along with Mary Daly) on feminist theology in the
USA from the very start and has since produced a first
"systematic" work on the subject.[3] The same basic orientation is shared by others, such as Hedwig Meyer-Wilmes,
Elisabeth Schüssler Fiorenza, and the American nun Anne
Carr, who attaches much importance (at least according to
her own testimony) to the link between feminism and Catholic tradition.[4] Writings from this so-called "moderate"
school of feminist theology will be used as preferred sources
of reference here, in order to make clear that the views
being presented are not just unusual, extreme examples.

An important aid to gaining information about feminist-
theological views has recently become available in the
Wörterbuch der Feministischen Theologie [Dictionary of
feminist theology], which appeared in 1991 under joint
editorship of three Catholic and three Protestant women
theologians. Particularly worth noting here are the Protestant Elisabeth Moltmann-Wendel and, on the Catholic side,
the (also earlier-mentioned) medievalist Elisabeth Gössmann, as well as Herlinde Pissarek-Hudelist, a professor of
catechetics and religious education. Pissarek-Hudelist has
been dean of the Jesuit Faculty of Theology in Innsbruck
since 1988. Almost eighty different women authors have
contributed to this dictionary.[5] As is often stressed in
related contexts,[6] confessional differences play no major
role here; the influence of particular church backgrounds
enters less into personal testimonies than into the kind of
thing opposed.

Particularly extreme "goddess feminism" will be considered only occasionally in the course of the following general assessment. Yet it cannot be totally omitted, since the
assertions by its adherents themselves often influence the

---

[3] Ruether, *Sexism,* publisher's cover text, German edition.

[4] Carr, 1–2.

[5] Wb, 5.

[6] For example, Halkes, "Theologie, feministische", in FLex, 1105.

nature of the general debate, and the boundary separating it from "moderate" feminism often fluctuates. The clearest example here is Mary Daly, whose basic work *Beyond God the Father* is repeatedly cited by feminist theologians and whose position constitutes an enduring source that cannot be overlooked.

2. Basic Characteristics of Feminist-Theological Anthropology

By the nature of its subject matter, feminist theology is first of all anthropology: the feminist image of man is applied in the area of theology and given an anchoring in transcendence. Crucial here is the already-described notion of an "androgynous utopia", which would have masculine and feminine traits combined, insofar as possible equally, in every individual person. Meanwhile, the word "androgyny" is increasingly avoided, and the relevant meaning is signified by the concepts of "wholeness", "comprehensiveness", or "totality". Halkes understands by this the "integration of the different polarities (woman/man; mind/body; and so on)" into a personal unity.[7] Ruether is more cautious about "masculine-feminine" labelling and demands that men and women should possess, to equal degrees, the whole of those psychological qualities that were, by tradition, previously divided into masculinity and femininity.[8] The

---

[7] Halkes, *Söhne,* 20.

[8] Ruether, *Sexism,* 111; similarly, Moltmann-Wendel, *Milch,* 162–65; Elisabeth Moltmann-Wendel, "Ein ganzer Mensch werden. Reflexionen zu einer feministischen Theologie" [Becoming a whole person: Thoughts for a feminist theology], EK 12 (1979): 340–42, 347. Donate Pahnke, *Ethik und Geschlecht. Menschenbild und Religion in Patriarchat und Feminismus* [Ethics and sex: Image of man and religion in patriarchy and feminism] (Marburg, 1991), 171–73, speaks here of a "substantial feminism", according to which there are no sex-specific qualities: what exists "substantially" are only the human ones. This sort of feminism is distinct from the gynocentric direction but also from "integrative feminism", which still

ideal of androgyny or "wholeness" is a basic principle of feminist theology that decisively stamps all its manifestations.

Even for gynocentric feminists, who reject the expression "androgyny", the notion of "wholeness" is the leading ideal. Forming the background of precisely this orientation is, once again, the depth psychology of C. G. Jung. According to Jung, wholeness, or the "self", is the most comprehensive psychological reality, in which the conscious and the unconscious, the masculine and the feminine, are conjoined. "Wholeness", then, means the integration of inherently polar psychological archetypes into a higher unity.[9]

Jung's disciple Erich Neumann holds that the achievement of psychological wholeness is easier for women: whereas a boy has to disengage himself, in the course of his development, from sexual identity with his mother, a girl can continue to identify with her mother. "This basic situation of the female", according to Neumann, "in which the process of 'finding oneself' corresponds to the primary form of human psychological relatedness, confers, from the start, the advantage of a natural wholeness and self-containedness that is lacking in the case of the male."[10]

The meanings attached to the terms "wholeness" or "comprehensiveness" are often, of course—as Moltmann-Wendel has to admit in the *Wörterbuch der Feministischen Theologie*—quite divergent. For example, striving for "wholeness" can mean: developing all the qualities inherent in being

---

assumes the existence of certain polarities and wants to see them integrated. This distinction between "integrative" and "substantial" is, however, more verbal than material; in either case, the goal is to eliminate the difference between the sexes to the greatest possible extent.

[9] Raimar Keintzel, *C. G. Jung: Retter der Religion? Auseinandersetzung mit Werk und Wirkung* [C. G. Jung: Savior of religion? An analysis of his work and influence] (Mainz and Stuttgart, 1991), 77–86.

[10] Erich Neumann, *Zur Psychologie des Weiblichen* [On the psychology of the feminine], 2d ed. (Munich, 1975), 14.

human; bringing together existing but otherwise separate qualities; achieving self-realization; or finding salvation.[11]

Regarding the ideal of "androgyny" or "wholeness", the following question arises: Does being a man or being a woman still have any value as such, or should the mutually complementary differences between the sexes be eliminated?

Catharina Halkes occasionally suggests that she by no means wants to achieve a "neutralization of the sexes".[12] At the same time, however, she dismisses any "two-sided anthropology" aimed at preserving a certain difference between men and women. She rejects both the formula "equal in value but different" and the idea that men and women should complement each other. Her so-called "transformative model" is based on the individual who, in the framework of a changed society, determines his personal attributes for himself.[13] That one's biological nature also affects the structure of one's psyche cannot, it is true, be denied, but since man is a mutable cultural being, "attributes based in nature and creation" cannot provide us with any "criteria of what livable . . . humanness is". Human sexual differentiation as a man or a woman is not, according to Schillebeeckx, among the anthropological constants.[14]

---

[11] Elisabeth Moltmann-Wendel, "Ganzheit" [Wholeness], in Wb, 136–42; cf. also H.-B. Gerl, "Ganzheitlichkeit" [Wholeness], in FLex, 399–404.

[12] Halkes, "Ebenbild Gottes", 96; *Suchen,* 112; *Das Antlitz der Erde erneuern: Mensch—Kultur—Schöpfung* [Renewing the face of the earth: Man—culture—creation] (Gütersloh, 1990), 168f.

[13] Halkes, "Ebenbild Gottes", 96; *Suchen,* 112; "Frau/Mann. B. Aus feministisch-theologischer Sicht" [Woman/man. B. From a feminist-theological viewpoint], in Peter Eicher, ed., *Neues Handbuch theologischer Grundbegriffe* 2, 2d ed. (Munich, 1991), 61; cf. *Antlitz,* 161f.; 168f.

[14] Halkes, *Antlitz,* 161f. Halkes refers here to Edward Schillebeeckx, *Christus und die Christen. Die Geschichte einer neuen Lebenspraxis* [Christ and Christians: The history of a new life experience] (Freiburg, 1977), 712–25. Surely no complete assessment of "anthropological constants" is to be given there (ibid., 715); as for the rest, the human body (which is not to be thought gender neutral) itself belongs, according to Schillebeeckx, to the aforementioned constants.

Halkes herself speaks positively here of a " 'singles' anthropology".[15]

This same rejection of the idea that men and women are mutually complementary can also be found in the other authors. For Ruether, "maleness and femaleness" survive now "solely as designations of reproductive roles".[16] Moltmann-Wendel caricatures the notion of "complementarity" as hopelessly antiquated and pleads for the "autonomy" of every individual person.[17]

Rejection of the idea that men and women are mutually complementary is, in fact, a common aspect of feminist theology. Only a few first signs are becoming evident that point in another direction. To cite an already-mentioned example: Hedwig Meyer-Wilmes, inspired by gynocentric feminism, once refers to being a man or a woman as an ontological, metaphysical reality.[18] But at the same time—and this view is more characteristic of her position—she constantly argues against any talk of an "essence" of woman, or against any "iconization" of the feminine.[19]

Elisabeth Gössmann—who is not necessarily typical of feminist theology—makes surprising reference to "the mysterious character of being human in two different forms of existence" and welcomes the formula "equality in difference". But this way of speaking, which contradicts her dominant equality feminism, is called into question by her very next sentence: "The openness of the theological image of man—as a consequence of insight into the always possible evolution of new essential traits for both sexes—

---

[15] Halkes, *Suchen,* 127. Here, the biographical context is perhaps noteworthy: Halkes has been separated from her husband since 1972: *Südwestpresse. Schwäbisches Tagblatt,* November 16, 1979.

[16] Ruether, *Sexism,* 111.

[17] Elisabeth Moltmann-Wendel, ed., *Frau und Religion: Gotteserfahrungen im Patriarchat* |Woman and religion: Experiences of God in the patriarchy| (Frankfurt, 1983), 31 (introduction); *Milch,* 17.

[18] Meyer-Wilmes, 91–93.

[19] Ibid., 53, 79, 141, passim.

means that this image can no longer be defined or circumscribed."[20]

The American Anne Carr is initially critical of the androgyne model: "While it is an attractive vision, it has problems as well, for it ignores the importance of human embodiment. . . . "[21] But she then goes on to align herself with a report issued by the Catholic Theological Society of America in 1978. This asserts that even though one-nature or single anthropology, which disregards the difference between men and women, can be criticized, it provides a sounder basis for theological debate than the dual anthropology.[22] Is not logic replaced by pragmatism here?

Carr then cites Karl Rahner, according to whom a static view of nature is false and persons must decide for themselves what the human being is and will become.[23] That the difference between the sexes and their being mutually complementary might be part of God's good creation, and would therefore need to be preserved, does not occur to the American nun. The continuing influence of Simone de Beauvoir's existentialism and of progressivist evolutionism is apparently stronger than the message of Genesis, according to which man was created as male and female (Gen 1:27).

At a certain point, however, the position that man can, and may, restructure his own nature without limit develops a large fissure: genetic engineering is also vigor-

---

[20] Elisabeth Gössmann, "Anthropologie", in Wb, 21.

[21] Carr, 124.

[22] Carr, 125–26. The allusion here is obviously to the struggle for ordination of women.

[23] Carr, 117, 131–33. The reference to Rahner here is quite problematic, however, since he definitely stresses the positive significance of the difference between the sexes, even if he strongly relativizes the enduring structures in this; cf. Karl Rahner, "Maria und das christliche Bild der Frau" [Mary and the Christian image of woman], in his *Schriften zur Theologie* 13 (1978), 358f.; Anita Röper, *Ist Gott ein Mann? Ein Gespräch mit Karl Rahner* [Is God a man? A conversation with Karl Rahner] (Düsseldorf, 1979), 58–60.

ously rejected by the theological feminists. The new technologies — according to the current position — represent a patriarchal abuse of power. Women must not be a party to making "their bodies" available for use "as vessels in which experiments are conducted and storerooms from which material is taken".[24]

The difference between men and women takes on a new cast in view of the problem of genetic engineering. This one point has not, however, been systematically integrated into the feminist position: apart from the case of goddess feminism, the difference between the sexes is almost exclusively regarded as an arbitrarily formable product of culture.

Now, if the difference between the sexes is of no value, the significance of marriage and the family also collapses, since those cannot be imagined apart from the mutual complementarity of husband and wife, father and mother. For the *Wörterbuch der Feministischen Theologie,* marriage is only *one* possible life-style among others in the area of sexuality and child-raising, and other forms of relationship must also be tried out. The criterion for behavior here is the "dismantling of relationships of dominance", which, however, is difficult to arrange: for the history of marriage reveals itself as a history of the incapacitation of women.[25] Female homosexuality is thus not called into question anywhere in the extensive dictionary (or in other similar contexts), although it is repeatedly noted and defended in a positive way.[26] As claimed in an article specifically devoted to lesbianism, the "abolition of forced heterosexuality is one of the most urgent tasks facing feminist theology."[27] This advocacy, or at least tolerance, of practical

---

[24] Ina Praetorius, "Gen- und Reproduktionstechnologien" [Genetic and reproductive technologies], in Wb, 151–53 (here 152).

[25] Regina Ammicht-Quinn, "Ehe" [Marriage], in Wb, 67–73.

[26] Wb, 38, 71, 219, 243–45, 257, 262, 293, 362, 371f.

[27] Eske Wollrad, "Lesbische Existenz" [Lesbian existence], in Wb, 245. This assistant of the Viennese pastoral theologian Zulehner even includes a relevant contact address: "Network of lesbian theologians in training"; Prüller, 212. Cf. also Barz, Leistner, and Wild (with a well-disposed

lesbianism is no mere coincidence resulting from some external situation but derives instead from the very core of feminist anthropology. Doris Strahm gets right to the point: "Women and men should, once and for all, stop complementing each other."[28]

The sharp rejection of any sort of complementarity of the sexes is based on recognition that the difference between partners in a marriage normally leads to a certain subordination of the wife and a more strongly developed leadership role for the husband.[29] In the perspective of feminism, however, any relation of superordination and subordination, any kind of "dominance" or "hierarchy", is the absolute incarnation of evil. The Marxist heritage reveals itself here with particular clarity. According to Moltmann-Wendel, the "crux of patriarchal theology" is "the dominance implied in the relationship between mind and body: will over the unconscious, history over nature, man over woman".[30] And Ruether: "Sexual symbolism is foundational to the perception of order and relationship that has been built up in cultures. The psychic organization of consciousness, the

---

foreword by Marga Bührig, a member of the highest executive committee in the World Council of Churches); Bernadette Brooten, "Liebe unter Frauen" [Love between women], in Sommer (1985), 351–57; Carter Heyward, *Und sie rührte sein Kleid an. Eine feministische Theologie der Beziehung* [And she touched his robe: A feminist theology of relationship], with an introduction by Dorothee Sölle (Stuttgart, 1986); Halkes, *Antlitz,* 159f., 178; contradictory: Schneider-Böklen and Vorländer, 113–16.

[28] Doris Strahm, *Aufbruch zu neuen Räumen. Eine Einführung in feministische Theologie* [Departure for new regions: An introduction to feminist theology] (Freiburg, Switzerland, 1987), 128; in agreement: Prüller, 102. This demand is not quite consistent, however, insofar as Strahm joins Luce Irigaray in speaking of an "open identity" of woman that will perhaps emerge in the future, for a female identity would be distinct from the male one. But precisely this is categorically rejected by Strahm in favor of an anthropology centered totally on the individual: Strahm, *Aufbruch,* 120–31.

[29] Halkes, "Frau/Mann", 61; Carr, 32–33, 49–51; Moltmann-Wendel, "Ganzheit" [Wholeness], in Wb, 136; cf. Sorge, 76; E. A. Johnson, "Jesus der Mann" [Jesus the man], *Concilium* 27 (1991): 522.

[30] Moltmann-Wendel, "Werkstatt", 34.

dualistic view of the self and the world, the hierarchical concept of society, the relation of humanity and nature, and of God and creation—all these relationships have been modeled on sexual dualism."[31] The implicit supposition here is that subordination and inferiority are identical[32] and that they signify "division" and "rape".[33]

This basic "antihierarchic" assumption and the criticism of any kind of "dualism"[34] are reflected in the way that the relationship between body and soul is defined. Also presupposed here is so-called "holistic thinking". Following Teilhard de Chardin, Ruether maintains that "spirit and matter are not dichotomized but are the inside and outside of the same thing."[35] "Material existence is ontologically inferior to mind"—this fundamental philosophical truth is "the root of moral evil" and is reflected in all other kinds of dominance relationships.[36] It is thus logically consistent that Ruether also radically denies immortality of the human soul.[37] "From the feminist viewpoint", according to the *Wörterbuch der Feministichen Theologie,* "the notion of an immortal soul is seen . . . as fundamentally hostile to the body and to women."[38]

Corresponding to the bodily is sense-based "experience", which alone ought to determine behavior.[39] For Moltmann-Wendel, "control over our bodies by the will and the understanding" is a kind of "rape".[40] The overvaluing of Greek logical and abstract thought has concretely resulted

---

[31] Ruether, *New Woman,* 3; cf. *Sexism,* 75ff.

[32] Ruether, *Sexism,* 94; Halkes, *Söhne,* 25.

[33] Moltmann-Wendel, *Milch,* 25.

[34] Cf. also Herta Nagl-Docekal, "Dualismus" [Dualism], in Wb, 64-67.

[35] Ruether, *Sexism,* 85.

[36] Ruether, *New Woman,* 189; cf. *Sexism,* 78.

[37] Ruether, *New Woman,* 211; *Sexism,* 257-58.

[38] Luise Schottroff and Dorothee Sölle, "Auferstehung" [Resurrection], in Wb, 35f.; criticism of this is expressed, however, by Elisabeth Gössmann, "Zukunft" [Future], in Wb, 440f.; cf. below, 190-92.

[39] On the concept of "experience", cf. above, 56-57.

[40] Moltmann-Wendel, *Milch,* 25.

in an objectified and technologized civilization, which is driving the world toward the brink of disaster. Halkes criticizes theological rationalism, which "is blind to the heart, the mystery, and the symbol with its many levels".[41]

As shown by concrete developments since Vatican II, criticism of an "overintellectualized" theology and liturgy, which has lost touch with the divine mystery and the realm of feeling, is currently shared by many sections of the Church, from the followers of the deceased Archbishop Lefèbvre to Eugen Drewermann.[42] However, the attack on "masculine" rationalism, which is recognized by many as justified, escalates among the feminists into an impassioned antagonism toward knowledge of trans-temporally valid truth per se. As previously indicated here, Moltmann-Wendel opposes experience-centered "theo-fantasy" to reason-guided "theo-logy", and Halkes calls for "less objectivity and more ambiguity".[43] Nelle Morton's programmatic address at the "sexism" conference of the World Council of Churches,[44] which was greeted enthusiastically by Moltmann-Wendel, speaks of "life's" having "to be taken as it is lived. Then there would no longer be that dichotomy on whose basis the mind constructs ultimately valid dogmas about matters of the body like . . . abortion, environment, and energy resources."[45]

Abortion appears here as a matter of the woman's body

---

[41] Halkes, *Söhne,* 114.

[42] In quite contrasting circles within the Church, for example, a positive reception was given to the book by the social psychologist Alfred Lorenzer, *Das Konzil der Buchhalter. Die Zerstörung der Sinnlichkeit, eine Religionskritik* [The council of book-keepers: The destruction of sensuality: A critique of religion] (Frankfurt, 1981).

[43] Cf. above, 57–58.

[44] Cf. above, 56; Elisabeth Moltmann-Wendel, "Sexismus in den siebziger Jahren. Ökumenischer Frauenkongreß in Berlin" [Sexism in the seventies: The Ecumenical Women's Congress in Berlin], EK 7 (1974): 484f.; *Frau und Religion,* 24.

[45] Nelle Morton, "Auf dem Weg zu einer ganzheitlichen Theologie" [On the way to a holistic theology], in Moltmann-Wendel, *Frau und Religion,* 203.

without any attention being given to the child's right to life. In an article from the *Wörterbuch* signed by Moltmann-Wendel and Ina Praetorius, the demand for penalty-free abortion is defended in terms of justified "autonomy over one's body".[46] As an example of "liberated bodily experience", the authors then refer to Rosemary Ruether's account of the "rituals" of the American "Women-Church", to the "liturgy" of the feminist "female church". Included there, among other things, is a "rite of healing from an abortion", which laments the need to decide between two evils, that is, favoring either potential life or existing life. By "potential life", the child is meant. The woman, in opting for abortion, has made a "hard choice" but has "made the best choice that she could make".[47] The same attitude recurs, with no mention of contrary views, throughout the book. Abstract principles—such as, for example, the child's right to life— are not to be applied to the problem of terminating a pregnancy.[48] Given this sort of stand in favor of abortion, it is not surprising that seventy feminist theologians in Germany have signed a petition supporting repeal of anti-abortion legislation.[49]

That human life must be guided, not by sensual impulses, but by the mind is not infrequently called into question. Moltmann-Wendel cautions against regarding "our passions, our feelings, our aggressions" "as needing to be controlled", for this is typical of patriarchy. Even rage and aggression must be lived out if psychological wholeness is to be achieved.[50]

The core of feminist-theological anthropology consists

---

[46] Elisabeth Moltmann-Wendel and Ina Praetorius, "Körper der Frau/ Leiblichkeit" [Woman's body/corporality], in Wb, 219.

[47] Rosemary R. Ruether, *Women-Church: Theology and Practice of Feminist Liturgical Communities* (San Francisco, 1985), 161.

[48] Wb, 224, 290f., 295.

[49] At the "4th feminist liberation-theological summer-school university in Hofgeismar" in 1990: *Evangelische Information* 35 (1990): 4.

[50] Moltmann-Wendel, *Milch,* 163.

less in any positive program than in rejection of the existing situation. Seen as the main reason for this is the mutual complementarity of man and woman that is anchored most visibly in the family. The complementarity of man and woman is regarded, in turn, as the expression of a worldview in which different realities are set against one another (God-world, mind-body, and so on) and which is termed "dualism". In contrast to this, the feminists call for the breaking down of such dualities. This levelling process extends from anthropology all the way—as will be shown later—to an androgynous image of God and the Church.

3. Critical Assessment

An axiom of Saint Paul's states: "Test everything; retain what is good" (1 Th 5:21). In that spirit, it is now time to meet the challenge of feminist theology by commenting, one by one and insofar as possible within the framework of this review, on the points that have been covered above.

That the questions of the feminists have a certain justification is suggested by the biblical sentence stipulating that man shall be "master" over woman (Gen 3:16). "Master" is probably meant here in the negative sense, as an oppressive subjugation.[51] The suppression of women is a consequence of sin that can also manifest itself within the Church. Whether, of course, that applies without distinction to any sort of "subordination" remains to be seen.

Another question is whether actual or presumed suppression of women can be placed at the center of one's thinking about the world. Precisely this constitutes the weak point of feminism, which, according to Ursula King,

---

[51] Pope John Paul II, apostolic letter *Mulieris dignitatem,* On the Dignity and Vocation of Women on the Occasion of the Marian Year (Boston: St. Paul Books, 1988); for exegetical questions, see Neuer (1993), 72–74.

is marked by a peculiar inconsistency: "There is a contradiction in its attitude toward female biology, which is repudiated as having no role-determining implications, yet also extolled, through bestowing the possibility of bearing and nourishing, as the source of female strength and experience."[52]

At least in "equality feminism"—which dominates the field in theology—it is in fact stressed, on the one hand, just how important, precisely in the case of women, experience is. Again and again, one hears the stereotyped comment that men are incapable of having anything to say about female concerns.[53] On the other hand, however, the experience of women is viewed as a limitlessly changeable product of culture. This fundamental contradiction runs through the whole of the relevant literature. Here, the thinking of "post-Christian" gynocentric feminism is essentially more consistent when it regards being female as an enduring ontological structure.

Fundamental to the "androgyny"-oriented mainstream in feminist theology is the thesis that every person combines in himself both "feminine" and "masculine" aspects. Here, it is seen as crucial to achieve a state of balanced "wholeness". The notion of an "androgynous utopia" derives to no small extent from the psychoanalysis of C. G. Jung. According to Jung, every person should also integrate into his psyche those aspects pertaining to the opposite sex, namely, the "animus" (for women) and the "anima" (for men).[54] This psychoanalytic approach corresponds to the general observation—which is backed up by biology (for example, the hormonal balance)—that, in a certain way, there is an interplay between "masculine" and "feminine" traits in every person. From the psychological viewpoint,

---

[52] King, 1283.

[53] Cf. below, 119.

[54] Jolande Jacobi, *Die Psychologie von C. G. Jung. Eine Einführung in das Gesamtwerk* [The psychology of C. G. Jung: An introduction to his work as a whole], 4th ed. (Zurich, 1959), 173–87.

"masculinity" and "femininity" are not qualities iden
with concrete male or female existence as such. To this
extent, feminism contains a core of truth when, for example,
it stresses that women should not stay out of traditional
"male domains" like the natural sciences, and, conversely,
that men should not allow their sensibilities to atrophy.[55]

This element of truth is taken too far, however, when
one demands an androgynous balancing of all qualities in
every person and regards any sex-specific emphasis as a
"halving".[56] Every person is, right down to the smallest
bodily cells, either a man or a woman.[57] No matter how
much one's concrete way of being a man or a woman is
stamped by cultural factors, all particular forms of this are
still contained within an antecedently biological framework.
The difference between men and women is no mere "designation of reproductive role" (Ruether) but goes much deeper.
The entire mental and physical being of a person is shaped
by this basic difference.[58] Gynocentric feminism's critique
of equality feminism seems justified in principle: biology,
psychology, and sociology cannot be separated from one
another. Social definition of the nature of the sexes is in many
respects flexible but is not also just pure invention that, as
it were, floats above the clouds with no physical anchoring.

---

[55] Strahm, *Aufbruch,* 128.

[56] "Being halved" is spoken of, for example, by a certain pastoral
theologian who, in streamlined accord with feminism, proclaims an
"androgynous future": P. M. Zulehner, *Pastorale Futurologie* [Pastoral
futurology] (Düsseldorf, 1990), 75–102; "Mann" [The male], in Hans
Rotter and Günter Virt, eds., *Neues Lexikon der christlichen Moral,*
(Innsbruck, 1990), 461f.

[57] Cf. the many varied essays in Sullerot.

[58] Cf. the conspectus, also including philosophy, in S. B. Clark, *Man
and Woman in Christ: An Examination of the Roles of Men and Women in
Light of Scripture and the Social Sciences* (Ann Arbor, 1980), 369–570;
Albrecht (1983), 29–43; Hauke, *Women in the Priesthood?,* 85–120; Neuer
(1993), 20–51; N. A. Luyten, ed., *Wesen und Sinn der Geschlechtlichkeit*
[Essence and meaning of sexuality], Grenzfragen 13 (Freiburg and Munich,
1985); Christof Gaspari, *Eins und Eins ist Eins — Leitbilder für Mann und
Frau* [One and one make one — Models for man and woman] (Vienna,
1985).

Even C. G. Jung—whose theoretical approach is, by the way, not undisputed[59]—has fully acknowledged the different natures of the sexes and has by no means lent support to the dissolution of specifically masculine or feminine identity. Feminist theologians apply their criticism to precisely this point[60] but nevertheless adopt the ideal of wholeness, which they then normally reinterpret as implying an equally balanced mixture of the male and female natures. The positive-sounding word "wholeness" obscures what is ultimately meant: the destruction of established identity. The goal is androgyny, in which anything specifically masculine or feminine must disappear. The Jungian disciple Barz, who is otherwise well-disposed toward feminism, regrets "that not even the concept of a complementarity of the sexes finds favor at the court of the feminists".[61] The gynocentric feminist Christa Mulack stresses, with much justification, that the androgynous ideal implies male-centeredness and hostility toward females.[62]

It is precisely from deepened reflection on the polarity and complementarity of the sexes that important impulses could emerge toward further development of the positive concerns in feminism. The psychologist and philosopher Philipp Lersch, for example, having evaluated countless well-founded particular facts, describes the "polarity" of

---

[59] For a critical assessment, cf. Clark, 633; Hauke, *Women in the Priesthood?*, 128–33; Albert Görres, "Erneuerung durch Tiefenpsychologie?" [Renewal through psychoanalysis?], in A. Görres and Walter Kasper, eds., *Tiefenpsychologische Deutung des Glaubens? Anfragen an Eugen Drewermann,* QD 113 (Freiburg i. Br., 1988), 140–47; Keintzel, publisher's cover text: "The works of the Zurich doctor Carl Gustav Jung have been well received mainly in esoteric, ecclesiastical, and theological circles; by contrast, they have been largely ignored within academic psychology."

[60] For example, Ruether, *New Woman,* 151–59; Brockmann; cf. also Ursula Baumgardt, "Anima/Animus", in FLex, 52–54.

[61] Helmut Barz, *Männersache: kritischer Beifall für den Feminismus* [Male business: Critical applause for feminism] (Zurich, 1984), 145.

[62] Cf. above, 39.

man and woman in a way that still remains exemplary.[63] According to him, men are more strongly marked by "eccentricity", which Lersch illustrates by the "symbol of a line emanating from the center of the subject and thrusting out into the world"; for the "centrality" of women, and their greater embeddedness in the rhythms of nature, he suggests "the image of a line circling around and enclosing its central point".[64] On the basis of the "centrality" or "centeredness" of women, one could, for example, argue that they have a greater aptitude for "seeing things in total perspective" as well as a stronger inclination to develop their talents less within a "pyramid of power" than within a readily comprehensible "circle".[65]

Feminists, of course, have a hopeless phobia about being tied down to "principles" as a result of adopting this sort of philosophical viewpoint, which transcends mere "role-oriented thinking". This fear is seen to be baseless if one considers that such phenomenological distinctions refer, not to firmly set "building blocks", but merely to accentuations or "prevalent tendencies".[66] Nothing exclusive is established in them. Despite vehement rejection of any talk of an "essence" of woman, feminists still constantly base their arguments on "female experience", which cannot be derived from "roles" that are understood as merely social. Here, Ingeborg Hauschildt observes critically: "All this amounts to a clear comment on just how insecure the

---

[63] Philipp Lersch, *Vom Wesen der Geschlechter* [On the nature of the sexes], 4th ed. (Munich and Basel, 1968); cf. the essays in Luyten, passim.

[64] Lersch, 62f.

[65] As suggested in Ute Knie, "Der Einfluß der Pfarrerin auf das Verständnis vom Pfarramt" [The influence of women pastors on the understanding of ministry], in Birgit Janetzky et al., eds., *Aufbruch der Frauen. Herausforderungen und Perspektiven feministischer Theologie* [The journey of women: Challenges and perspectives of feminist theology] (Münster, 1989), 180f.

[66] The expression "prevalent tendencies" was apparently first used by Theoderich Kampmann: *see* Mörsdorf, 399.

consciousness of female identity is today".[67] And Hanna-Barbara Gerl: "What would be desirable is an understanding in which independence and an allowance for complementarity belong together."[68]

If one begins with the assumption that there is a different accentuation of certain qualities in each of the sexes, it is quite allowable to speak, philosophically, of the "essence" of man or woman, even if no satisfactory "definition" seems possible. The ways in which reality is sexually stamped are too rich to be captured in any philosophical paraphrase. This does not mean, however, that classificatory attempts are senseless or that the reality underlying such efforts may be overlooked.[69] As Barbara Albrecht puts it, "self-realization apart from acknowledgement of reality", apart from acknowledgement of a female nature, is a senseless and presumptuous proposition. Measuring oneself against an objective "archetype" of woman (or man) does not imply alienation but, rather, the defining of one's individual being.[70]

According to traditional Christian understanding, what is at issue in the debate about the "essence" of the sexes is no mere demarcation dispute between biology and sociology. Being a man or a woman is not the defective chance product of an ever-advancing evolutionary process but the creative gift of a good God. In the very first chapter of Holy Scripture, we read: "God created man in his image; in the divine image he created him; male and female he created them. . . . God looked at everything that he had made, and he found it very good" (Gen 1:27, 31).

As images of God, man and woman are equal in value

---

[67] Hauschildt, "Feministische Theologie", 14.

[68] H.-B. Gerl, *Wider das Geistlose im Zeitgeist: 20 Essays zu Religion und Kultur* [Against the spiritless in the Age of the Spirit: 20 essays on religion and culture] (Munich, 1992), 50.

[69] A noteworthy recent attempt, summarizing the data from the human sciences in tabular form, is presented in Gaspari, 142f.

[70] Albrecht (1983), 33f.

but not equal in kind. Anyone who wishes to aboli: distinction between male and female places hims opposition to the will of the Creator and the nature of man, which is not something neutrally sexless. Rebellion against one's own nature as male or female is ultimately grounded in the atheistic delusion of being able to create oneself. The ideas of Sartre, as appropriated by de Beauvoir, continue to exert their influence here, even when there is still formal talk of "God" or "creation". The conceptual system in Christian feminist theology is largely determined, not by belief in God the Creator, but by an existentialist imperative that could be termed "structural atheism". If it is true, as Ursula Erler thinks, that revolt by women against their own female nature is virtually the norm today,[71] then what we are faced with here is an alarming godlessness of major proportions. The currently pressing task, therefore, is not primarily to overcome false stereotypes about roles, although such undoubtedly exist, but to foster healthy self-awareness of the specifically masculine or feminine natures. In view of the countless attacks against "sex roles" that occur in the Church's educational work, nothing is more appropriate than the following characterization from C. S. Lewis' *Screwtape Letters:* "The game is to have them all running about with fire extinguishers whenever there is a flood, and all crowding to that side of the boat which is already nearly gunwale under."[72]

By rejecting the idea of an antecedently given nature of woman, the equality feminists ultimately turn against themselves. For whoever would like to see his own identity as man or woman vanish into a greater wholeness cuts at the very roots of his personal wholeness. The actual result of

---

[71] Ursula Erler, *Zerstörung und Selbstzerstörung der Frau. Emanzipationskampf der Geschlechter auf Kosten des Kindes* [Destruction and self-destruction of women: The emancipatory struggle between the sexes at the expense of the child] (Stuttgart, 1977), 88.

[72] C. S. Lewis, *The Screwtape Letters* (New York, 1946), 129.

the sorts of striving that are supposed, in feminist theology, to lead to "wholeness" is broken human existence.

The inner distractedness of feminist theology can, at times, almost be "seen". On the title page of the new standard text by Hedwig Meyer-Wilmes, *Rebellion auf der Grenze* [Rebellion on the borders], there is a color illustration of a female figure, which is described as follows in the catalogue for an exhibition of feminist art:[73]

> A self-confident young woman.... The shoulders ... are broad and powerful, her features are angularly accentuated ... she moves ... actively toward the observer, challenges him. Draped like a stole around her neck, shoulders, and arms, is a reddish-colored serpent, whose tail and head, with its darting tongue, she holds securely in her grasp, like a snake-charmer in a circus. No impression is created that the serpent could threaten the female figure ... rather, it seems to exist in concord with her, to be bound to her in a playful dance. Woman and serpent form a harmonic unity.

Whether this androgynous image really exudes "harmony" may be left to the observer's own judgment. A question may well also remain (assuming a Christian interpretation of Genesis 3) as to just who holds whom in his grasp here.

The androgynous ideal ultimately makes women (and men) incapable of marriage. For marriage is always inherently linked to the complementarity of one partner with the other. Men and women are dependent on each other, not simply interchangeable. A warning sign of broken human existence is the earlier-noted tolerance, or even encouragement, of lesbianism. The inability to view man and woman as a mutually complementary couple results in existences without futures, condemned to extinction on biological

---

[73] Andreas Mertin, "Der Griff zur Freiheit. Die 'andere Eva' im Blick der Kunst" [Reaching for freedom: The "other Eve" in the view of art], *forum religion* (3/1987): 22. The exhibition was organized by the Protestant "Institute for Present-Day Church Construction and Religious Art", Marburg, 1985–1986, under the title "The Other Eve: Transformations of a Biblical Image of Woman".

grounds alone. Whoever tampers with the institutii the family effectively deprives mankind of its future. N ness and femaleness were conceived by the Creator, no suspect components of a class-war structure, but as sources of an inexhaustible richness of mutual complementarity. Men have need of women, and vice versa. Along with similarity, it is precisely the differences between people that provide a basis for mutual exchange. The aim of achieving a hermaphroditic, androgynous "autonomy" is at odds with the ideal of "community", which draws its existence from the harmonious interaction of differing talents.

Feminist theology is so vehement in its opposition to the differing natures of man and woman because it recognizes in this a certain ordering structure. The "eccentricity" of men and the centeredness of women[74] can be seen with particular clarity in the example of the family: as a mother, the wife is normally tied more closely to the children and the home, whereas the husband more often tends to assume leadership of the family. Although that is not the case exclusively, the contrasting tendencies are nevertheless there. In this sense, the husband is more the "head" of the family, and the wife, as its "heart", more "subordinate" — even if contemporary developments have brought their respective tasks closer together. Pope Pius XI, in his encyclical *Casti connubii,* on marriage, refers to this ordering structure as a "fundamental law enacted and upheld by God himself", although its concretely applicable form may, of course, be variable "in accordance with differing personal and geographical and temporal circumstances".[75] Vatican II repeatedly cites this encyclical as a definitive authority whose assertions it presupposes without restating them in their full breadth.[76] On the occasion of the

---

[74] Cf. above, 103.

[75] Encyclical *Casti connubii,* no. 27f.; AAS 22 (1930): 549f.

[76] Pastoral constitution *Gaudium et spes* (The Church in the Modern World), nos. 48–51.

reform of German marriage and family law in 1953, the German bishops declared: "Whoever denies, in principle, the responsibility of the husband and father as head of the wife and family places himself in opposition to the gospel and the teaching of the Church."[77]

There is no corresponding declaration in the writing of the German bishops in 1981 on the position of women. The general, more open main concept is worded: "Mutual partnership".[78] The ideal of an equal partnership is often presented as being contrary to the biblical structural order; in the author's opinion, however, both belong together.[79]

In 1988, Pope John Paul II published his apostolic letter on the dignity and vocation of women, *Mulieris dignitatem.* In it, he offers a brief interpretation of Ephesians 5:21–33, where the relationship of husbands and wives in marriage is compared to the bond between Christ and the Church. The Pope emphasizes here that there is, in marriage, not just the subjection of the wife to the husband, but also a mutual subjection (Eph 5:21).[80] In this, the Pope sees the new element in the gospel, whose effect is to exclude any desire for domination by either party and to transform from within the patriarchal structure of the Judaism of the time.

This central and decisive viewpoint on mutual submission should always be borne in mind, along with the fact that the submission acquires, for each partner respectively,

---

[77] "Hirtenwort der deutschen Erzbischöfe und Bischöfe zur Neuordnung des Ehe- und Familienrechts vom 20.2.1953" [Pastoral statement by the German archbishops and bishops on the revision of marital and family law of February 20, 1953], *Amtsblatt für die Diözese Augsburg* 63 (1953): 72.

[78] *Zu Fragen der Stellung der Frau in Kirche und Gesellschaft* [On the question of the position of women in Church and society], Die Deutschen Bischöfe 30 (Bonn, 1981).

[79] On the subject of "partnership", see Eugen Kleindienst, *Partnerschaft als Prinzip der Ehepastoral* [Partnership as the principle of the pastoral letter on marriage] (Würzburg, 1982); Hauke, *Women in the Priesthood?,* 111, 345–51 (German ed.).

[80] *Mulieris dignitatem,* no. 24.

a specifically masculine or feminine coloring. In the masculine symbol of the bridegroom, John Paul II sees an allusion to God's love, who was "first" to love,[81] while, in the case of the wife, he emphasizes a special receptive "sensitivity" as the essential characteristic of her femininity.[82] The unity of male and female (Gal 3:28) does not cancel out their diversity.[83] The document on the ordination of women issued by the Sacred Congregation in 1976, to which the Pope refers, had already viewed the images of "bridegroom" and "head" in terms of a natural analogy between Christ and an official priesthood consisting of men.[84]

As a component of the relationship between the sexes (namely, in marriage), this "head"-structure is seen by many recent theologians as hopelessly antiquated and as having been superseded by the Council.[85] Nevertheless, precisely as a result of the controversy with feminism, Catholic[86]

---

[81] Cf. 1 Jn 4:19; *Mulieris dignitatem,* no. 25.

[82] *Mulieris dignitatem,* no. 16.

[83] Ibid.

[84] Declaration of the Congregation for the Doctrine of the Faith on the Admission of Women to the Ministerial Priesthood, no. 5; cf. Hauke, *Women in the Priesthood?,* 59f. On the ordination of women, cf. *Mulieris dignitatem,* no. 26.

[85] For example, Wolfgang Beinert, "Theologie und kirchliches Frauenbild", in his *Frauenbefreiung und Kirche* [Women's liberation and the Church] (Regensburg, 1987), 51f. In the wake of feminist theology, some authors have begun describing the relevant statements in the New Testament, and the still relatively recent papal documents, as instances of "structural sin": one example is Hans Schilling, "Frauen im Kirchen- und Gemeindedienst: Hilfskräfte oder Partnerinnen der Männer?" [Women in church and community service: Auxiliary workers or partners of the men?], MThZ 39 (1988): 99; another is: Gutting, *Offensive,* 47, 52. Both theologians presuppose here the popular Marxist theory of a prehistoric matriarchate (Schilling, 99; Gutting, *Offensive,* 50f., 63; Gutting also claims support from the physicist (!) F. Capra, one of the main protagonists of the New Age movement (ibid.).

[86] For example, Clark, passim; Albrecht (1980), 32f.; (1983), 42; Burggraf (1986), 26f.; W. E. May, "Marriage and the Complementarity of Male and Female", *Anthropotes* 8 (1992): 58–60.

and Protestant[87] theologians (both female and male) have reflected, in a new and deepened sense, on that basic tenet of biblical anthropology, and recent research in the humanities has contributed a variety of material to this.[88] Such activity is not directed toward "patriarchalism", social "discrimination", and historical "regression", but toward a structured conception that can shape the future.

Fundamental here is the recognition that subordination is not the same as inferiority. This holds true, in a certain way, of the relationship that exists among the three Divine Persons: when they are enumerated, the Father is always named first, as the one from whom the Divine Life emanates. The Father sends the Son and the Spirit into the world, but not vice versa. The order inherent in the relationship grounds the difference between Father, Son, and Spirit yet does not annul the unity and equality of the Divine Nature. By reason of their origin, as Persons, in the Father, the Son and the Spirit are subordinate, in their redemptive-historical role, to the Father; but they are not therefore diminished in their Divine Being.

An American woman theologian, Joyce A. Little, draws a comparison between the feminist anthropological notion equating subordination with diminished selfhood and the Christology of the heretic Arius, which was condemned by the Council of Nicaea (325): Arius had regarded Jesus as subdivine because, even as the preexisting Son, he is subor-

---

[87] For example, Beyerhaus, *Aufstand,* 10, 44f., 48f., 53f.; Hauschildt, "Feministische Theologie", 52; *Versuchung,* 24; Neuer (1993), 72–74 (cf. also the commentary by Christa Meves [1985], publisher's cover text); "Frau (c) systematisch-theologisch" [Woman (c) systematic-theologically], ELTG 1 (1992): 632–34; Dieperink, *Feministische Theologie,* 35; *Vrouw,* 29–32; John Piper and Wayne Grudem, eds., *Recovering Biblical Manhood and Womanhood: A Response to Evangelical Feminism* (Wheaton, Illinois, 1991).

[88] As examples, just the following may be noted here: Clark, 369–506; Wigand Siebel, ed., *Herrschaft und Liebe. Zur Soziologie der Familie* [Governance and love: On the sociology of the family], Soziologische Schriften 40 (Berlin, 1984); Anne Moir and David Jessel, *Brainsex* (Düsseldorf, 1990), 132f., 209–25.

dinate to the Father. Arius was—to formulate the point in terminology of a later time—unable to reconcile (1) the idea that the Person of the Eternal Logos could be subordinate to the Father (as his origin) with (2) the idea that there is an equality in the Divine Nature. The theologians of the Council of Nicaea, by contrast, recognized that Jesus' being obedient to the Father (which is consistent, at the human level, with his being the Eternal Son) does not preclude his having fully equal worth by virtue of his divinity. Asymmetry in relationship does not, of itself, imply a higher or lower degree of worth. Something similar holds true of the way that the relationship between the sexes is structured: being of equal worth and being subordinate are not antitheses.[89]

Here, of course, "superordination" and "subordination" are not universal principles applicable to all situations but function-related qualifications of the more fundamental male or female natures, by which a mutual subordination is also implied (Eph 5:21). Without any ordering structures— which always contain elements of superordination and subordination—social institutions are utterly inconceivable.[90] This applies not least to marriage and the family. The Dutch theologian Martie Dieperink directed this humorous point at feminism: A ship with two captains—that couldn't go well for long.[91] Also, the husband's responsibility in marriage is comparable, from the Christian viewpoint, not to the model of an authoritarian "overlord" or brutal

---

[89] Cf. J. A. Little, "Sexual Equality in the Church: A Theological Resolution to the Anthropological Dilemma", *The Heythrop Journal* 28 (1987): 169. On the christological question, cf. also Wolfgang Marcus, *Der Subordinationismus als historiologisches Problem* [Subordinationism as a historiological problem] (Munich, 1963); "Subordinationismus" [Subordinationism], LThK, 2d series, 9 (1964): 1138f.; Dietrich Wiederkehr, "Entwurf einer systematischen Christologie" [Outline of a systematic Christology], *Mysterium Salutis* 3, no. 1 (1970): 562f., 568f.; Wolfhart Pannenberg, *Systematische Theologie* 1 [Systematic theology 1] (Göttingen, 1988), 298–305, 352–55, 455; Franz Courth, *Der Gott der dreifaltigen Liebe* [The God of trinitarian love] (Paderborn, 1993), 3, II, 3, b.

[90] Siebel, 14–19.

[91] Dieperink, *Feministische Theologie,* 35.

"macho" man, but to the devotion of Jesus, who gave up his life for the Church (Eph 5:21–32). "To be the head means, following Christ's example, to give oneself for the woman."[92] To reject any kind of superordination, caricaturing it in late-Marxist tones as "domination", can only mean being greatly out of touch with reality, which is not without consequences for the social sphere.[93] "Being master" (Gen 3:16) in the sociological sense, as "acting under mandate from and on behalf of some social unity",[94] is not the same as "being master" in the sense of oppressing. This ambiguity is not taken into account in many discussions.

It would, of course, be inappropriate to define the relationship between the sexes in terms of the partial aspect of "subordination". If married couples love each other and assume responsibility for each other, there is no wrangling over areas of competence. The more comprehensive view-

---

[92] Joseph Ratzinger, "Die Frau, Hüterin des Menschen. Versuch einer Hinführung zum Apostolischen Schreiben 'Mulieris Dignitatem' " [Woman: The protector of man: Attempt at an introduction to the apostolic letter *Mulieris dignitatem*], in *Die Zeit der Frau. Apostolisches Schreiben "Mulieris dignitatem" Papst Johannes Pauls II.* [The era of woman: The apostolic letter *Mulieris dignitatem* of Pope John Paul II] (Freiburg, 1988), 116.

[93] Clark (442f.) cites, for example, the following "achievements" of the egalitarian ideology:

(1) The family is weakened because the wife pursues her career independently of her husband and children and because the husband is less ready to assume responsibility for his family. Weakened families, in turn, produce children with greater personal problems.

(2) Sexual relations are thrown into confusion (impotence in men; "blossoming" of homosexuality).

(3) The women lose their sense of self-esteem and come under greater pressure to compete with men.

(4) Feminine talents, like providing a personally stamped source of care within the family, are neglected.

(5) There is also a functional decrease in areas for which the main responsibility is usually assumed by the husband: order, discipline, and protection.

(6) Men and women become psychologically unstable. The more influential the feminist movement—as Clark claims with reference to various relevant studies—the greater the psychological problems.

[94] Siebel, 18.

point on the relationship between men and women is that of mutual complementarity in unity and difference. The divinely willed differentness and complementarity of the sexes is the "watershed" that separates feminism and Christian anthropology. One can thank the *Catechism of the Catholic Church* for clearly underlining the element of complementarity: "Man and woman . . . are equal as persons . . . and complementary as masculine and feminine."[95]

The Pauline passage stating that there is neither male nor female in Christ (Gal 3:28) needs to be judged in the context of the theology of baptism. Through baptism, male and female are "one" in Christ, having been equally granted the life of divine grace. Here, according to Pauline theology, the Holy Spirit acts, not as a "leveller", but in the fullness of Christ's body, which consists of different parts (1 Cor 12). In particular, the Spirit does not subvert the order of creation but works it into his activity. Even the Pauline statements on the "headship" of the husband (1 Cor 11), offensive to some, are grounded, not in the fall—as, for instance, Moltmann-Wendel thinks—but in creation.[96]

The power of women is surely not less than that of men, even if it tends to be exerted behind the scenes and in ways that are not obvious. Oda Schneider, a pioneering figure in the Catholic lay apostolate, wrote penetratingly on this as early as fifty years ago.[97] That it seems sensible today for women to participate more widely in tasks formerly thought suited only to men need not be disputed here.[98] Pope Pius XII had already emphatically encouraged women to assume a greater public role, and we know that Pope

---

[95] CCC, no. 372.

[96] Clark, 166–82; Neuer (1993), 102–7; Hauke, *Women in the Priesthood?*, 345–56.

[97] Cf. above, 9.

[98] Something treated with foresight by: Edith Stein, "Das Ethos der Frauenberufe" ["The ethos of Women's Professions"] (1930), in her *Die Frau. Ihre Aufgabe nach Natur und Gnade,* Werke 5 (Louvain, 1959), 1–15 (English ed.: *Woman* [Washington, D.C.: ICS Publications, 1987]).

John XXIII spoke in this connection of a clear "sign of the times".[99] Inside the Church, too, scope for activity by women can certainly still be expanded. But is it really auspicious to identify the redemption of mankind with gaining totally equal and undifferentiated access (fifty-fifty) to every sort of task?[100] This already somewhat "hoary" utopia would sound more convincing if the process of human gestation were—as some radical feminists demand[101] —completely technologized. Whether that would be beneficial has, in the meantime, come to be seen as doubtful even by most feminists.

It seems that feminist theologians, despite their protestations to the contrary, often introduce an ideal model oriented toward male structures (or nonstructures). Mary Daly, for example, dedicates her *Gyn/Ecology* to "big, strong women" and puts on the first page the image of a double-bladed ax, with which she would like, in untrammeled rage, "to cut down" all opposition with "imperial might".[102] Could a deep-seated inferiority complex have been influencing her pen here?

In any case, it hardly attests to feminine self-confidence when women start calling for "androgyny", or "man-womanliness". Is not the logical implication of such thinking a feminization of men and a masculinization of women?

There is also a peculiar paradox in the fact that, on the one hand, feminism celebrates its tender bond with everything living, while, on the other, it has, from the very start, promoted the cause of abortion. Feminist theology often adopts this paradoxical attitude to its fullest extent. Un-

---

[99] Cf. Hauke, *Women in the Priesthood?*, 55f.

[100] Not the least of those active along these lines is Rita Süssmuth, "Partnerschaft" |Partnership|, in FLex, 883–90 (cf. above, 21); according to her own statements, Süssmuth, who is known to regard Simone de Beauvoir as her model (see above, 23) has meanwhile, in the wake of Mary Daly, begun "to take up arms" for feminist theology: *Publik-Forum*, January 29, 1988, 16.

[101] Cf. above, 36f.

[102] Daly, *Gyn/Ecology*, xiv, 405.

restricted abortion is endorsed,[103] or at least not criticized. The maternal womb is regarded as the source of a new spirituality, while, at the same time, it becomes a slaughterhouse. A more brutal form of "domination of man by man"—the charge brought against patriarchy by feminist theology—hardly seems conceivable.

Properly understood, wanting to combine body and soul into a harmonious "whole" is certainly a praiseworthy concern. The same applies to the relationship between "head" and "heart", between reason and feeling. In modern Western culture, one can, indeed, observe an extreme "top-heaviness" (resulting to no small extent from the so-called "Enlightenment") that fails to do justice to the whole person. The fact that tendencies of this kind have become particularly widespread in the postconciliar Church— as rightly noted in Halkes' critique—needs to be decisively counterbalanced. An indicative example of "masculine" rationalism can probably be found in the (provisional first) ecumenical translation of Luke 2:19, 51: the notion of "keeping in her heart" becomes, at the beginning of the 1970s, "keeping in her memory" or "reflecting on".[104] This kind of "overintellectualization" can lead, in the political sphere, to a purely technico-rational calculation of power that plunges the world into the abyss. Here, the more strongly "holistic" faculties characteristic of women can provide an important counterweight, assuming that they are applied with a sound awareness of pertinent identity.

But does direction of the body by the soul, of everchanging "experience" by the mind, amount, as such, to "rape"? Must not a "democratization" of body and soul lead to dictatorship by the body? To irrational capriciousness? It is in the spiritual soul, moreover—which also

---

[103] For example, Daly, *Father*, 110–14; *Gyn/Ecology*, 57ff.; *Lust*, 323; Moltmann-Wendel, *Milch*, 99; *Frau und Religion*, 203 (Morton); cf. the references in Hauschildt, "Feministische Theologie", 13.

[104] Ecumenical translation of Holy Scripture: *The New Testament* (Stuttgart, 1972).

survives the body's decay—that man's unique personal identity is grounded. Only for this reason are infants in the womb, the aged and weak, or the handicapped endowed with a dignity over which no one may exercise arbitrary control. Must not any abandonment of this personal core of the human being prepare the way for a destructive, death-dealing barbarism?

The soul has priority, ontologically, over the body. At the same time, both an intimate connectedness and a mutual interaction are to be assumed between them. It is, of course, inappropriate to identify the relationship between man and woman with that between body and soul. At best, it makes sense to attempt a cautious analogy here.[105] Man and woman share the same level of being, which is precisely not the case with body and soul. The "dualism-critique" advanced by feminist theology effectively confuses different levels of being.

Anthropology provides the decisive, substantial point of departure for feminist theology. All other areas are viewed and defined from its perspective. The revolutionary outlook, understood, not as a supplement to traditional theology, but as something radically new,[106] is ultimately justified on anthropological grounds. The demands of feminism, in order that they be felt even more emphatically, are carried over into areas bound up with the image of God and the Church. Feminist theology, according to Eva Schmetterer, thus becomes an "appendix to feminist anthropology". It appears "as an extending of feminist anthropology into the sphere of the transcendent but no longer as an *original* speaking about God himself".[107] In the end, the decisive point is not to see "feminine" traits as being actively copresent in the image of God or to replace "brothers" as a

---

[105] Cf. Hauke, *Women in the Priesthood?*, 113–15.
[106] Halkes and Meyer-Wilmes, in Wb, 102.
[107] Schmetterer, *Frau,* 153; cf. Axmacher, 13.

form of address in liturgical texts with "brothers and sisters". Rather, what is crucial for feminist theology is the expansion into the theological sphere of an anthropology that resolves the tension-filled interrelatedness of man and woman into a colorless oneness: "androgyny". This sort of fundamental estrangement from the message of creation is perpetuated in every other area that feminist theology addresses. At best, then, dialogue with feminist theology can be carried on about one or another problematic aspect but not about this largely dominant basic approach. What presents itself in new dress here, it would seem, is the ancient challenge of Gnosticism, according to which God created man, not as male and female, but as a man-woman, as an androgyne.[108]

---

[108] On the connection between Gnosticism, feminism, and feminist theology, which is recognized and affirmed by some female theologians themselves, cf. (from a positive viewpoint) Elaine Pagels, *Versuchung durch Erkenntnis. Die gnostischen Evangelien* [Temptation through knowledge: The Gnostic gospels] (Frankfurt, 1981); from a critical viewpoint: Hauke, *Women in the Priesthood?*, 158–65; Heine, *Frauen,* 117–35; Sudbrack, *Neue Religiosität;* and Padberg, *New Age* (topic: "Gnosis").

VI. THE EXPERIENCE OF WOMEN AS "FORMAL PRINCIPLE"

1. "Material" and "Formal" Principles of Theological Feminism

In order to characterize the basic concern underlying Protestantism, a distinction is drawn, in denominational studies, between a substantial and a formal point of departure, between a "material" and a "formal" principle. The material principle is the man's justification before God. This comes about solely through faith (*sola fide*) and solely through grace (*sola gratia*). The criterion of knowledge, or the formal principle, is solely Holy Scripture (*sola scriptura*), in which God's revelation is presented to man.[1] In contrast to this, the Catholic Church stresses that man also plays a role in his justification and that works of love cannot be separated from faith. Divine revelation is mediated not only through Holy Scripture but also through Church tradition.[2]

Such talk of a "material" and a "formal" principle can also be applied, in a certain way, to feminist theology. If "material principle" refers to the substantial, central concern, then that can be identified here as the previously

---

[1] In present-day ecumenical theology, this distinction is utilized only rarely, since it is usually seen as too strongly emphasizing a systematic point. Still, it retains its value as a basic conceptual determinant requiring further, more concrete elaboration.

[2] Fundamental here is the Dogmatic Constitution of Vatican II on divine revelation, *Dei Verbum.*

described ideal of "wholeness" or "androgyny".[3] It shows itself most clearly in anthropological contexts and runs, like a central theme, through statements in all other areas. The formal starting point, on the other hand, and the decisive criterion for evaluating all theological statements, is female "experience". Feminist theologians are largely agreed about the validity of this general characterization. The only disputed aspect is the degree of exclusivity attaching to the criterion of "experience": the "female way of seeing" either becomes the sole principle of theology — according to "post-Christian feminism" — or is to be linked to the larger body of Christian thought — according to the "moderate" female theologians.[4]

2. "Experience" and Revelation

Putting an emphasis on "experience" does not suffice to explain just what, concretely, is to be understood by that concept. Also needing to be clarified is whether "female experience", as a generally valid criterion, even exists at all and how its relation to revelation is to be construed.

The concept of experience itself is more often presupposed than positively investigated.[5] A formal definition is not to be found, even under the entry for that topic, in the *Wörterbuch der Feministischen Theologie*.[6] Theological feminists are one in regarding the experience of women, which they see as having been unjustly neglected in the androcentric theology of the past, as their main concern.

---

[3] The ideal of "wholeness" is described as a "central" and "fundamental" category in, for example, Moltmann-Wendel, "Ganzheit", in Wb, 136, 139.

[4] Schmetterer, *Frau,* 39–41.

[5] Ibid., 147f.

[6] Wb, 73–78.

But what is this experience of women?[7] According to Moltmann-Wendel, what is involved here—much as in liberation theology—is the "experience of social oppression".[8] The earlier-mentioned elements of "contextuality" and "partiality" are repeatedly emphasized. Dorothee Sölle gets particularly concrete here: God is "red-green and a woman".[9] In the *Wörterbuch,* this is put somewhat more soberly: "Orientation toward the experiences of women requires decisiveness, partisanship, and the renunciation of claims to neutrality and general validity."[10] The aim is quite conscious adoption of an angle of vision oriented toward the interests of female "liberation". As is occasionally stressed with reference to Jürgen Habermas, there is no objective, neutral perspective.[11] Habermas' monograph *Erkenntnis und Interesse*[12] is one of the best-known philosophical works of the neo-Marxist "Frankfurt School".

The claim that experience can have general validity is renounced; and yet, in relation to the experience of women, such validity is usually presupposed. A problem is caused here by the fact that feminists often evaluate women's experiences in quite opposing ways. In the USA, a feminist theology linked to black women has emerged: the so-called "womanists",[13] who separate their own experiences off from those of whites. With an at times remarkably positive view of the experience of Islamic women,[14] even the

---

[7] Cf. the survey in Schmetterer, *Frau,* 148–50; Christine Schaumberger, "Erfahrung" [Experience], in Wb, 75–77.

[8] Moltmann-Wendel, *Milch,* 77.

[9] According to: *idea,* no. 58/59 (June 22, 1989): 6.

[10] Schaumberger, "Erfahrung", 75f.

[11] Moltmann-Wendel and Kegel, 191 (resolution of female theologians in Würtemberg).

[12] Jürgen Habermas, *Erkenntnis und Interesse* [Knowledge and interest], 3d ed. (Frankfurt, 1975).

[13] Wb, 438–40.

[14] For example, Rita Rieplhuber, "Islam", in FLex, 515–24; Monika Fander, "Reinheit/Unreinheit" [Cleanliness/uncleanliness], in Wb, 350; more critical: Iris Müller, "Frauen in Weltreligionen. IV. Islam" [Women in world religions. IV. Islam], in Wb, 123–26.

institution of the harem can occasionally be favorably evaluated, as a prototype of feminist self-experience groups, by committed feminists[15]—though this is hardly likely to be a view shared by all their comrades-in-arms. Moreover, circumstances in German-speaking countries have meanwhile led to coinage of the technical term *"Schwesternstreit"*, or quarrel among sisters.[16] Just what "female experience" does, and does not, concretely mean is thus anything but clear.

The phrase "experience of women" can refer to women not only as the subjects of experience but also as its objects.[17] In this second sense, the central focus is on self-experience. Catharina Halkes (in an earlier-noted context) observes that "rebellious women" are not only the subjects but also the subject matter of feminist theology.[18] Strictly considered, the concern here is no longer with God but with women. Rosemary Ruether, by contrast, speaks with greater subtlety: " 'Experience' includes experience of the divine, experience of oneself, and experience of the community and the world in an interacting dialectic."[19]

"Orientation toward experience" is a formal concept that admits of broad interpretation. But its import becomes quite concrete in the context of attempting to evaluate what Christian tradition calls "revelation". The most fundamental document of revelation—which is accepted, at least in principle, by all Christians—is Holy Scripture. The relationship between subjective "experience" and "revelation"

---

[15] Vittoria Alliata, *Harem. Die Freiheit hinter dem Schleier* [Harem: The freedom behind the veil] (Munich and Gütersloh, 1981).

[16] For example, Birgit Cramon-Daiber et al., *Schwesternstreit. Von den heimlichen und unheimlichen Auseinandersetzungen zwischen Frauen* [Dispute among sisters: On the secret and uncanny disagreements among women] (Reinbek, 1990).

[17] Schmetterer, *Frau,* 149.

[18] Cf. above, 57; Catharina Halkes, "Maria, die Frau. Mariologie und Feminismus" [Mary, the woman: Mariology and feminism], in Walter Schöpsdau, ed., *Mariologie und Feminismus* (Göttingen, 1985), 47f.

[19] Ruether, *Sexism,* 12.

in biblical interpretation thus needs to be clarified somewhat more precisely through relevant examples.

"History is . . . nothing other than a compilation of the
statements that were made by murderers about their vic-
tims and themselves." This quote from Simone Weil is
applied directly to the interpretation of Holy Scripture by
Elisabeth Schüssler Fiorenza.[20] Her exegetical commen-
taries are endorsed to the greatest possible extent by Halkes,
Ruether, and Moltmann-Wendel.[21] This American exegete,
of German origin, has meanwhile become something like a
feminist "Church mother", cited enthusiastically by most
feminist theologians. In frequency of citation in the *Wörterbuch der Feministischen Theologie,* she is surpassed only
by Mary Daly and comes just ahead of Rosemary Ruether.[22]
Schüssler Fiorenza thinks "that revelation and truth are
present only in those traditions and texts that evaluate and
transcend their patriarchal culture and androcentric religion".[23] As a means of recognizing "revelation", she makes
use of a four-stage method:

1. A *"hermeneutics of suspicion",* which is supposed to
purge biblical texts of patriarchal influences. Accordingly,
Holy Scripture must be regarded critically from the very
outset, since it originated in an androcentric culture.

2. A *"hermeneutics of historical recollection",* which is
aimed at bringing to light lost aspects of relevant history.
Here, it is presupposed that the activity of women has been
suppressed in biblical texts.

3. A *"hermeneutics of proclamation",* according to which

---

[20] Elisabeth Schüssler Fiorenza, "Die Rolle der Frau in der urchristlichen
Bewegung" [The role of women in the original Christian movement],
Concilium 12 (1976): 4.

[21] Cf., for example, Halkes, *Suchen,* 35f.; Ruether, *Sexism,* 33; Moltmann-Wendel, *Milch,* 89f.; Moltmann-Wendel, *Eigener Mensch,* 10f.

[22] Wb, index.

[23] Elisabeth Schüssler Fiorenza, "Für eine befreite und befreiende
Theologie: Frauen in der Theologie und feministische Theologie in den
USA" [For a liberated and liberating theology: Women in theology and
feminist theology in the USA"], *Concilium* 14 (1978): 202; cf. her *In
Memory of Her,* 29–35.

"patriarchally oppressive texts should no longer be proclaimed as the word of God". That, for example, the husband is the "head" in a marriage, as stated in the Pauline letters, cannot be the word of God and must be excluded from what is proclaimed as such.

4. A *"creative hermeneutics"*, which is aimed at contributing to women's "struggle for liberation" "by means of a retelling of biblical texts and a recreating of biblical figures".[24] History thus needs to be rewritten for the purpose of furthering the ideals of feminism.

Schüssler Fiorenza illustrates all this with a striking example, namely, an interpretation of the story of Mary and Martha (Lk 10:38-42):

1. "Hermeneutics of suspicion": The "patriarchalism" of the evangelists is "exposed": "The story places the *Kyrios* and his authority at the center of the action. Since he is characterized in terms of masculine concepts, it is clear that this story is linguistically androcentric, that is, grammatically male-centered. . . . Beyond that, the story justifies Mary, the silently listening woman, whereas Martha, who speaks in defense of her interests, is made to fall silent."

2. The "hermeneutics of recollection": "As mistress of the house and head of a home-based church, Martha welcomes the *Kyrios* to her house. The text contains not a single word to indicate that Martha is in the kitchen preparing the meal. Rather, it stresses that she is occupied with *diakonia* and *diakonein,* concepts that were already in use at Luke's time to designate a 'leading office' in the Church."

3. The "hermeneutics of proclamation": The text, as it appears in the Gospel, is not "God's word" but "Luke's word".

4. The "creative hermeneutics": The story is rewritten:

I am Martha, the founder of the church of Bethany and the sister of Mary, the evangelist. Various men are trying to

---

[24] Elisabeth Schüssler Fiorenza, "Biblische Grundlegung" [Biblical foundations], in Maria Kassel, ed., *Feministische Theologie* (Stuttgart, 1988), 25f.

collect stories about Jesus and to write them down, but they are not doing this properly. Some even make use of our own names to argue against women's having leading roles in the movement. Our great-great-granddaughters must learn our true story if the succession of equals is to endure.... Jesus asked me to sit at the head of the table for the breaking of bread and invited Susanna to say the blessing and explain the day's biblical passage. The men grumbled a bit, to be sure, but we women were quite enthused about the new possibilities that God had opened up to us.[25]

With this "hermeneutics", Schüssler Fiorenza effectively adopts a middle position on a scale defined by three broad tendencies:

1. The "Bible and its symbols are 'nonsexist' ".[26] If one only interprets the text precisely enough, its concern is found to correspond to that of feminism. This probably more ideal sort of model was still thought possible by Halkes in 1980[27] but was discarded a year later.[28]

2. The "Bible is partly sexist and partly nonsexist". This is the position of most "moderate" feminists.

3. The Bible is to be dismissed entirely as "hopelessly sexist"—the position of Daly and "post-Christian feminism".[29]

What one "selects" from the Bible is the decisive factor.[30]

---

[25] Schüssler Fiorenza, "Grundlegung", 35f., 43f.

[26] R. G. Hamerton Kelly, "Gott als Vater in der Bibel und in der Erfahrung Jesu. Eine Bestandsaufnahme" [God as Father in the Bible and in the experience of Jesus: A summary review], *Concilium* 17 (1981): 247.

[27] Halkes, *Söhne,* 64: "The question of whether the Bible is a patriarchal and androcentric book I don't want . . . to answer yet. . . . Perhaps in 25 years . . . we will have to acknowledge, after all, that the Bible is an androcentric book."

[28] Catharina Halkes, "Motive für den Protest in der feministischen Theologie gegen Gott den Vater" [Motives for the protest in feminist theology against God the Father], *Concilium* 17 (1981): 260: "As regards the Bible and tradition, I do not . . . believe that these . . . can be entirely purged of sexism."

[29] Hamerton Kelly, 247.

[30] Catharina Halkes, "Feministische Theologie. Eine Zwischenbilanz" [Feminist theology: An interim assessment], *Concilium* 16 (1980): 298.

The Protestant Moltmann-Wendel claims support here from Martin Luther, who rejected the Letter of James as a "dry epistle" because it contradicts his doctrine of justification by faith alone.[31] Such a view necessitates finding some principle that is more significant than Holy Scripture (and tradition). This repeatedly sought principle now turns out to be "experience". The *Wörterbuch der Feministischen Theologie* stresses that the "experience of women" is the "source of, and criterion for, feminist theology".[32] Or Schüssler Fiorenza: Feminist theology begins, "not with statements about God and revelation..., but with the experience of women".[33]

The statements in the Bible—with their claim to being revealed truth—and the so-called experience of women are thus set against each other. Something similar is done by the three authors, who can be regarded as particularly exemplary in the present context. Halkes allows that the biblical message retains a certain independent value whenever "revelation" and "experience" can generate critical perspectives on each other.[34] Nonetheless, the greater weight attaches to experience, by force of which we "judge whether these biblical ideas are still at all sound and make sense".[35] In actual fact, the Bible is a "loathsome book" for women, first, because the Old Testament opposes the cult of the goddess and, second, because it stems from a patriarchal culture.[36] Whenever use is made of liturgical

---

[31] Moltmann-Wendel, *Milch,* 204f.

[32] Schaumberger, "Erfahrung", 75; cf. 73.

[33] Elisabeth Schüssler Fiorenza, "Für Frauen in Männerwelten. Eine kritische feministische Befreiungstheologie" [For women in men's worlds: A critical feminist theology of liberation], *Concilium* 20 (1984): 34. cf. her *Brot statt Steine. Die Herausforderung einer feministischen Interpretation der Bibel* [Bread instead of stones: The challenge of a feminist interpretation of the Bible], 2d ed. (Freiburg, Switzerland, 1991), 18–20, 103–109.

[34] Halkes, *Suchen,* 25f.

[35] Ibid., 25.

[36] Halkes, *Söhne,* 55.

"texts hostile to women", women should get up and walk out of the church.[37]

The possibility of completely rewriting the Bible has to be kept open[38]—a process that has already been initiated in the USA. In so-called "nonsexist" translations of the Bible, "Father" and other "masculine" symbols are either expunged or supplemented by "feminine" ones; the personal pronoun "he" is neutralized as "he/she". At the instigation of the National Council of Churches in the USA, a "lectionary" was issued for use in church services according to which, for example, Christ (in Gal 4:6) is no longer sent by his "Father" but by "his Mother and his Father" (in reference to the first Divine Person). In the same biblical verse, the "Son of God" becomes the "Child of God". This is regarded as "inclusive" language, that is, as language that includes women (*Inclusive Language Lectionary*).[39]

In Ruether's case, the significance of Holy Scripture is even more strongly circumscribed than for Halkes. "The critical principle of feminist theology is the promotion of the full humanity of women."[40] The "experience"[41] that flows from this makes use of the Bible merely as one intellectual model among others.[42] Of equal importance, for example, are the movements of ancient Gnosticism or the Canaanite fertility cult.[43] "In the Bible", the teachings of Jesus have already been "falsified", and the canon of

---

[37] Ibid., 56.

[38] Ibid., 58f.

[39] The relevant sources are cited in Teresa Berger, "Women and Worship: a Bibliography", *Studia liturgica* 19 (1989): 96–110.; typical examples are given in William Oddie, *What Will Happen to God? Feminism and the Reconstruction of Christian Belief,* (San Francisco, 1988); D. G. Bloesch, *Battle for the Trinity: The Debate over Inclusive Language,* (Ann Arbor, 1985). Going beyond the official bounds of American denominations is Ruether's *Women-Church.* Cf. below, 148.

[40] Ruether, *Sexism,* 18.

[41] Ibid., 12f.

[42] Ibid., 17, 21.

[43] Ibid., 14, 34f.

Holy Scripture is a product of the "victors" that wrongly excludes heresies.[44] For Ruether, "revelation" amounts to "breakthrough experiences" that are found in all religions.[45]

Halkes protests against the idea that revelation was concluded with the coming of Jesus,[46] while Moltmann-Wendel insists that what is decisive has already been realized in Jesus. On the basis of her protest, Halkes later prefers to speak of an "unfolding" of revelation as opposed to an "ongoing revelation";[47] in the new edition of her monograph, however, this "correction" is not taken into account.[48] The relevant statements by Herlinde Pissarek-Hudelist in the *Wörterbuch* remain obscure: a so-called "older, static model for understanding revelation", described in a caricatured way, is contrasted with a so-called "dynamic" model.[49]

Halkes and Moltmann-Wendel, despite their reference to the revelation of Christ, also attempt to incorporate, for example, the Canaanite fertility goddess in the present-day image of God.[50] Moltmann-Wendel refers favorably to a certain theologian who wishes to achieve a "synthesis" between Yahweh and Astarte,[51] namely, Helgard Balz-Cochois. Balz-Cochois takes a stance "*against* 'the prophet' Hosea", who adhered all too conservatively to the First Commandment, and "*for* Gomer", his wife, who had participated in the mother-cult of the goddess of love. The

---

[44] Ibid., 14, 18.

[45] Ibid., 13.

[46] Halkes, "Zwischenbilanz", 297; *Söhne,* 60. Support for the view that revelation has "taken place repeatedly throughout the whole of history" is claimed from Vatican II in Carr, 73f. In the Dogmatic Constitution on Divine Revelation (*Dei Verbum*), however, nothing consistent with that can be found.

[47] According to Krattiger, 81f., based on an oral report of conference proceedings; cf. Halkes, "Protest", 260.

[48] In Halkes, *Söhne,* 60, both positions occur in an unreconciled way.

[49] Herlinde Pissarek-Hudelist, "Offenbarung" [Revelation], in Wb, 307–10.

[50] Halkes, *Söhne,* 55; Moltmann-Wendel, *Milch,* 62.

[51] Moltmann-Wendel, *Milch,* 113f.; Balz-Cochois, 55.

whore, Gomer, "appears as a pious woman, and Hosea, by contrast, as an eccentric, . . . a tyrant".[52]

The methodology for dealing with Scripture is even termed by some feminists *"Hexegese"* [a German contraction turning "exegesis" into "witch-egesis"], or "wild exegesis".[53] A serious claim (which is no less problematic for all that) underlies the image of the "primal Church" that Schüssler Fiorenza describes as the "egalitarian primal-Christian movement".[54] "Most" of this rich tradition, to be sure, has "probably been lost"[55] in the New Testament, but it still glimmers through in Galatians, according to which there is neither male nor female in the community of Jesus (Gal 3:28). This passage signifies "the annulment of social and religious distinctions".[56] In primal Christianity, "class distinctions were annulled or disregarded, and there were neither fixed structures nor an institutionalized leadership."[57] At the same time, it is nevertheless stated that there were female leaders of the community—in particular, the apostle Junia, who was only later interpreted as having been a man.[58] Through later accretions to the New Testament, however, patriarchalism and the principle of subordi-

---

[52] Balz-Cochois, 41, 55.

[53] Elisabeth Moltmann-Wendel et al., eds., *Feministische Theologie—Praxis. Ein Werkstattbuch* [Feminist theology—practice: A workshop book], Arbeitshilfen 3 (Bad Boll, 1981), 34–42.

[54] Elisabeth Schüssler Fiorenza, "Der Beitrag der Frau zur urchristlichen Bewegung. Kritische Überlegungen zur Rekonstruktion urchristlicher Geschichte" [The contribution of women to the original Christian movement: Critical thoughts on reconstructing original Christian history], in W. Schottroff and W. Stegemann, eds. *Traditionen der Befreiung,* vol. 2: *Frauen in der Bibel* (Munich, 1980), 80.

[55] Schüssler Fiorenza, "Rolle", 4.

[56] Ibid., 5.

[57] Ibid.

[58] Ibid., 6; the originator of this hypothesis is Bernadette Brooten; cf. her " 'Junia . . . hervorragend unter den Aposteln' (Rom 16,7)" ["Junia . . . prominent among the apostles" (Rom 16:7)], in Elisabeth Moltmann-Wendel, ed., *Frauenbefreiung. Biblische und theologische Argumente* [Women's liberation: Biblical and theological arguments], 2d ed. (Munich and Mainz, 1978), 148–51.

nation once again descended upon Christianity, even though Gnostics and Montanists had maintained the egalitarian approach to roles.[59] The idea that Gnostic circles had preserved the real nature of primal Christianity is also found in Moltmann-Wendel, Ruether, and Halkes.[60]

3. Critical Commentary

This is not the place for a detailed evaluation of the feminist theological interpretation of Scripture. Through strong concentration on female biblical figures, certain aspects can be brought to light that can be integrated into a responsible scholarly exegesis. The sensitive point is "biased interpretation" of Scripture,[61] which critics characterize as "rape".[62] The feminist worldview is used more or less as a sieve through which the biblical texts are "sifted". Of course, as the philosopher H. G. Gadamer notes, the oft-cited notion of "experience" is one of our "least-explained concepts",[63] and is hardly capable of providing an objective criterion; consequently, feminist theologians can sometimes arrive, on the basis of their "experience", at quite differing conclusions.

For purposes of critical analysis, "experience" can be defined, in a very general sense, as "practically useful knowledge gained through a long period of 'having to do' with people and things".[64] Generally, the concept of "experience" is characterized by an inherent link to the individual,

---

[59] Schüssler Fiorenza, "Rolle", 8; "Beitrag", 73; above all in: *In Memory of Her.*

[60] Moltmann-Wendel, *Eigener Mensch,* 13; Ruether, *Sexism,* 36, 214; Halkes, *Suchen,* 36.

[61] Uwe Gerber, *Die feministische Eroberung der Theologie* [The feminist conquest of theology] (Munich, 1987), 92.

[62] Beyerhaus, *Aufstand,* 35.

[63] H. G. Gadamer, *Wahrheit und Methode* [Truth and method], 2d ed. (Tübingen, 1965), 329.

[64] Josef de Vries, "Erfahrung" [Experience], in Walter Brugger, ed., *Philosophisches Wörterbuch,* 14th ed. (Freiburg, 1976), 88.

which, although it can be combined with "science", is precisely not identical with that.[65] An approach that remains
inside the sphere of feminine subjectivity is both self-
contradictory and incapable of grounding a "scientific"
discipline, which is concerned with universally valid knowledge that can be understood by women and men equally.
"Feminist theo-logy ... does not place subjectivity at the
service of knowledge but declares that it is itself the arbi-
ter and criterion of truth."[66] One can thus no longer speak
of a "science" here.[67] Eva Schmetterer rightly asks: "How
is experience—which is, of course, fundamentally and immediately someone's own particular experience—to be criticized? At most, one can say 'I have a different experience';
then it is just one experience against another."[68]

The "formal principle" of feminist theology is not only
logically senseless but also contradictory to the elementary principles of a theology that accepts the word of God
as its decisive criterion. Theology's proper source and
definitive standard is divine revelation, which has its
unsurpassable center in Jesus Christ, the Son of God who
became a man. Feminist theology, as pursued by its leading
authors, turns this point of departure upside down. Theology's source and criterion is no longer God himself but
the individual needs of this or that woman. If theology is
understood as a "discourse about God" that is grounded in
divine revelation, then what is involved in the feminist
conceptions is no longer theology.[69]

---

[65] Hans Wissmann et al., "Erfahrung" [Experience], TRE 10 (1982):
83–141.

[66] Schmidhäuser, 111.

[67] Schmidhäuser, 112: feminist theology is no longer a theo*logy* —as
some feminists willingly admit; cf. above, 57.

[68] Schmetterer, *Frau,* 145.

[69] Cf. Schmetterer, *Frau,* 151f., 198; Susanne Heine, "Feministische
Theologie—Theologischer Feminismus. Über die Bedeutung des Aus-
tauschs der Adjektiva" [Feminine theology—theological feminism: On
the significance of the exchange in adjectives], in Winfried Böhm and
Martin Lindauer, eds., *Mann und Frau—Frau und Mann. Hintergründe,
Ursachen und Problematik der Geschlechterrollen* [Man and woman—

The insistence on "experience" does have its gra
truth, namely, in the importance of the concrete per
whose belief in Christ (according to the Catholic view) is
logically preceded by a natural cognition and a readiness
of the will. In order to be able to accept revelation, man
must recognize its credibility. Among the *praeambula fidei*
— the knowable conditions that materially precede supernatural faith — are, for instance, the existence of God and
the testimony that the miracles provide to Jesus' divine
claim. A fundamental anthropological understanding also
precedes, or is coincident with, belief in revelation: for
example, the distinctive natures, and mutual needs for
complementarity, of man and woman; the positive worth
of motherhood and the family; and the specific responsibility of a father. What has been revealed by God must then
be appropriated by means of human reason and brought
into conceptual unity by theologians. Only here, at the
point of subjective appropriation of revelation, does specifically "masculine" and "feminine" experience come into
play. And at this point it is also possible, if need be, to
criticize the way in which people in the Church (or also
"the men") have given formulation to revelation. To a
certain extent, however, such criticism defeats its own
purpose if that revelation which occurred once and forever
in Jesus Christ, and was transmitted by the apostles, is no
longer acknowledged as the enduring standard. Otherwise,
theology becomes just a "projection screen" for subjective
needs.

An individualistic subjectivism is, in fact, evident in the
way that feminism treats the Christian religious heritage.
Ruether calls the Christian tradition just one, equally valuable perspective among others, from which she proposes

woman and man: Background, motives, and problems of gender-based
roles] (Stuttgart, 1992), 174; Motschmann, "Selbstversorgerinnen", 292;
Schmidhäuser, 118f. Reminders that the starting point for Christian theology is not "experience" but revelation are otherwise repeatedly given by
critics of feminist theology, e.g., Schneider-Böklen and Vorländer, 134f.;
Dieperink, *Feministische Theologie,* 30.

to select at will. Jutta Burggraf describes "syncretism", or the intermixing of religions, as "a characteristic feature" of feminist theology[70] — a reproach that crops up repeatedly, and not without justification, in the critical literature.[71] This corresponds to the similar "department-store mentality" that leads some devotees of the "New Age" to attempt to piece together a religion of their own. Here, faith is no longer grounded in listening to God's word but is dissolved into "gnosis", into seeming "knowledge".

The most severe criticism of this syncretism is directed at the view held by some feminists that "the female divinities in Israel's cultural environment, which the prophets opposed on the basis of the First Commandment, appear as manifestations of the true God."[72] The relevant memorandum of the Confessing Communities speaks of a "regression to archaic natural paganism".[73]

In Christian understanding, "revelation" refers, not to "trail-blazing experiences" of humans (Ruether), but to the self-disclosure of God. Holy Scripture is human "experience" only insofar as it presents God's revelation in a binding way. In so doing, it also takes a critical stance against other "experiences" that it rejects as heresy. Further, the qualitative shift from the Old to the New Testament must not be ignored. The complete and unsurpassable revelation of God occurs in Jesus Christ, who corrects the incomplete aspects of the Old Covenant. This corrective is also beneficial precisely to women, as is clear from Jesus' behavior and his prohibition of divorce.[74] It is not our "experience" that is the measure of God's self-revelation in Jesus Christ, but vice versa.

---

[70] Burggraf (1986), 16.

[71] For example, Hauschildt, "Feministische Theologie", 20; *Gott eine Frau?,* 26; Beyerhaus, *Aufstand,* 23, 41. Also substantially relevant are: Padberg, *Feminismus,* 144; Dokumentation (= nordelbische Bischöfe), 104 (5.); Axmacher, 6.

[72] Dokumentation (= nordelbische Bischöfe), 105 (6.); cf. Hermisson (1982).

[73] Beyerhaus, *Aufstand,* 43.

[74] Hauke, *Women in the Priesthood?,* 326–29.

To construe the history of the Church, already at the stage of the New Testament, as a history of decline (Schüssler Fiorenza) is at odds with New Testament evidence that Jesus cannot be separated from the community of the Church. Apart from the processes of Church tradition, none of the biblical writings would be available at all. It was the Church that first delimited the scope of the Bible and, for example, left out the fantastic texts of the Apocrypha and the myths of the Gnostics. Are we to disqualify as a piece of "androcentric editing" Jesus' promise that the Holy Spirit would stand by the Church and guide her to all truth?[75] Without the community of the Church, which is led by the Pope and the bishops, faith in Christ would be exposed to the sway of limitless caprice.

An authentic critique of the suppression of women can proceed only within an objectively authoritative context such as is provided by Scripture and tradition in the doctrinal office of the Church. Otherwise, charges and countercharges based on "feminist" or "masculinist" experiences of every possible kind can be thrown back and forth endlessly.

The construct of an "egalitarian Jesus movement", which is played off against two thousand years of Church history, is all too reminiscent of the popular Marxist "myth of the matriarchy". More detailed commentary on this may be deferred until the topic of "ecclesiology" is discussed later.[76] The feminist image of the past, according to the historian Lutz von Padberg, expresses "less about the nature of early times than about the hopes of feminists for the future".[77] Again, Schüssler Fiorenza complained bitterly when her intended contribution to an exegetical volume honoring her academic teacher was rejected.[78]

---

[75] Jn 14:26; 16:13.
[76] Cf, below, 207–9.
[77] Padberg, *New Age,* 58.
[78] Schüssler Fiorenza, "Beitrag", 83f.

The violence done to history by relentless imposition of certain favorite feminist theories, such as that of a matriarchy or an egalitarian primal Church, is the exact opposite of the gentleness and carefulness that the same authors demand in our treatment of the animal and plant worlds.[79] Mary Daly calls explicitly for "Methodicide", evidencing a rapacious mentality that rightly outrages Susanne Heine;[80] and Ulrich Schmidhäuser, not without reason, compares feminist hermeneutics to the "blood and soil" ideology of fascism.[81] At that time, "German Christians" caused great damage in the Protestant sphere. "Feminist Christians" are well on the way to repeating those same mistakes, this time in the ecumenical community. Mistakes, moreover, that should not be perpetuated but rather corrected.

---

[79] On this see below, 184.
[80] Daly, *Father,* 7–12; Daly, *Gyn-Ecology,* 23; Heine, *Frauen,* 12.
[81] Schmidhäuser, 124.

VII. THE IMAGE OF GOD

1. The Link to Feminist Anthropology

As explained earlier, the feminist image of man appears in two different variations: the "gynocentric" feminists orient themselves on the female nature, which they think deserves priority in society, while the "equality" feminists aim to achieve a balanced mixture of "masculine" and "feminine" traits in every individual person: the ideal of "wholeness" or "androgyny". Correspondingly, then, these two anthropological goals are adapted and transferred to the image of God. The "woman-centered" approach is reflected in "goddess feminism", whose adherents have largely abandoned Christianity as "irretrievably patriarchal"; the most prominent example here is Mary Daly.[1] Equality feminism, by contrast, requires the image of God to contain an "androgynous" mixture of masculine and feminine symbols. Regarding the image of God (as in other contexts), the boundaries between these two currents are fluid, since it is not unusual for talk of God as the "Father" or "Lord" to strike even "moderate" feminists as suspect.

The rejection of the biblical image of God, with its predominantly "masculine" symbolical stamp, must not be seen in isolation here: just as sharply rejected is the analogy between the marriage relation and the tie between God and men, in which the people of Israel, or the Church, appear as a "bride" and God as a "bridegroom". That Christian tradition gives precedence to the feminine for

---

[1] Cf. above, 78–86.

purposes of representing the position of mankind before God (which is also definitive for males) is branded by feminists of every shade as institutionalized female oppression. On this point, "equality" and "goddess" feminists are in the widest possible agreement. (This will be discussed in more detail later when the image of the Church and Mariology are examined.)

Equal inclusion of "masculine" and "feminine" traits in the image of God also occurs in philosophical and theological positions that do not presuppose feminist anthropology but that assume a complementarity, or polarity, of the sexes.[2] An "androgynous" image of God had been clearly developed in ancient Gnosticism and also appears in the world religions that flourished at the time, such as Hinduism[3] (which, however, contrasts with feminism by not at all neutralizing the difference between the sexes). Reference to these historical precedents for a "feminization" of the image of God is frequently made by feminists.[4] Despite its actual dependence on the "androgynous ideal" in anthropology, the feminist image of God is therefore to be regarded as having a certain character of its own.

---

[2] As apparently in H.-B. Gerl, *Die bekannte Unbekannte: Frauen-Bilder in der Kultur- und Geistesgeschichte* [The familiar unfamiliar: Images of women in cultural and intellectual history], (Mainz, 1988), 147-60.

[3] Cf. Hauke, *Women in the Priesthood?,* 152-65.

[4] On Gnosticism: Referring to Pagels, e.g., Ruether, *Sexism,* 34-35; Christa Mulack, "Gnosis (Verdrängte christliche Erkenntnis)" [Gnosis (suppressed Christian knowledge)], in M. Kassel, ed. (1988), 227-56; more cautious: Schüssler Fiorenza, *In Memory of Her;* Luise Schottroff, "Gnosis", in Wb, 156-58; on Hinduism: Ursula King, "Frauen in Welt-religionen I. Hinduismus" [Women in world religions I. Hinduism], in Wb, 113f.; Wb, 47; Marianne Katappo, *mitleiden — mithandeln. Theologie einer asiatischen Frau* [Suffering with — acting with: Theology of an Asian woman] (Erlangen, 1981).

2. Typical Positions

Mary Daly's key work *Beyond God the Father* has become
definitive of efforts to "depatriarchalize" the image of God.
The so-called "moderate" feminist theologians (who are
the primary focus of attention here) would like, at least in
principle, to combine "masculine" and "feminine" images
of God. Mary Daly, however, thinks differently: she radically rejects any talk of a "Father" and—especially since
the appearance of her work *Gyn/Ecology*[5]—is concerned
solely with worship of the "Goddess". A similar case, in
the German-speaking realm, is the Protestant theologian
Elga Sorge, who mocks the "Our Father" and opposes it
with a polemical "Our Mother".[6] Christa Mulack, in
particular, calls for a "matriarchal image of God".[7] How
difficult it would be to ignore the "goddess feminists" is
shown by the mere fact that Elga Sorge and Christa Mulack
appeared as speakers at the Protestant Church Congress
[*Evangelischer Kirchentag*] in 1991 and received enthusiastic applause.[8]

The "moderate" writers tend to distance themselves from
"goddess feminism"[9] and its exclusion of masculine symbols, which they see as simply reversing the previous
polarization.[10] Nonetheless, Halkes, Ruether, and Moltmann-Wendel regard the "matriarchal" symbol of the god-

---

[5] Cf. above, 84.

[6] Sorge, 3, 90f.

[7] Christa Mulack, *Die Weiblichkeit Gottes. Matriarchale Voraussetzungen des Gottesbildes* [The womanliness of God: Matriarchal suppositions in the image of God] (Stuttgart, 1983).

[8] *Idea spektrum*, no. 24 (1991): 27.

[9] M.-T. Wacker, "Die Göttin kehrt zurück. Kritische Sichtung neuerer
Entwürfe" [The goddess returns: Critical survey of recent conceptions],
in her *Der Gott der Männer und die Frauen* (1987), 11–37; Heine,
Göttinnen; Ruether, "Symbole"; Denise Dijk, "The Goddess-Movement
in the U.S.A. A Religion for Women Only", *Archiv für Religionspsychologie*
18 (1988): 258–66.

[10] Halkes, *Suchen,* 74; Ruether, *Sexism,* 39, 52; "Symbole"; Moltmann-
Wendel, *Milch,* 15, 103.

dess as the more fundamental,[11] even if they differ in their interpretations of just how the feminine has priority in the image of God. Catharina Halkes sees the feminine more as an emblem of God's immanence, of his nearness and presence in this world; in transcendence, which is symbolically expressed more in masculine images, she sees God's distance from the world and his self-containedness.[12] She wants to keep both combined yet also argues that at least provisional priority should be given to immanence.[13] Emphasis should be placed on the "mutuality of relationship between God and man . . . , the fact that God is tender, vulnerable, and close".[14] Whenever the image of the divine Father is experienced as oppressive, it should be discarded.[15]

Ruether, by contrast, repudiates divine transcendence altogether. "The divine is not 'up there', as abstracted ego, but beneath and around us as encompassing source of life."[16] In absolutely no case should one regard the divine as something that already existed prior to the world.[17] She rejects the "paternal" image of the "heavenly Father", which she views as a product of early Oriental nomadic culture,[18] and "our preferred images of the absolute are the Primal Matrix, the mother the earth,[19] the birth-giving "world egg", or the maternal "source".[20]

Moltmann-Wendel's position tends in the same direction. "As opposed to the masculine divine heaven, from

---

[11] Halkes, *Suchen,* 37; Ruether, *Sexism,* 2, 47; Moltmann-Wendel, *Milch,* 64 f., 187.
[12] Halkes, "Ebenbild Gottes", 94.
[13] Halkes, *Suchen,* 74.
[14] Halkes, "Zwischenbilanz", 296.
[15] Halkes, *Suchen,* 76.
[16] Ruether, *Sexism,* 49; cf. 52, 70–71.
[17] Ibid., 54.
[18] Ibid., 53.
[19] Ruether, *New Woman,* 211; *Sexism,* 50, 76, 266.
[20] Ruether, *New Woman,* 12; *Sexism,* 48, 70.

which a God reigns over us, the goddess represents for
women a kind of inner-worldly principle: she is the world,
manifest in every woman."[21] The relationship with God
must not be seen as "asymmetric and hierarchic" but as a
"love of like for like".[22] "Abba", the intimate form in which
Jesus addresses God, is interpreted by Moltmann-Wendel
as "disrespectful", and she characterizes "obedience" to
God as a "traumatic formulation".[23] Agreeing with Christa
Mulack, she thinks that there are ultimate matriarchal
roots to the term "Abba".[24] Mulack herself appeals here to
the esoteric tradition of Judaism, the Cabbala: "From the
purely outward side, 'Abba' represents something male; yet
the inner value is female: the maternal character *aleph* (A)
encloses the double . . . female character *beth* (B)."[25] In a
similar way, Moltmann-Wendel interprets the Trinity of
Father, Son, and Spirit as "a badly concealed product of
patriarchal overpainting", which was preceded by "a female
trinity".[26] This original trinity lives on in popular representations of Mary, the Child, and St. Anne.[27]

Other female theologians speak of a trinity of "girl,
mother, and old woman" (Mary Grey), or refer to the
"three-form *protennoia*" of Gnosticism (Christa Mulack).[28]

Hildegunde Wöller—Protestant theologian and publisher's
editor—urges that the "earth" should also be included in
the image of God. Here, she feels inspired by the psycho-

---

[21] Moltmann-Wendel, *Milch,* 62.

[22] Ibid., 185. The author agrees here with the psychoanalyst H. E.
Richter, who zealously opposes the "God-complex".

[23] Ibid., 107.

[24] Ibid., 109. Elga Sorge maintains, in all seriousness, that Jesus had
called out not only to the heavenly Father but also to a divine earth-
mother: Sorge, 119.

[25] Mulack, *Weiblichkeit,* 333. (Parenthetical letters added.)

[26] Moltmann-Wendel, *Milch,* 187.

[27] Ibid., 190.

[28] Herlinde Pissarek-Hudelist, "Trinität" [Trinity], in Wb, 425–27; cf.
Sorge, 26.

analyst C. G. Jung, who wanted to expand the Trinity, through inclusion of the devil or, alternatively, of Mary, into a quaternity.[29] The deification of "Mother Earth" would be in line with the worship of "goddesses" but also with "eco-feminism", which remains to be discussed as such here.[30]

The ultimate reason for transforming the image of God is indicated quite pointedly by Mary Daly, whose oft-quoted saying is: "If God is male, then the male is God."[31] The image of God is seen as providing transcendent anchoring for a certain subordination of women to men. In order to break down this relationship, there is a readiness to do away even with subordination to God.

That this animosity extends to wishing to dissolve God's identity as distinct from the world was made clear especially by Ruether. But even Halkes—the "most conservative" of our three representative authors—has reasons for "anxiety about being all too quick to characterize God as a person".[32] Since God's personhood is expressed primarily through the use of nouns ("Father", "King", "Lord" . . .), Halkes joins Daly in urging that the divine be identified instead through locutions based on verbs, for example, the "calling into being".[33] The descriptions of the divine favored by these theologians are transpersonal ones, such as the "ground of being", whose "earthing ground" is the "community".[34]

---

[29] On Wöller: Gerber, *Eroberung,* 39; on Jung: Herbert Unterste, *Theologische Aspekte der Tiefenpsychologie von C. G. Jung* [Theological aspects of C. G. Jung's psychoanalysis] (Düsseldorf, 1977), 107, 126–28, 140f.; Keintzel, 102–4.

[30] Cf. below, 232–38.

[31] Daly, *Father,* 19.

[32] Halkes, *Söhne,* 38.

[33] Halkes, *Söhne,* 37; *Suchen,* 74.

[34] Halkes, *Söhne,* 37; Ruether, *Sexism,* 49; Elisabeth Moltmann-Wendel, "Gottesbilder durch Frauen überprüfen" [Have images of God reviewed

As a means of breaking down the established image of God, with its predominantly masculine symbols, considerable use is made of the Bible itself. There, as we know, God is compared in several passages to a mother,[35] on which basis calls are made for at least a "parity" of masculine and feminine traits in the present-day image of God. There is a special liking for references to the Hebrew word for "showing mercy", *rechem,* which signifies "maternal womb",[36] and to the "feminine" figure of wisdom, which, after the appearance of Jesus as a man, was unfortunately suppressed by the "masculine" image of the divine Word, the "Logos".[37] Pope John Paul I is cited as having said that God is more mother than father.[38]

A favorite argument is based on man's createdness in the image of God. Herlinde Pissarek-Hudelist, for instance, says in the *Wörterbuch:* " 'Male and female he created them' (Gen 1:27) *must* mean that both masculine and feminine elements are contained in God. There can be nothing outside of God that was not first present within him."[39]

Although the general concern is to emphasize female

by women], in *Seid fruchtbar und wehrt Euch. Frauentexte zum Kirchentag* [Be fruitful and defend yourselves: Women's texts for Church congresses] (Munich, 1986), 64, 71.

[35] Esp. Is 49:14f.; 66:13.

[36] Halkes, *Söhne,* 38, 58; Ruether, *Sexism,* 56; Moltmann-Wendel, *Milch,* 103.

[37] Halkes, "Ebenbild Gottes", 94; Ruether, *Sexism,* 58f.; Moltmann-Wendel, *Milch,* 105. An extended example of the feminist approach to exegesis is provided by Virginia Mollenkott, *Gott eine Frau? Vergessene Gottesbilder der Bibel* [God a woman? Forgotten images of God in the Bible] (Munich, 1985); an appendix to this was written by Moltmann-Wendel.

[38] Halkes, "Ebenbild Gottes", 94; Moltmann-Wendel, *Milch,* 103.

[39] Herlinde Pissarek-Hudelist, "Gott/Göttin I. Praktische Theologie" [God/goddess I. Practical theology], in Wb, 161; cf. Helen Schüngel-Straumann, "Gottebenbildlichkeit I. In der biblischen Überlieferung" [Being in the likeness of God I. In biblical tradition], in Wb, 176; Wb, 45; Halkes and Meyer-Wilmes, "Feministische Theologie", in Wb, 104, 172.

aspects in the image of God, this does not apply without qualification to the mother symbol. Ruether is suspicious about possible insinuation of a relational model that subordinates man, that sees him as a child and thus makes him a "minor".[40] That Jesus views being a "child" before God as the ideal (Mk 10:13-16) is repeatedly treated with suspicion by other writers as well and is supplanted by emphasis on one's being an "adult" or on a "partnership" with God based on equal rights. Anne Carr even claims to find support for this in Thomas Aquinas—although without justification, since the cited passage concerns mutual love (*mutua amatio*) but by no means "friendship based on equal rights".[41]

Halkes and Meyer-Wilmes stress that "taking leave of God as the omnipotent Father is superseded by an emphasis on the reciprocity between . . . man and God."[42] Denial of divine omnipotence has meanwhile become a "fundamental principle" in feminist theology, to be found among all the important writers. For example, in connection with Whitehead's earlier-mentioned "process philosophy" (as appropriated by Mary Daly),[43] Anne Carr rejects any possibility of God's intervening in the course of history. Without human collaboration, God is helpless and suffers (as God) along with us. He is placed neither above us nor opposite us, but ahead of us as "future".[44] The *Wörterbuch* contains repeated references to the American Carter Hey-

[40] Ruether, *Sexism,* 69f.; cf. Dorothee Sölle, "Vater, Macht und Barberei. Feministische Anfragen an autoritäre Religion" [Father, power, and barbarism: Feminist questions for authoritarian religion], *Concilium* 17 (1981): 227; Claudia Lueg, " 'Vater unser'—ein Gott für Frauen?" ["Our Father"—a God for women?], *Katechetische Blätter* 112 (1987): 591.

[41] Carr, 150, 235n. 43 (on Thomas Aquinas, STh II-II q 23 a 1); cf. 135-41, 143; Gerber, *Eroberung,* 39-41; Prüller, 104; Wb, 171.

[42] Halkes and Meyer-Wilmes, "Feministische Theologie", in Wb, 104; cf. Halkes, *Antlitz,* 185.

[43] Cf. above, 82.

[44] Carr, 153-57.

ward, a professor of theology who was among the first
women ordained as "priestesses" (in 1973) in the Anglican-
like Episcopal Church. Heyward speaks of God as a process of "becoming God" ("godding") and of a "mutual
redemption" of God and man.[45] Dorothee Sölle—a vet-
eran of the "God-is-dead theology" of the 1960s—similarly
stresses that God has need of man. God comes into being
only by degrees and is himself in need of redemption.[46]
The latter proposition is also affirmed by Moltmann-
Wendel.[47] Hence, obedience to God, Sölle maintains, must
be replaced by mutual solidarity.[48] From this sort of perspective, there is no longer any place for the biblical practice of referring to God and Jesus Christ as "Lord".[49]

"More than to the Father and the Son", Halkes writes,
"feminist theologians have access to God the Spirit, who
embodies the relational (the connected) and the dynamic,
and kindles the spark in the things that occur between
people."[50] A feminist theology would have to be "primarily a pneumatological theology".[51] "As long as . . . it is
only asserted that Christ is the Lord of the Church, that he
is her pinnacle, while the Spirit appears to be secondary,
the situation of women in the Church is not good."[52]

The Holy Spirit's way of working coincides with the
feminist emphasis on how we "can experience the divine
more *within* us".[53] Moltmann-Wendel cites a Russian pro-

---

[45] Dorothee Sölle, "Gegenseitigkeit I. Theologisch" [Reciprocity I.
Theological], in Wb, 142; Elisabeth Moltmann-Wendel, "Gegenseitigkeit
II. Feministische Diskussion" [Reciprocity II. Feminist discussion], in Wb,
145; Heyward.
[46] Sölle, "Gegenseitigkeit", in Wb, 142; "Kreuz" [The Cross], in Wb,
235.
[47] Moltmann-Wendel, "Gegenseitigkeit", in Wb, 145.
[48] Sölle, "Vater".
[49] Cf. above, 72.
[50] Halkes, *Söhne,* 42.
[51] Halkes, "Zwischenbilanz", 297.
[52] Halkes, *Suchen,* 163.
[53] Ibid., 171; cf. "Ebenbild Gottes", 94.

verb that similarly emphasizes the Spirit's "immanence": "In the earth dwells the Holy Spirit."[54] The Holy Spirit, who was designated in Hebrew by the feminine word *ruah,* first became neuter in Greek, then masculine in Latin—a "masculinization" that must be exposed as such.[55] Both Halkes and Moltmann-Wendel (following the Swiss reformed theologian Kurt Marti) therefore see it as necessary today to speak of the "Holy Spiritess".[56]

A special case is put by the Swiss theologian Silvia Schroer, who argues for "feminine" characterization of the divine Spirit on the basis of the Gospels' account of the baptism of Jesus. The voice from heaven was not that of the divine Father but that of the goddess of love, Sophia. To justify this interpretation, she cites the Gnostic gospel of the Hebrews and the oriental goddesses of love, who were accompanied by a dove.[57]

Ruether, to be sure, has fears that a "Holy Spiritess" could only make the situation even worse. For in the classical doctrine of the Trinity, the Holy Spirit is subordinate to the Father and the Son, which means that the patriarchal split would then be introduced into the divine sphere as well.[58]

Jürgen Moltmann attempts to circumvent such fears by eliminating the "hierarchy" even within the Trinity. He claims that the biblically sanctioned formula "to the Father through Christ in the Holy Spirit" (especially Eph 2:18) is merely secondary; decisive are the reciprocal interpenetra-

---

[54] Moltmann-Wendel, *Milch,* 113.

[55] Halkes, *Söhne,* 61; Moltmann-Wendel, *Milch,* 106; similarly Ruether, *Sexism,* 59–60.

[56] Kurt Marti, *Zärtlichkeit und Schmerz* [Tenderness and pain], 4th ed. (Neuwied, 1980), 109; Halkes, *Suchen,* 159–73; Moltmann-Wendel, *Milch,* 202.

[57] Silvia Schroer, "Der Geist, die Weisheit und die Taube . . . " [The Spirit, wisdom, and the dove . . .], *Freiburger Zeitschrift für Philosophie und Theologie* 33 (1986): 197–225; "Gott/Göttin III. Neues Testament" [God/goddess III. New Testament], in Wb, 165.

[58] Ruether, *Sexism,* 61.

tion of the Persons (*perichoresis*) and the formula "with the Father and the Son", which no longer implies any element of subordination.[59]

The broad trend is not so much toward exclusive "feminization" of the Holy Spirit as toward equalized endowment of all three Divine Persons with female attributes—unless, that is, any mention of a Trinity is avoided altogether. Along the latter lines, Ruether speaks of God solely as the "Holy Spirit", the "Ground of Being of creation", and rejects the image of the Father;[60] the title "Spirit" can also apparently be omitted.[61] Even when Halkes and Moltmann-Wendel talk of a "priority" of the Holy Spirit, it seems questionable whether they are adhering to a trinitarian image of God or assuming a modalistic conception in which a single divine entity expresses itself through different images. In any case, what is stated by an American woman theologian about the doctrine of the Trinity seems not untypical, namely, that it is irredeemably patriarchal and "has become (except for some theologians, bishops, and fundamentalists) totally irrelevant".[62] Pissarek-Hudelist[63] surveys various attempts at "re-imaging" the doctrine of the Trinity, only to end by proposing that the troublesome Father-Son relation be supplemented by "matriarchal" approaches.

Usually, "the Divine" is to be viewed, not as a transcendent reality distinct from man, but—recalling the view

---

[59] Moltmann, "Vater"; "Die Gemeinschaft des heiligen Geistes. Zur trinitarischen Pneumatologie" [The community of the Holy Spirit: On trinitarian pneumatology], ThLZ 107 (1982): 714; *Der Geist des Lebens* [The spirit of life] (Munich, 1991), 303–20; on the christological question, cf. below, 166–67.

[60] Ruether, *New Woman,* 80.

[61] Ruether, *Sexism,* 70–71.

[62] Julie Hopkins, "Sind Christologie und Feminismus unvereinbar?" [Are Christology and feminism incompatible?], in Doris Strahm and Regula Strobel, eds., *Vom Verlangen nach Heilwerden. Christologie in feministisch-theologischer Sicht* [On the longing to be saved: Christology in feminist-theological perspective] (Fribourg and Lucerne, 1991), 204f.

[63] Pissarek-Hudelist, "Trinität" [Trinity], in Wb, 423–28.

taken by Tillich[64] — as the deepest dimension of this world. Denial of God's separate personal reality is a characteristic aspect of all "post-Christian feminism"[65] and predominates even in the writings of so-called "moderate" authors who would claim to be Christian. To a large extent, even "Christian" feminism denies basic tenets of the Christian teaching on God (for example, distinctness from the world, immutability, omnipotence, being the "Lord").

An important touchstone is whether creation of the world out of nothing is accepted or not. Anyone who rejects *"creatio ex nihilo"* as something "patriarchal" has broken with the biblical image of God, even if this break with Christianity is not described as such. Whoever rejects creation out of nothing, while also assuming the existence of something "divine", necessarily identifies God with the world. Asserting the identity of God and the world is usually designated in theology as "pantheism", or, if "God" still exceeds the totality of the world in some way, as "panentheism". Hence, just what relationship feminist theology has to pantheism (or panentheism) is a decisive question.

If the subject of "creation out of nothing" is broached at all, directly or indirectly, it is in a negative way. The *Wörterbuch* holds that there is an "older" story of creation, with which the authors obviously sympathize. According to it, the earth, viewed as divine, generates everything itself. Only the present, later texts "show a God (imagined as male) who created everything through forms (Gen 2) or through the Word (Gen 1)".[66] According to Halkes, " 'God' did not create out of nothing, nor did she give birth, but dealt lovingly and creatively with what presented itself to her." The world is, so to speak, God's "body", in which he

---

[64] Cf. above, 82.

[65] Ulrike Wiethaus, "Gott/Göttin IV. Theologiegeschichte/Mittelalter" [God/goddess IV. History of theology/Middle Ages], in Wb, 168.

[66] Ina Praetorius, Luise Schottroff, and Helen Schüngel-Straumann, "Schöpfung/Ökologie" [Creation/ecology], in Wb, 357.

expresses himself and makes himself vulnerable.[67] Halkes
refers here to Jürgen Moltmann and an American woman
theologian, and herself describes this image of God as
"panentheism".[68] The image of the cosmos as the "body"
of the divine world-soul can be found already in ancient
Stoic pantheism[69] — a fact which does not, however, seem
known to Halkes. It is not surprising that the *Wörterbuch
der Feministischen Theologie* explicitly urges that there is
a need to break down the "fear" of pantheism.[70]

The backdrop to Halkes' writings is ultimately the ideal-
istic philosophy of Hegel, which is also a starting point for
Moltmann: in Hegel, man becomes a transient factor in the
history of God's development. Hegel's image of God can
already be most aptly described as "panentheism".[71] Moltmann's position does not seem quite clear: on the one
hand, causal thinking is to be expunged from the doctrine
of creation,[72] but, on the other, the *"creatio ex nihilo"* is

---

[67] Halkes, *Antlitz,* 180–85; quote: 183; similarly Elisabeth Moltmann-
Wendel, *Wenn Gott und Körper sich begegnen. Feministische Perspektiven
zur Leiblichkeit* [When God and body meet: Feminist perspectives on
corporeality], 2d ed. (Gütersloh, 1991), 46.

[68] Halkes, *Antlitz,* 112.

[69] Eduard Schweizer, "Soma . . . ", *Theol. Wörterbuch zum NT* 7 (1964):
1034; Max Pohlenz, *Die Stoa I/II* [The Stoics I/II], 5th ed. (Göttingen,
1978–1980).

[70] Ina Praetorius et al., "Schöpfung/Ökologie", in Wb, 355f.; cf.
Wiethaus, in Wb, 168. Also expressly self-characterized as "pantheistic"
is Sorge, 35, 40f., 66, 93.

[71] Walter Brugger, *Summe einer philosophischen Gotteslehre* [Summa
of a philosophical theology] (Munich, 1979), 430–32; Ludger Oeing-Hanhoff,
"Hegels Trinitätslehre. Zur Aufgabe ihrer Kritik und Rezeption" [Hegel's
doctrine of the Trinity: On the task of criticizing and appropriating it],
Theologie und Philosophie 52 (1977): 378–407; Peter Koslowski, "Hegel —
der Philosoph der Trinität? Zur Kontroverse um seine Trinitätslehre"
[Hegel — the philosopher of the Trinity? On the controversy surrounding
his doctrine of the Trinity], *Theol. Quartalschrift* 162 (1982): 123; Jörg
Splett, *Die Trinitätslehre G. W. F. Hegels* [G. W. F. Hegel's doctrine of
the Trinity], 3d ed. (Freiburg, 1984).

[72] Jürgen Moltmann, *Gott in der Schöpfung* [God in creation] (Munich,
1985), 28.

nevertheless still valid.[73] Moltmann speaks of "compassion" and of God's self-transformation through the influence of creatures.[74] Christian theism and pantheism are to be reconciled,[75] in which connection the word "panentheism" also crops up,[76] although (and this seems to be overlooked by Halkes) it is interpreted critically: God's transcendence of the world is lacking even in "analytically subtle" panentheism.[77]

A pan(en)theistic position has far-reaching implications. The relationship to God then no longer culminates in loving worship by man, who, for his part, knows himself to be the recipient of divine love, but, rather, constitutes a naturally given state of affairs. According to Christa Mulack, the aim of feminist "liturgy" is therefore, "not to achieve contact with a 'supernatural' reality, but to effect a shift in levels of consciousness".[78] Rosemary Ruether's compilation of the "rituals" of the American "Women-Church"—which one might regard as the best-known feminist "prayer book"—also advocates, in effect, a radical hominism, a deification of the human person. Instead of prayer, there are practical exercises designed to incite anger, to bolster self-esteem, and to exorcise the evil spirits of patriarchalism. For purposes of example, one need cite only Ruether's commentary on feminist "baptism": "The transcendence of grace is not beyond the human nature given to us in biological birth. Rather, it is beyond cultural consciousness and the system of unjust power that have shaped us."[79]

---

[73] Ibid., 91.

[74] Ibid., 28f., passim.

[75] Jürgen Moltmann, *Trinität und Reich Gottes* [Trinity and Kingdom of God] (Munich, 1980), 122.

[76] Ibid., 120; *Gott,* 114f.

[77] Moltmann, *Gott,* 115.

[78] Christa Mulack, "Ritual/Magie" [Ritual/magic], in Wb, 352.

[79] Ruether, *Women-Church,* 126.

It might be stressed once again here that Ruether belongs to the "moderates" within theological feminism and that Meyer-Wilmes regards her as the "most Catholic" of the American feminists.[80]

3. Critical Commentary

"If God is a male, then the male must be God" (Daly). Such a remark betrays a failure to appreciate the characteristic nature of all talk about God. Images like "Father" for the first Divine Person, and "Son" for the second, must always be interpreted as analogies. They merely express an element of similarity, while that of dissimilarity always remains greater. This holds true of all human assertions about God.[81]

Ancient Israel, very much in contrast to the pagan world around it, had already avoided attributing any sexual traits to God: "Yahweh was situated . . . beyond the polarity of the sexual, and this meant that Israel was not able to regard the sexual as a sacred mystery. It fell outside the realm of religion because it was a creaturely phenomenon."[82]

Man's being made in the likeness of God is also not to be understood with a view to his sexuality but pertains to his specific nature as surpassing the rest of creation that can be sensibly experienced and assuming responsibility for it (Gen 1:26ff.). The crucial ontological ground of man's likeness to God is his personal spiritual soul, which is not, as such, sexually stamped.[83] The argument that sexual attributes must exist in God because they are present in

---

[80] Meyer-Wilmes, 216.

[81] Fourth Lateran Council (1215): "For no similarity can be asserted between the Creator and any creature without a greater degree of dissimilarity always being implied" (Neuner-Roos 280 = DS 806).

[82] Gerhard von Rad, *Theologie des Alten Testaments* 1 [Theology of the Old Testament 1], 7th ed. (Munich, 1978), 40f.

[83] On likeness to God, cf. Hauke, *Women in the Priesthood?*, 199f.;

creation (Pissarek-Hudelist) rests on the failure to appreciate the analogical nature of discourse about God. According to the classical rules of theology, God, in the literal
sense, can have no qualities attributed to him whose essence
contains any limitedness or incompleteness but only the
so-called "pure perfections", for instance, "being", "truth",
and "goodness". The so-called "mixed" perfections, whose
essence contains something limited or incomplete—for
instance, God's "seeing" and "hearing"—can be applied to
God only in the figurative or metaphoric sense.[84]

The feminist recommendation that the Old Testament
image of God should be enriched by adding the attributes of
the Canaanite fertility goddess is regarded by the Old Testament scholar H.-J. Hermisson simply as a "regression" "to
deification of worldly phenomena".[85] What is characteristic of Jewish and Christian discourse about God consists
precisely in the fact that God is not identical with the
world but has, out of his free love, called it into being from
nothing. This idea of an act of creation—rejected by Ruether
as "patriarchal"[86]—presupposes the supernatural transcendence of God, who infinitely surpasses the world.
God's "nearness", his immanence, is meaningful only on
the basis of his transcendence.

God's being merely immanent—an assumption brought
to the fore in feminist theology—would imply a retraction
of God's transcendence and a questioning of his personhood.
But if God is no longer a person, then he is downgraded to

347–49; Leo Scheffczyk, *Einführung in die Schöpfungslehre* [Introduction
to the doctrine of creation], 3d ed. (Darmstadt, 1987), 105–11.

[84] Franz Diekamp and Klaudius Jüssen, *Katholische Dogmatik nach
den Grundsätzen des hl. Thomas* 1 [Catholic dogmatics based on the
principles of St. Thomas 1], 12/13th ed. (Münster, 1958), 136; Brugger,
Gotteslehre, 93, 284f.

[85] Hermisson, "Rückschritt", 294; cf. his "Zur 'feministischen' Exegese
des Alten Testaments" [On the "feminist" exegesis of the Old Testament],
Theol. Beiträge 22 (1991): 126.

[86] Ruether, *New Woman,* 14.

the status of the mere "ground of being".[87] It is logically consistent that God appears in Daly's conception as a verb predicated of *man* (as the substantive).[88] Is not God actually replaced here by man?

If God were only the "deepness" of the world, there would be no problem in calling, with Dorothee Sölle, for a "democratization of the image of God".[89] Masculine and feminine traits would then have to be applied symbolically to the "divine" in equal ways. In the ancient Oriental fertility religions, precisely this was the case, and such "democratic parity" was a recognized feature of the pagan cultural environment of the New Testament and the early Church. The Stoics, for instance, in whose pantheistic system God and the world are identical, can quite "impartially" characterize "God" as "both father and mother".[90] The same applies to Gnosticism, which is praised by feminist theology and which Gilles Quispel describes as a "mythic projection of (human) self-experience".[91] Today, a pantheistically unified vision is also offered not least notably by Hinduism, which has no problem at all in addressing God equally as "father" and "mother".[92]

Human speech about God is merely analogical. Nevertheless, it is not a matter of indifference which images and symbols we give preference to—and particularly not when the humanly central sphere of the God-created polarity of

---

[87] Cf. Franz Courth, "Zum Gottes- und Menschenbild der Feministischen Theologie" [On the images of God and man in feminist theology], *Kath. Bildung* 87 (1986): 674.

[88] Daly, *Father,* 34, 36, 198.

[89] As in the plenary session of the World Council of Churches, 1983, in Vancouver: Uwe Gerber, "Feministische Theologie. Selbstverständnis—Tendenzen—Fragen" [Feminist theology: Self-understanding—directions—questions], ThLZ 109 (1984): 574.

[90] Cf. Augustine, *The City of God* bk 7, no. 9; Hauke, *Women in the Priesthood?,* 166f.

[91] Gilles Quispel, *Gnosis als Weltreligion* [Gnosticism as a world religion] (Zurich, 1951), 17.

[92] Hauke, *Women in the Priesthood?,* 152–58.

the sexes is involved. Man's sexual structure goes deeper than the social stamping upon which the theological wing of equality feminism builds its theories. The symbolism that is rooted in these primary facts about man comprehends, in essence, the bases for assertions that have lasting significance.

How to make an appropriate selection in this realm of "images" is determined essentially, not by subjective taste, but by divine revelation. "That the Bible speaks of God as the Father, the Son, and the Spirit is part of its unalterable testimony about God, who has seen fit to reveal himself in that, and no other, way."[93]

This applies especially to Jesus' addressing God as "Abba", "Father". It was not until the revelation of the New Covenant that reference to God as Father became notably prominent; what we find here is the "very heart of the New Testament understanding of God".[94] Cardinal Ratzinger rightly stresses that "we (are) not authorized to transform the 'Our Father' into an 'Our Mother'."[95]

In the image of the Father, the elements of goodness and authority are combined. These two are held together in the New Testament, whereas feminist theology weakens or dissolves God's authority in favor of a "maternal" image of God, according to which God supposedly accepts man "unconditionally".[96]

Any redefining of the image of God entails a fundamental alteration not only of its symbolic structure but also of belief in God itself. Representatives of feminist theology allude repeatedly to this themselves: "Religion is a coher-

---

[93] Dokumentation, 105.

[94] Courth (1986), 674; cf. Joachim Jeremias, *Abba. Studien zur neu-testamentlichen Theologie und Zeitgeschichte* [Abba: Studies in New Testament theology and cultural history] (Göttingen, 1966); Pannenberg, 284–87.

[95] Ratzinger, *Report,* 97. The revelatory character of Jesus' addressing God as "Father" is also stressed by many other critics of feminist theology, e.g., Burggraf (1986), 23f.; Courth (1986), 674; Dieperink, *Feministische Theologie,* 28.

[96] Cf. below, 169–70.

ent totality amounting to conferment of ultimate meaning
in the language of images and symbols, and one cannot
arbitrarily remove one of these images and symbols and
replace it with another (for example, replacing 'father' by
'mother') without endangering the totality."[97] Feminist
theology is aimed at achieving, not cosmetic changes in
hymnbooks to bolster female self-confidence, but a new
religion. The Anglican lay theologian C. S. Lewis saw this
danger more than twenty years ago: "If all these supposals
were ever carried into effect we should be embarked on a
different religion"; and "a child who has been taught to
pray to a Mother in Heaven would have a religious life
radically different from that of a Christian child."[98]

Of course the image of God also contains "feminine"
aspects. All creaturely perfections have their ultimate ground
in God. The idea expressed by Pope John Paul I when he
says, with reference to Isaiah 49:15, that God is also a
mother to us is by no means alien to the Christian tradition.[99] But this observation, correct in principle, is often
taken to grotesque extremes in feminist theology.[100]

---

[97] Halkes, *Suchen*, 73.

[98] C. S. Lewis, "Priestesses in the Church?", in his *Undeceptions: Essays on Theology and Ethics* (London, 1971), 193f.

[99] That God is "more" "mother" than "father" cannot be inferred from the Pope's words; cf. *L'Osservatore Romano*, September 11/12, 1978, 1. How so much significance could be attached to a minor comment on the "Angelus" prayer can really be explained only as the result of a certain oversensitivity; cf. Hauke, *Women in the Priesthood?*, 229, n. 94; see also CCC, no. 239.

[100] Also, the widely popularized interpretation of the term "mercy" (*rechem*) in the Isaiah passage is, in the correspondingly translated form ("tenderness"), not correct. For critical assessment of the "feminine" traits in the image of God, cf. in particular: Hauke, *Women in the Priesthood?*, 228-39, 271-76, 277-96, 309-12; on the Old Testament: Werner Berg, "Die Mütterlichkeit Gottes im Alten Testament" [God's motherliness in the Old Testament], in Josef Scharbert, *Ausgewählte Themen der Theologie des ATs I. Gott im AT*, Skripten des Lehrstuhls für Theologie des ATs, no. 5 (Munich, 1982), 185-97; Urs Winter, *Frau und Göttin. Exegetische und ikonographische Studien zum weiblichen Gottesbild im Alten Israel und in dessen Umwelt* [Woman and goddess: Exeget-

Fundamental to the biblical understanding of God is precisely an accentuation within the symbolism of the sexes that differs radically from what is found in paganism. "Feminine" symbols like "mother", "bride", and "virgin" are by no means excluded. However, they acquire a different sort of status in the context of revealed religion. The image of the "bride" does not signify a goddess but, rather, the people of Israel and the Church.[101] Mystical reference is thus made to man's position before God, that is, one of open receptivity and cooperative striving for salvation. Receptivity and cooperativeness do not imply "passivity", as feminist theology often suspects, but require the engagement of one's whole person and all one's powers. It is not, however, usual in Christian mysticism to depict the position of one's own soul before God in the image of a "bridegroom".[102]

The "eccentricity" (outward-directedness) of the male seems the more suitable symbol for suggesting God's powers of effective action, which are expressed in two main aspects of the monotheistic religions: his creation out of nothing and his revelation within history. Conversely, the "centeredness" of the female is more readily suggestive of divine immanence in the world and man's position before God.[103] The "feminine" position before God is ultimately definitive

---

ical and iconographic studies on the female image of God in ancient Israel and its surrounding cultures], 2d ed. (Fribourg and Göttingen, 1987) (on "Erbarmen": 531-35); Siegfried Kreuzer, "Gott als Mutter in Hosea 11?" [God as mother in Hosea 11?], *Theol. Quartalschrift* 169 (1989): 123-32. Kreuzer is critical of Helen Schüngel-Straumann, who insinuates a "feminist" critique into Hosea 11:9: in the statement "I am God and not man" (Hebrew: isch), her German version substitutes "*Mann*" [male person] for "*Mensch*" [human].

[101] Hauke, *Women in the Priesthood?*, 252-56.

[102] Ibid., 304; cf. Pierre Adnes, "Mariage spirituel" [Spiritual marriage], *Dictionnaire de spiritualité* 10 (1980): 388-408; Gerda von Brockhusen, "Brautsymbolik" [Bridal symbolism], in Christian Schütz, ed., *Praktisches Lexikon der Spiritualität* [Practical lexicon of spirituality] (Freiburg, 1988), 172-74.

[103] On this pair of concepts, coined by P. Lersch, cf. above, 102-3.

not only of women but also of men. Here, female symbolism is given a priority whose significance is not fully appreciated in feminist theology.[104]

This biblical accentuation within the symbolism of the sexes does not imply a devaluation of women. For the male is not God; the "masculine" images only represent something with which they are not identical. The female, by contrast, herself embodies the meaning of what the "feminine" images suggest, and men, too, must take this as their standard.

The feminist image of man, in which masculine and feminine elements are undifferentiatedly combined, parallels the image of God. This parallelism is concretely exemplified in the Protestant parish church at Dornbusch in Frankfurt, a church whose interior has been decorated by feminist artists. A human figure, half male and half female, is interpreted there as "God/dess".[105] If the observation is correct that "masculine" images are more illustrative of God's relationship to man, and "feminine" ones, of man's relationship to God—must not, then, an androgynous fusing of these images ultimately lead to a fusing of God and man? To a confusing, which deprives both God and man of their identities? Which, as it were, intermixes the divine and the human in the way claimed by pantheism?

"One is, in fact, reminded of earlier pantheistic theology" —as even a reviewer who is himself sympathetic to feminist theology has commented.[106] Feminists themselves also sometimes expressly refer to their image of God as "pantheistic" or "panentheistic".[107] W. Schulze, who completed doctoral

---

[104] Cf. below, 197–98.

[105] "Feministische Kunst. Den Altar in Watte verpackt" [Feminist art: The altar wrapped in cotton wool], *Publik-Forum,* no. 16 (August 14, 1987): 18f.

[106] Gerber, "Feministische Theologie" (1984), 585; somewhat more cautious: his *Eroberung,* 52–54; Axmacher criticizes Ruether's monistic pantheism, 10–13.

[107] Cf. above, 146–48.

research in 1939 on "the androgynous ideal and the Christian faith", observed tersely: "Behind almost every claim that God is androgynous lies an emanationist conception of creation."[108] "Emanation" means that the world was not created by God in an act of free will but "flows" necessarily forth from the divine nature. The identity of God and world (pantheism) is based on this notion of emanation. The inner dynamics of feminist theology would thus impel it toward a pantheism in which the divine and the human are equally dissolved.

One must also ask whether the "parity" in the image of God, as usually postulated theoretically, is even consistently maintained. The imagery surrounding "heaven", which is more strongly aligned with the "Father", is not really agreeable to feminist theology; whereas the "motherly" earth is given much prominence, along with the similarly toned symbolism of the source and the cycle.[109] On the whole, this peculiar paradox seems to play a role in pantheistically inclined forms of religion: the "androgyne" is "born" of a mythical primal mother.[110] This mythic nexus extends all the way to the just-mentioned androgynous image in Frankfurt, which depicts the man-woman emerging from an egg—an ancient symbol of birth.[111] The seemingly "democratic" image of God, when examined more closely, is weighted in favor of the feminine. Consciously neo-pagan "goddess feminism" displays great consistency of thought here. Elga Sorge, for example, critically questions Halkes and Moltmann-Wendel about why, in view of their relevant positions, they continued to speak of "God"

---

[108] W. Schulze, *Das androgyne Ideal und der christliche Glaube* [The androgynous ideal and the Christian faith] (Lahr-Dinglingen, 1940; extract from a dissertation, Heidelberg, 1939), 38.

[109] On this, see N. E. Auer Falk, "Feminine Sacrality", in Mircea Eliade, ed., *The Encyclopedia of Religion* 5 (New York and London, 1987): 302–12; Hauke, *Women in the Priesthood?*, 134f., 137–41.

[110] Hauke, *Women in the Priesthood?*, 138.

[111] Ibid.

instead of the "goddess"? Didn't this show that they still accorded predominance to the male?[112]

The preponderance, or parity, of the feminine in the image of God is intended, in the feminist view, to reinforce the worth of women. The only question is whether this actually leads to furtherance of that aim. All forms of pantheism reject the person-like reality of God. But when it is denied that God is a personally acting being, the God-created personality of man also disappears.[113] Then the person, just like God, is reduced to the level of a multifactorial material process, and death means the end of any individual life. This consequence is, in fact, accepted by not a few theologians.[114] But what results is the collapse of the unexchangeable, unique worth of every person.

The question of whether the goals that feminist theology sets for itself can actually produce what they promise also applies to the struggle against real, or assumed, suppression of women. In the end, what is effective in opposing suppression is not wordy protests but only concrete power— even if it be a matter of the power of love. That God is the "Lord", the omnipotent and everlasting, is of benefit to precisely the disadvantaged and the oppressed.[115] Celebrating, on the one hand, the delivery out of Egypt as the paradigm of feminist theology, while, on the other hand, shackling the might of the divine Liberator to the impotence of man, do not go well together. A God who intervenes in history, who judges men and is leading up to a new creation, can be "used" much better for the purposes of "liberation" than can an apersonal "deepness" of one's own frangible being. Repudiation of God as the almighty Lord redounds most strongly on the repudiators themselves.

An important concern of theological feminism is self-

---

[112] Sorge, 49.
[113] Dieperink, *Feministische Theologie,* 51.
[114] Cf. below, 239–40.
[115] Cf. Schneider-Böcklen and Vorländer, 34, 125.

realization, or "autonomy". A woman should not be reduced to her very womanliness—and this is a justified goal—but should be recognized as a unique individual human being. On the other hand, it is not solely the representatives of goddess feminism who cast longing glances back at the mother goddesses of ancient times, especially when they are intent upon discovering there the primal paradise of the "matriarchy".

Yet precisely the most ancient evidence yields female figures that are obviously important, not because of their personalities, but because of their wombs. Here, "one should note that the return to a supposed 'matriarchal' religion would involve not only a fundamental denial of God's transcendence—for then the primal, birth-giving womb would be equivalent to God (Goddess)—but also a retrogressive abandonment of the true emancipation and worth of women, achieved on the basis of the preaching of Jesus Christ, in favor of the prepersonal sexual and birth-giving factor."[116]

Again, there is a certain justification in asking whether the symbolism of the Holy Spirit does not contain "feminine" traits. Here, however, reference to the grammatically feminine Hebrew word *ruach* seems rather unproductive. For one thing, what is involved in the Old Testament is an impersonal force of God, a "neutrum", and not a proper person. Also, from the linguistic viewpoint, the situation is, in general, essentially more complex than feminist theology takes it to be.[117] Not until the New Testament, on the basis of the revelation of Jesus, does a (masculine) personal pronoun appear alongside the (in Greek) neutrally used term (Jn 16:8, 13f.). On the other hand, the existence of "feminine" traits in the Holy Spirit could be inferred

---

[116] Sudbrack, *Neue Religiosität*, 121.
[117] Hauke, *Women in the Priesthood?*, 277; cf. Heine, *Göttinnen*, 35f.: "sword" and "virility" are, for example, "feminine" in Hebrew; and in German, also "power" and "force".

from his identity as the "divinely receptive", his "immanence", and his characterization as a mediatory "relational being".[118] As Ruether is probably right in fearing, the results of studies in this area are likely to prove less than satisfactory to feminist theology. Moreover, the "feminine" symbolic elements constitute only a partial aspect and point more in the direction of ecclesiology and Mariology.[119]

Applying the term "mother" to the Holy Spirit is questionable in any case, since the Holy Spirit does not produce the eternal Logos. Hence, recourse to the pagan concept of a divine family seems just as dubious as the thesis put forward in the eighteenth century by Count Zinzendorf, who characterized the Holy Spirit as the "Mama" within the Trinity.[120]

It would also be theologically monstrous to remove the Holy Spirit from the structure of the Trinity. To "emancipate" him or to bring him to the fore, instead of the Father or the Son, would diametrically contradict the most elementary testimonies of Scripture and tradition. The authenticity of the Holy Spirit reveals itself in the prayer that does not begin with "Come, creative Spirit", but with "Abba, Father!"[121]

Anyone who overlooks the basic thrust of this runs the

---

[118] Hauke, *Women in the Priesthood?*, 277-96; "Die Diskussion um die weibliche Symbolik in der Pneumatologie" [The debate about feminine symbolism in pneumatology], in Johannes Stöhr, ed., *Der dreifaltige Gott und das Leben der Christen* (St. Ottilien, 1993), 130-50; Yves Congar, *Der Heilige Geist* [The Holy Spirit] (Freiburg, 1982), 424-32; F. X. Durwell, *Der Geist des Herrn. Tiefe Gottes—schöpferische Weite* [The Spirit of the Lord: Depth of God—breadth of creation] (Salzburg, 1986), 211-18; Anton Ziegenaus, "Maria als Abbild der Person des Hl. Geistes nach M. J. Scheeben" [Mary as a figuration of the Person of the Holy Spirit according to M. J. Scheeben], in A. Ziegenaus, ed., *Maria und der Heilige Geist,* Mariol. Studien 8 (Regensburg, 1991), 25-38.

[119] On this, cf. also Hauke, "Pneumatologie", 147-50; cf. below, 199-201.

[120] Cf. Moltmann, "Gemeinschaft", 711; Peter Zimmerling, *Gott in Gemeinschaft. Zinzendorfs Trinitätslehre* [God in community: Zinzendorf's doctrine of the Trinity] (Gießen, 1991), passim.

[121] Gal 4:6; Rom 8:15, 26.

danger of confusing the Spirit of God with self-experience in the focal mirror of group dynamics, with the short-winded "dynamics" of his own spirit.

VIII. CHRISTOLOGY AND THE DOCTRINE OF REDEMPTION

1. The Meaning of the Central Christian Message

Along with belief in the divine Trinity, the main characteristic of Christianity that distinguishes it from all other religions is its message that God became man. Already in the First Letter of John, acknowledgment of the Incarnation is regarded as the most important criterion for distinguishing true from false prophets: "Every spirit that acknowledges Jesus Christ come in the flesh belongs to God, and every spirit that does not acknowledge Jesus does not belong to God" (1 Jn 4:2f.). In opposition to Arianism, which viewed Jesus as God's supreme creature but not as God, the early Church stresses that God himself became man in order that we men might be granted participation in the Divine Life. Apart from the divinity of Jesus, our redemption is not assured.

Hence, whether feminist theology is prepared to endorse this acknowledgment of Jesus Christ as God's Son is an important question. Who Jesus Christ is becomes clear, of course, through his redemptive works, especially his death and Resurrection. So we must ask here: What role is played by the expiatory event of the Cross, through which Jesus sacrifices himself for the sins of man? Is the Resurrection accepted as a concrete occurrence, in which the Lord's body is released from the tomb and transmuted into a new form of existence?

161

2. The Feminist Image of Jesus

Precisely the central Christian message, namely, that God's eternal Son became man for the purpose of our redemption, appears, in large part, suspect to feminist theology. A precedent was set here by Mary Daly: "The idea of God's unique incarnation in the form of a man, of the God-man of the 'Holy Trinity', is sexist to the core and opens the way for oppression. Christ-worship is idol-worship."[1] No one can ignore the fact that "Christ is a male symbol and therefore actually excludes woman on this plane."[2] This "peculiarity" goes much deeper than, for instance, the fact that he was young or Semitic. The notion of a unique male redeemer legitimizes male superiority, particularly when the female figure of Mary is used to exemplify the human who worships God. If one is to continue to speak of an "incarnation", then it should only be in the sense that the "power of being" is inherent in all humans. Similarly, it would be necessary to "castrate" the "myth of sin" and the "myth of redemption, which are just two different symptoms of the same disease", namely, male arrogance.[3] In any case, the doctrine that Jesus offered himself up for the salvation of mankind must be rejected, since this "scapegoat syndrome" encourages women to emulate Jesus' self-sacrificing love.[4]

The decisive question is this: What approach do the so-called "moderate" feminists take to this sort of critique? Is Christ still recognized as the eternal Son of God whose Incarnation is unique and unrepeatable? How is his maleness interpreted? What status is attached to the redemptive events of the Cross and the Resurrection? What meaning is given to "redemption"?

---

[1] Mary Daly, "Der qualitative Sprung über die patriarchale Religion" [The qualitative leap beyond patriarchal religion], in E. Moltmann-Wendel, *Frau und Religion,* 110.

[2] Ibid., 99.

[3] Ibid., 90.

[4] Daly, *Father,* 75–77.

Inge Wenck writes that "God has not been well served by maleness"; "and I must agree with her", says Halkes.[5] Contrary to the Roman declaration on women in the priesthood, she regards Jesus' maleness as a purely temporally conditioned fact.[6] To appeal to it, Anne Carr holds, is "heretical", "evil", and "violent".[7] In Halkes' opinion, "God's Incarnation" does not involve just one historical figure but "extends farther". Feminist theology "believes in a still-continuing Incarnation, to be manifest in the rebirth of all the oppressed".[8] Moreover, he requires female images for the accomplishment of his work, for example, the hen who takes her chicks under her wing, or the woman who seeks the lost coin.[9]

Halkes and Moltmann-Wendel also cite Hanna Wolff, a theologian and psychologist linked to the school of C. G. Jung, who has played a key role in feminist Christology in German-speaking countries.[10] In line with the Protestant theosophist Jakob Boehme,[11] she characterizes Jesus as "androgynous".[12] Jesus lived out the feminine side of his personality, the "anima", as an integral part of his psychic totality; he was the first "anima-integrated male in world history".[13] Jesus' androgynous nature influenced his "notion of God", which is also "androgynous";[14] in fact, even more: "Jesus allows feminine ontological values to

---

[5] Halkes, *Suchen,* 73; Inge Wenck, *Gott ist im Mann zu kurz gekommen. Eine Frau über Jesus von Nazareth* [God has not been well-served in maleness: A woman on Jesus of Nazareth] (Gütersloh, 1982).

[6] Halkes, *Söhne,* 69.

[7] Carr, 178.

[8] Halkes, "Zwischenbilanz", 297; cf. *Söhne,* 41.

[9] Halkes, *Söhne,* 69.

[10] Brockmann, 55.

[11] Hanna Wolff, *Jesus der Mann. Die Gestalt Jesu in tiefenpsychologischer Sicht* [Jesus the man: The figure of Jesus from the psychoanalytic viewpoint], 2d ed. (Stuttgart, 1976), 53, 70.

[12] Wolff, 47; on Wolff's relation to Jung, cf. Brockmann, 55–82.

[13] Wolff, 70.

[14] Ibid., 51.

dominate in the image of God!"[15] God does not pass judgment and does not require reconciliation.[16] Instead, what is decisive for Jesus are: "keeping and protecting, attending and caring, helping and healing".[17]

It is no wonder, then, that feminist artists (male and female) occasionally depict a "Jesa Christa" on the cross—as occurred, for example, in the largest North American cathedral, the Episcopalian "Saint John the Divine" in New York. (The Episcopal Church is among the most significant promoters of the ordination of women in the Anglican world.) Meanwhile, a theosophical sect has heralded Christ's Second Coming as a woman, using the image of an Episcopal-like "Jesa Christa".[18]

Inge Wenck (quoted above) differs from Hanna Wolff in contesting the perfection of Jesus. Even Jesus was "male, all-too-male", and was "careful to make a big detour around . . . anything unpleasant".[19] Through his "maleness", "God's cause . . . has been impeded", and "disadvantage, constraint, and rejection" have resulted for women.[20] Here, God's Incarnation as a male is quite openly perceived as offensive, as it is in general by decidedly anti-Christian "gynocentric feminism".

For Halkes, Jesus is a "prophet and messiah".[21] Is he also God's Son, truly God and truly man, in the sense of the Council of Chalcedon? Given the comments on the "Incarnation" by Halkes that have been cited here, that can hardly be assumed, even if the Dutch theologian seems, in her German-language publications, to avoid any formal

---

[15] Ibid., 121.
[16] Ibid., 36f.
[17] Ibid., 122.
[18] Cf. Wanda Marrs, *New Age Lies to Women* (Austin, Tex., 1989), 20. The same image, produced by Edwina Sandys, is on the title page of Oddie (1988).
[19] Wenck, 83f.
[20] Ibid., 126.
[21] Halkes, *Söhne,* 43.

denial of Jesus' divinity.[22] The American Ruether, on the other hand, takes a clear stand against Jesus' being God's Son. The Council of Chalcedon, she thinks, contradicts Jesus' own view of himself.[23] The "myth of Jesus as the Messiah or divine Logos" must be overcome.[24] "Jesus, the homeless Jewish prophet", is himself "one who was redeemed", as is shown in his baptism by John.[25] Here, the ancient Gnostic heresy of the "redeemed Redeemer"[26] is newly "resurrected". Quite obviously, Jesus is not God's last word,[27] and his being a male certainly has nothing more than a kind of "social symbolic significance" that is no longer valid today.[28] When Ruether speaks of "Christ", what she means is, "not . . . the immutable perfection of one individual person . . . who lived two thousand years ago", but "liberated humanity" as a whole.[29]

For Moltmann-Wendel, too, Christ is no "miracle worker who holds, independently of mankind, some divine mystery in himself". The power to work miracles would "be gained . . . by humans themselves".[30] He is no "unemotional

---

[22] Rather enigmatic, for example, are the statements by Halkes, "Maria", in Wb, 272; Jesus, accordingly, was called the Son of God because he was so filled with the spirit of God that, through his life and person, he made God visible. Is it too farfetched to think here of the Jesuology of Hans Küng and the Dutchman Schillebeeckx (often quoted by Halkes), according to which Jesus was only an especially blessed human being? For a brief commentary on these authors, cf. Johann Auer, *Jesus Christus— Gottes und Mariä "Sohn"* [Jesus Christ—Son of God and Mary], KKD, vol. 4, no. 1 (Regensburg, 1986), 61-63. Dieperink, *Feministische Theologie,* 59, who is well-versed in Halkes' original Dutch works, misses in them the acknowledgment of Jesus Christ as the only begotten Son of God who became man in order to reconcile us with God. A "Christology from below" is also advocated by Carr, 199, 202, 216f.; for her, the Incarnation is obviously not a reality but a "symbol" (188).

[23] Ruether, *Sexism,* 116.

[24] Ibid., 135.

[25] Ibid., 138.

[26] Kurt Rudolph, *Die Gnosis* [Gnosticism], 3d ed. (Göttingen, 1990), 141f.

[27] Ruether, *Sexism,* 121-22.

[28] Ibid., 137.

[29] Ibid., 138.

[30] Moltmann-Wendel, *Milch,* 129.

Son of God", but a complete human being.[31] This theologian praises a representation of the crucifixion that depicts Christ as "without hope", "earthly"; "with this Jesus", who suffers and perishes, "humans can have something in common".[32]

The main article on "Jesus Christ" in the *Wörterbuch der Feministischen Theologie,* written by the Swiss Catholic theologian Doris Strahm, is not lacking in explicitness. A Christology that does justice to feminist criteria "must relinquish the claim that Jesus Christ's significance for the self-revelation of God ... or the redemption of mankind has uniqueness and final validity. Accordingly, Jesus is 'relativized' in most christological conceptions by feminist theologians and, in fact, in a twofold sense: (1) he is the incarnation of God, but not the only one ..., a messianic prophet, but not the final Messiah (Radford Ruether); (2) he is thus brought into relation/connection with other messianic figures, and not least with us ourselves. ..."[33]

This author also states quite clearly how feminist theology reaches these conclusions: the "starting point"—as also, for example, in the Christologies of Schillebeeckx, Boff, and Moltmann—is "not dogma but the historical Jesus or the biblical Jesus traditions, which are now, however, read and interpreted from the *viewpoint of women*".[34] In the end, then, the "historical Jesus" amounts here to the exegesis of liberal Protestantism, which has been crystallized above all in Rudolf Bultmann's continuingly influential "demythologization" program: any direct influence by God on this world—for example, natural wonders or bod-

---

[31] Ibid., 133.

[32] Ibid., 132.

[33] Doris Strahm, "Jesus Christus", in Wb, 204; cf. her *Aufbruch,* 71-96; Strahm and Strobel.

[34] Strahm, in Wb, 201.

ily resurrection—is rejected from the first.[35] This, in effect, undermines the divinity of Jesus, which cannot be demonstrated apart from the criterion of the miraculous. According to this liberal "dogma", "resurrection" then means—as stated in the same "Jesus Christ" article—"the experience that what his life signified could not be destroyed, that he lived on in his female successors. . . . "[36]

On the basis of the pantheistic image of God that is usually assumed, such a position is only consistent: if God is identical with the world, then of course he can effect nothing in this world beyond its own forces. Apart from the powerful deeds of Jesus, to which he himself refers,[37] his claim (documented in the New Testament) to be the Messiah and eternal Son of God is left hanging in mid-air.

The feminist need for self-importance is so strong in some female theologians that they try to derive Jesus' authority from women. Elisabeth Schüssler Fiorenza's major work has the title *In Memory of Her*. This refers to the woman who anointed Jesus with spikenard oil before the Passion. Her name, according to Schüssler Fiorenza's critique, was suppressed by Mark, although even the name of the betrayer, Judas, was recorded for posterity. What had been suppressed for two thousand years needs to be rediscovered now: a woman had anointed Jesus as Messiah and given him the name Christ.[38]

With even greater powers of imagination, Christa Mulack embellishes this bold claim. Whereas the Gospel of John records that the anointer was Mary of Bethany, Mulack

---

[35] For a critical view on this: Scheffczyk, *Gott-loser Gottesglaube?,* 108–12; Richard Kocher, *Herausgeforderter Vorsehungsglaube. Die Lehre von der Vorsehung im Horizont der gegenwärtigen Theologie* [Challenged faith in providence: The doctrine of providence in the context of present-day theology] (St. Ottilien, 1993), 180ff.

[36] Strahm, in Wb, 205.

[37] Esp. Mt 11:2-6 par.

[38] Schüssler Fiorenza, *In Memory of Her,* xiii–xiv.

identifies Lazarus' sister with Mary of Magdala; as a priest-ess of the oriental mother-goddess, she had run a secret academy of the mysteries in Bethany. In a way reminiscent of Egyptian myths in which the god Osiris is reawakened to life by the goddess Isis, Mary Magdalen, a representative of the goddess, had anointed her beloved as Messiah, consigned him to the realm of death, and finally assisted him to new life. Here, for Mulack, "resurrection" does not involve the body but signifies a visionary experience within the disciples, which, to be sure, presupposes the continued existence of Jesus' soul.[39] In support of the thesis that Mary Magdalen had been a member of a secret society of women, the Protestant theologian cites a neo-Gnostic strongly influenced by the Jewish Cabbala, Otfried Eberz.[40] Being anointed by a woman corresponds to the primal matriarchal worldview, "in which the female sex is experi-enced as the creator and sustainer of all life, whereas the male is seen as having been created by the female. . . . "[41]

Mulack's theses are not necessarily representative of the broad spectrum of feminist theology. They certainly provide a particularly extreme example of the denial of Jesus' divinity: the sending of Jesus derives, not from the heavenly Father, but from an oriental fertility goddess—which will supposedly bolster feminine self-confidence. With most of the other "moderate" feminists, Mulack agrees that Jesus Christ is not the eternal Son of God who became man for our salvation but merely an unusually exemplary man. This denial of the Incarnation is a constantly recur-ring strand within feminist "Christologies".

---

[39] Christa Mulack, *Jesus—der Gesalbte der Frauen. Weiblichkeit als Grundlage christlicher Ethik* [Jesus—anointed by women: Womanliness as the foundation of Christian ethics] (Stuttgart, 1987), 271f.; cf. below, 188.

[40] Mulack, *Jesus,* 104-28. On Eberz, cf. Hauke, *Women in the Priest-hood?,* 270.

[41] Mulack, *Jesus,* 126.

3. The Denial of the Expiatory
Sacrifice on the Cross

With this diminished image of Jesus, the New Testament doctrine that Christ shed his blood representatively, for the many, also collapses. Again and again, feminists emphasize that one must not understand Jesus' death as an expiation for our sins.[42] In Hanna Wolff's view, God is no "insufferable patriarchal monster . . . who has to sacrifice the blood of his own Son . . . in order to be able to let 'grace' reign again"[43] — that is the redemption doctrine of "patriarchal consciousness". Instead of it, "the feminine scale of values is definitive" "in Jesus' conception of love"; "God 'seeks' no sort of reparation for his wounded majesty."[44]

In a quite similar vein, Moltmann-Wendel talks of how God would never distance himself from man but, like a mother, would "unconditionally" accept even the immoral person.[45] This theologian thinks that guilt feelings can be purged with statements like: "I am good. I am whole. I am beautiful."[46] There is no such thing as "universal sinfulness".[47] Women's only sin consists in seeking attachment rather than autonomy. The reverse tendency, which is at the basis of the biblical notion of sin, is, by contrast, typical of males. The typical sin of females is not pride but the renunciation of their own self-realization.[48] This reinter-

---

[42] Ruether, *Sexism,* 122; Moltmann-Wendel, *Milch,* 157, 180; Schüssler Fiorenza, *In Memory of Her,* Wb, 130; 225-27; Strahm and Strobel, 52f., 56f., 59f., 148f., 182.

[43] Wolff, 36.

[44] Ibid., 124.

[45] Moltmann-Wendel, *Milch,* 156; cf. 104, 155, 178.

[46] Ibid., 155, 158-69.

[47] Ibid., 148.

[48] Ibid., 169. On Moltmann-Wendel, cf. Lucia Scherzberg, *Sünde und Gnade in der Feministischen Theologie* [Sin and mercy in feminist theology] (Mainz, 1991), 45-50.

pretation of the "basic sin" is characteristic of feminist theology as a whole.[49]

Feminist theology's position on the redemptive process in Christ shows itself with particular clarity in its statements about the Cross. Feminist theology, the *Wörterbuch* says, "has fundamentally criticized the Christian theology of the Cross from the very start".[50] Following Mary Daly,[51] the Cross is either replaced by the tree of life or—because the notion of sin is rejected—explained as something that occurs in a similar way for all sufferers.[52] Depicting a Jesa Christa in place of the Crucified then no longer poses a theological problem. The Protestant minister Jutta Voss is logically consistent in objecting to the emphasis on the blood of Christ: it is homicidal blood and can be understood as the mystery of transubstantiation only symbolically. Female menstrual blood, however, is both real and the most important thing in the life of mankind.[53]

4. The Reinterpretation of the Resurrection

Although biblical concepts like "Incarnation", "Crucifixion", or "Resurrection" are often retained, a new meaning is attached to them. Catharina Halkes, for instance, holds: "For me, two . . . paradigms . . . retain their status as unique

---

[49] Scherzberg, 18f.; Evi Krobath, "Sünde/Schuld III. Feministisch-theologische Diskussion" [Sin/guilt III. Feminist-theological debate], in Wb, 387–89.

[50] Luise Schottroff, "Kreuz I./II." [Cross I./II.], in Wb, 226.

[51] Cf. above, 84.

[52] Schottroff, 229; "Die Crux mit dem Kreuz. Feministische Kritik und Re-Vision der Kreuzestheologie" [The crux of the Cross: The feminist critique and re-vision of the theology of the Cross], EK 25 (1992): 216–18; Regula Strobel, "Feministische Kritik an traditionellen Kreuzestheologien" [Feminist criticism of traditional theologies of the Cross] and "Das Kreuz im Kontext feministischer Theologie. Versuch einer Standortbestimmung" [The Cross in the context of feminist theology: An attempt to assess the current situation], in Strahm and Strobel, 52–64; 182–93.

[53] Voss, 50f.: cited in Schneider-Böklen and Vorländer, 102.

revelation, namely, the voice that summons to liberation from slavery (Old Testament); and the man, Jesus of Nazareth, God's image and Incarnation, who lived out his path in life through suffering and death, paradigmatically and redemptively, so that we might attain constantly renewed resurrection (New Testament)."[54]

"Resurrection" is obviously meant here in an inner-worldly sense, which is also suggested elsewhere: as "coming to experience, through suffering, cross, and death, the call to resurrection and rebellion".[55] The "eschatological hope" is identical with that universal "wholeness" in which there is no longer any distinction between man and woman.[56] "Resurrection", the *Wörterbuch* says, refers to something effected *before* death and to living on in other persons.[57] An especially strong influence was exerted by Rosemary Ruether's idea that dying involves becoming absorbed into the earth, a process that is unfortunately obstructed by the use of steel coffins.[58] In place of a hope that reaches beyond this earthly life, Ruether puts the goal of a "redeemed humanity": "recovery of holistic psychic capacities and egalitarian access to social roles".[59]

The "Resurrection" of Jesus, according to Dorothee Sölle, pertains to Jesus' "cause", but not to any special process of reviving Jesus himself.[60] Opinions like Sölle's are not the exception but the rule. Schneider-Böklen and Vorländer, who would like to integrate feminism into Christianity, note with consternation that, for almost all feminist theologians, the possibility "of experiencing the living, resurrected Christ as a reality" remains an empty

---

[54] Halkes, *Suchen,* 48.

[55] Ibid., 21.

[56] Ibid., 20.

[57] Strahm, "Jesus Christus", in Wb, 205.

[58] Luise Schottroff and Dorothee Sölle, "Auferstehung" [Resurrection], in Wb, 34f.

[59] Ruether, *Sexism,* 113. On Ruether's "doctrine of redemption", cf. Scherzberg, 58-75.

[60] Sölle, in Wb, 236.

one. Although they like to emphasize that Mary Magdalen was the first witness to the Resurrection, they fail to take her experience seriously. This is "an uncharted area on the map of feminist theology".[61]

5. The Distortion of Sacred History

It is not only the Incarnation, Cross, and Resurrection that are reinterpreted or blurred over but, in conjunction, the whole of sacred history. This becomes particularly clear from the view taken of the first and the last times.[62] As in the Marxist approach, the Christian doctrines of a sacred relationship to God during the first times, and of a regeneration of the world after the Second Coming, are converted into worldly, and supposedly "scientific", categories. The hoped-for final age corresponds roughly to the paradisal "primal state", whose role is filled, for feminist theologians, by the prehistorical "matriarchy"[63] or the "egalitarian Jesus movement".[64] Following it came, as it were, the "fall" into patriarchy, which led to the "original sin of sexism".[65]

Things that appear as negative in the biblical account of the fall are not infrequently regarded as positive. The title page of the representative *Wörterbuch der Feministischen Theologie* is resplendent with a monumental female figure who triumphally extends toward the reader a serpent she is holding. Moltmann-Wendel sees the "apple" as a "symbol of the world's sensuousness and wholeness", while, on the other hand, the "serpent" and the "dragon" signify "the

[61] Schneider-Böklen and Vorländer, 130.

[62] On eschatology, cf. below, 239–44.

[63] Moltmann-Wendel, *Milch,* 64f.; Ruether, *Sexism,* 47f.

[64] Halkes, *Suchen,* 35f.; Ruether, *Sexism,* 33; Moltmann-Wendel, *Milch,* 89f. In this sense, see also Schüssler Fiorenza, *In Memory of Her.*

[65] Ruether, *Sexism,* 182; cf. earlier, Daly, *Father,* 72.

world of wisdom, knowledge, and sensual desire".[66] For Halkes, too, the serpent is a sign of "knowledge and self-renewing eternal life".[67] Hence, Moltmann-Wendel speaks of "Eve, the first Protestant".[68] It is appropriate to this perspective that, at the Protestant Church Congress in Frankfurt in 1987, a large stand for books in feminist theology was set up under the proud banner: "Fruits from the Tree of Knowledge".

These statements may be scandalous, but they are not new. Ancient Gnostics had already enthusiastically welcomed the original sin as an act of supposed "knowledge". The serpent, sin, and even the fratricidal Cain are praised, while God is blasphemed as the cause of evil.[69] Similar elements occur in nineteenth-century German Idealism.[70]

6. Critical Commentary

Feminist theology's attempts at androgynization are especially problematic in relation to the figure of Jesus Christ, whose masculine nature has to be declared coincidental or even dangerous. An urgent question also arises about the transhistorical significance of Jesus. If Christ is not the eternal Son of God, but only a "prophet", then his revelation is also, in principle, surpassable; new "knowledge" ("gnosis") could still present itself that is even "more

---

[66] Moltmann-Wendel, *Milch,* 117, 119; cf. 57, 115f.

[67] Halkes, *Suchen,* 41. The serpent is also regarded as an "old friend" of women by the long-time head of the KFD: Lissner (1993) 71.

[68] Moltmann-Wendel, *Frau und Religion,* 33.

[69] Norbert Brox, *Offenbarung, Gnosis und gnostischer Mythos bei Irenäus von Lyon* [Revelation, gnosis, and gnostic myth in Irenaeus of Lyons] (Salzburg, 1966), 50–53.

[70] Heinrich Köster, *Urstand, Fall und Erbsünde. Von der Reformation bis zur Gegenwart* [Primal state, fall, and original sin: From the Reformation to the present], HDG II, 3c (Freiburg, 1982), 149, 151, 153, 166f. (Schelling, Kant, Schiller, Hegel).

complete". Apart from acceptance of the divinity of Christ, Christianity becomes a kind of general religious market-place ("New Age") and ultimately disintegrates.

It is supremely regrettable that feminist theology either denies Jesus' divinity or at least attaches no discernible weight to it. The same thing applies to the question of Jesus' true humanity. Whoever does not wish to make a "dream-figure" out of Jesus[71] cannot escape the fact that the Son of God took on his human nature within a specific culture and in a specific sexual form. The Letter to the Galatians, so fondly cited by feminists, speaks of the "fullness of time" (Gal 4:4), in relation to which Christ marks a midpoint determined by divine providence.

Certainly God's becoming man is of more importance than the fact that Christ was a male. But can one really portray Jesus' maleness as a historical accident by tracing it back exclusively to the "patriarchal conditions" in ancient Israel? Are not maleness and femaleness rooted in some-thing deeper than socio-cultural circumstance?

What God has created is not to be destroyed even after the new creation. In our existence after resurrection, we will be, in the words of the Gospel, "like the angels", who neither marry nor are given in marriage (Mk 12:25 par.). Our bodily nature will be "transfigured", changed, but not dissolved. In antiquity, the abstruse speculations of the Origenists postulated that man would have to be resurrected in the form of a sphere, since that is the most perfect geometric form. In one of his myths, Plato had already described androgynous primal man as "spherical".[72] The Church has defended herself energetically against this sort of estrangement from the message of creation. Augustine declared that "he who established the two sexes will restore them both."[73] Elisabeth Gössmann, herself a feminist,

---

[71] The critical remark by Gerber, "Feministische Theologie" (1984), 583.

[72] *Symposium,* 189d–191e; cf. Hauke, *Women in the Priesthood?,* 160–61.

[73] Augustine, *The City of God,* bk. 22, no. 17 (CChr.SL 48:836); cf. on all this Hauke, *Women in the Priesthood?,* 250f.

regards precisely this hope as favorable to women; the Church is thereby disburdened of the accusation of being "hostile to the body".[74]

With respect to revelation, is it really a matter of complete indifference that Christ was a man and Mary a woman? It would seem difficult to answer yes to this question while also affirming, in theology, that being man and being woman constitute *the* fundamental human situation.

Susanne Heine arrives at a critique of feminist theology precisely from her "feminist" starting point:

> It is not without significance that a man has set himself against the seductions of power. . . . A woman could not serve to represent the downtrodden, because she always finds herself in the same situation as they. . . . Jesus, a man, turns the top-most into the bottom-most. Jesa, a woman, would already be at the bottom. . . . Thus Jesus Christ and not Jesa Christa. . . . What would Jesa Christa be? No salvation for women, and a temptation for men to cast down God.[75]

The feminist Elizabeth Johnson, who devotes an entire essay to Jesus' maleness, has something similar to say. She thinks that "the main problem (is) by no means Jesus' 'masculinity'; rather, it lies in the fact that most males are just not like Jesus." Still, Johnson speaks only of a "social" significance to Jesus' maleness and avoids drawing any further conclusions.[76]

Christology and the doctrine of redemption correspond to each other. At the center of the Christian doctrine of redemption is release from sins and participation in the Divine Life. Jesus' representative intercession on our behalf as a man, and his redemptive power as God, are both presupposed in this. If human beings, be they men or women, were without sin, then Christ would have been an

---

[74] Elisabeth Gössmann, "Zukunft", in Wb, 441.

[75] Heine, *Göttinnen,* 156f., 162.

[76] E. A. Johnson, "Jesus der Mann", *Concilium* 27 (1991): 523f.

idiot to pursue his goal of dying for our sins.[77] According to everything we find in the Gospels, it was precisely this that he regarded as the essence of his mission.[78] The Lutheran bishops of the Northern Elbe region stressed in 1985: "There is no human existence without sin, and no experience of salvation apart from forgiveness of sins. When 'feminist theology' interprets emancipation and integration as self-liberation, and blurs over sin in relation to women ('I am good, I am beautiful'), an image of man is implied that is at odds with the one in the Bible."[79]

Although the existence of "sin" is acknowledged by "moderate" feminists,[80] it is given a new "definition". Pointedly summarized, feminist theology sees power-seeking and pride as temptations for men yet holds that precisely the same dispositions are to be cultivated by women. It must be acknowledged, of course, that—like everything else in human life—the phenomenon of "sin" has its masculine and feminine "colorings". For example, the temptation to misuse one's own physical power is, by nature, stronger for men than for women. It is not by chance that the passages exhorting husbands, in the Letter to the Ephesians, to model their behavior toward their wives on Christ's selfless sacrifice for the Church are almost twice as long as those directed at wives (Eph 5:21–33). Conversely, women more often tend to suffer from inferiority complexes or deficiencies in self-confidence, and they therefore have need of a healthy sense of self-trust. Love of others presupposes love of oneself (cf. Mt 7:12).

But "pride", as classical theology describes it, is an attitude of mind that is found, with differing shadings, in men *and* women. As the "inordinate striving for self-

---

[77] Cf. 1 Jn 1:8–10.

[78] Cf., for example, Mk 10:45 par.; 14:22–24 par.; Heinrich Schürmann, *Jesu ureigener Tod* [Jesus' uniquely own death] (Freiburg, 1974); *Gottes Reich—Jesu Geschick* [God's Kingdom—Jesus' destiny] (Freiburg, 1983).

[79] *Dokumentation*, 104.

[80] Cf. Krobath, in Wb, 387–90; Scherzberg.

excellence",[81] pride gives every person cause for con-science-searching. The original sin, involving man's aspir-ing to become like God by his own efforts (Gen 3:5), illustrates with special clarity what occurs in every sin: man posits some creaturely good as absolute and thereby turns away from God.[82] Women and men may employ differing strategies for placing themselves or some created reality at the center of things, but the spiritual core of the sin remains the same. The earlier-noted demands, for instance, for political "positions of power" (quota ratios of fifty-fifty or seventy-thirty [Mulack] in favor of women) would not necessarily seem to suggest that feminists are less power-seeking than other people. What Mary Daly calls for can quite certainly be endorsed without any qualms by most of her comrades in arms: "The revolutionary women's movement is aimed at achieving... *power* and a redefinition of power."[83] Here, that "readiness to serve" which the New Testament by no means demands only of women is turned upside-down.

Regarding the goal to be striven for, the same criterion that applies to liberation theology also applies to feminist theology: "A clear distinction must be made between the 'freedom for which Christ set us free' (Gal 5:1) and the liberation of women in the sense of a comprehensive trans-formation of their social role."[84] There is, no doubt, a genuine relation between redemption and liberation, inas-much as being redeemed also means being set free from the things of this time and world.[85] The "wholeness" of

---

[81] Thomas Aquinas, STh II–II q 162 a 2: "inordinatus appetitus propriae excellentiae". Cf. Josef Weismayer, "Hochmut" [Haughtiness], in Karl Hörmann, ed., *Lexikon der christlichen Moral* (Innsbruck, 1976), 795–98.

[82] Thomas Aquinas, STh II–II q 162 a 6; cf. Karl Hörmann, "Sünde" [Sin], in Hörmann, *Lexikon* 1534.

[83] Daly, "Sprung", 111 (emphatic italicization hers); cf. Monika Maassen, "Macht/Bemächtigung" [Power/empowerment], in Wb, 262–65.

[84] Dokumentation, 104.

[85] Sacred Congregation for the Doctrine of the Faith, "Instruction on Certain Aspects of the Theology of Liberation", August 6, 1984.

being redeemed within the harmony of grace cannot, however, be identified with the psychological androgyny of a feministically imagined future. Non-Christian feminists thus occasionally observe that feminist theology has turned religion into psychology.[86] In feminist theology, redemption is transformed into an androgynous "liberation" from inner-worldly relationships. The "paradise" of the "matriarchate" and the "egalitarian Jesus movement" of the past correspond here to the utopia of the future. A similar estrangement from sacred history is found, as we know, in Marxism: the "domination-free" state of the primal horde corresponds to the future classless society under communism, in which, according to Marx, all "domination of man by man" will have been abolished. In this respect, feminism and Marxism are as alike as two eggs in a basket.

The inner-worldly focus of the hope leads to an expectation that the androgynous liberation will come, not from God, but from one's own efforts. Redemption is, in any case, superfluous if God—according to Moltmann-Wendel—already loves us "unconditionally" anyway. For Halkes, there is at least still an element of divine assistance (not more precisely described) in the liberation process. Effective "redemptive power", according to the basic drift of many feminist writings, inheres in those "feminine" forces that will automatically lead to a "wholeness" of man and world if they can just be set free from the slavery of "sexism". Jutta Burggraf—like Ingeborg Hauschildt and Barbara Albrecht—thus characterizes feminist theology as "a modern doctrine of self-redemption that exhibits clear anti-Christian features".[87] Or, more politely formulated: feminist theology would have to defend itself against the charge of Pelagianism.[88]

---

[86] Cf. Halkes, *Suchen,* 47, 57.

[87] Burggraf (1986), 18. Cf. Hauschildt, "Feministische Theologie", 19; *Gott eine Frau?,* 31f.; Beyerhaus, *Aufstand,* 36; Albrecht (1983), 56; Axmacher, 14.

[88] Gerber, "Feministische Theologie", in Schöpsdau (1985), 130f.

Beyond this, the memorandum of the Confessing Communities detects a "regression to demonic relationships", not least "in the silly assumption of the witch role".[89] Christa Mulack, in the *Wörterbuch der Feministischen Theologie,* defends the so-called "white magic" of the witches movement, which is assumed to have a healing function.[90] "Practicing" witches like Starhawk have collaborated in the "liturgy" of the "Women-Church" and given "courses" at Catholic educational institutions in the USA.[91] By contrast, a commentator familiar with the occult scene rightly stresses: "You would be better off keeping a pet rattlesnake in your home than becoming involved with occult practices."[92] Apart from the blasphemous aberrations of Daly, the sympathy that even "moderate" feminists show for the "serpent", in the account of the fall, has an at least repugnant effect. Is it any wonder that, instead of confessions of one's own guilt, enraged indictments of the "evil" forces of "patriarchy" come to the fore in the rites of the feminist "Women-Church"?[93] The feminists themselves refer to this as "exorcism". But may it not be, as Cornelia Ferreira thinks, the very opposite that occurs here?[94]

---

[89] Beyerhaus, *Aufstand,* 42; cf. Ruppert, *Hexen.*

[90] Mulack, in Wb, 352f.

[91] Ferreira (1987), 10–12.

[92] U. Bäumer, *Wir wollen nur deine Seele* [We only want your soul], 2d ed. (Wuppertal, 1985), 90; writing from her own bitter experience: Dieperink, *New Age;* see also Egon von Petersdorff, *Dämonologie* 2 [Demonology 2], 2d ed. (Aschaffenburg, 1982), 170–215.

[93] Ruether, *Women-Church,* passim.

[94] Ferreira (1987), 11.

IX. MARY—MOTHER OF GOD OR DOMESTICATED GODDESS? ON THE IMAGE OF MARY IN FEMINIST THEOLOGY

1. Introduction

Mary, the virginal Mother of God, is a kind of central point at which the main lines of the Catholic Faith come together.[1] Since it is impossible to conceive of sacred history without her, she points in a unique way toward the mystery of Christ and the Church. By virtue of that position, she also becomes a criterion against which new theological conceptions must be measured. Mary's criteriological significance is of supreme value when assessing feminist theology, which puts forward demands for fundamental changes in religious life.[2]

This chapter consists largely of material from a lecture of the same title that the author gave in 1992 at the World Mariological Congress in Huelva (and that will soon be published among the official records of that congress). That is the explanation for the repetition of some points made earlier in the present work.

[1] Cf. *Lumen gentium,* no. 65.

[2] A selection of works presenting feminist standpoints on Mariology: Joan Arnold, "Maria—Gottesmutterschaft und Frau" [Mary—Mother of God and a woman], *Concilium* 12 (1976): 24-29; K. E. Børresen, "Maria in der katholischen Theologie" [Mary in Catholic theology], in E. Moltmann-Wendel, H. Küng, and J. Moltmann, eds., (1988), 72-87; Carr, 237-43; Daly, *Father,* 82-92; *Gyn/Ecology,* 83-85, 86-89, 231; *Lust* (see Index); Gössmann, *Schwestern,* 99-104; "Maria und die Frauen" [Mary and women], *Lebendiges Zeugnis* 43 (1988): 54-63; "Mariologie", in Wb, 279-83; Elisabeth Gössmann and D. R. Bauer, eds., *Maria—für alle Frauen oder über allen Frauen?* [Mary—for all women or above all women?] (Freiburg, 1989); Catharina Halkes, "Eine 'andere' Maria" [A

180

2. Mary Daly's Critique of Mariology

2.1 The Basic Objection: Mary as Domesticated Goddess

The decisive impulse to theological feminism's critique of Mariology came in 1973, from Mary Daly's *Beyond God the Father.* [3]

"different" Mary], *Una sancta* 32 (1977): 323-37; *Söhne,* 92-118; "Maria/Mariologie. B. Aus der Sicht feministischer Theologie" [Mary/Mariology. B. From the viewpoint of feminist theology"], in Peter Eicher, ed., *Neues Handbuch Theologischer Grundbegriffe* 3, 2d ed. (Munich, 1991), 315-23; "Maria, die Frau. Mariologie und Feminismus" [Mary, the woman: Mariology and feminism], in W. Schöpsdau, ed., (1985), 42-70; *Suchen,* 81-99; "Maria—inspirierendes oder abschreckendes Vorbild für Frauen?" [Mary—an inspiring or intimidating model for women?], in Moltmann-Wendel, Küng, and Moltmann (1988), 113-30; "Maria", in Wb, 268-75; E. A. Johnson, "Mary and the Female Face of God", *Theological Studies* 50 (1989): 500-526; Maria Kassel, "Maria—Urbild des Weiblichen im Christentum?" [Mary—a prototype of the feminine in Christianity?], in Moltmann-Wendel, Küng, and Moltmann (1988), 142-60; Maria Clara Lucchetti Bingemer, "Frau: Zeitlichkeit und Ewigkeit. Das ewige Weib und das weibliche Antlitz Gottes" [Woman: Temporality and eternity: Eternal woman and the feminine face of God], *Concilium* 27 (1991): 514-20; Els Maeckelberghe, *Desperately Seeking Mary: A Feminist Appropriation of a Traditional Religious Symbol* (Kampen, Netherlands, 1991); Moltmann-Wendel, *Milch,* 198-202; Elisabeth Moltmann-Wendel, Hans Küng, and Jürgen Moltmann, eds., *Was geht uns Maria an?* [What does Mary have to do with us] (Gütersloh, 1988); Christa Mulack, "Maria und die Weiblichkeit Gottes—Ein Beitrag feministischer Theologie" [Mary and the womanliness of God—an essay in feministic theology], in Wolfgang Beinert et al., eds., *Maria—eine ökumenische Herausforderung* (Regensburg, 1984), 143-70.; *Maria—die geheime Göttin im Christentum* [Mary—the secret goddess in Christianity] (Stuttgart, 1985); Ruether, *New Woman,* 36-59; *Mary—The Feminine Face of the Church* (Philadelphia, 1977); *Sexism,* 139-58; Eva Schirmer, *Eva—Maria. Rollenbilder von Männern für Frauen* [Eve—Mary: Role images by men for women] (Offenbach, 1988); Schöpsdau; Marina Warner, *Alone of All Her Sex: The Myth and the Cult of the Virgin Mary* (New York, 1976).

[3] The same assessment is made by Elisabeth Gössmann, "Mariologische Thesen in der Feministischen Theologie. Darstellungen und Kritik" [Mariological theses in feminist theology: Outline and critique], in Gössmann and Bauer (1989), 168; René Laurentin, "Marie dans la per-

Already in 1968, Daly had published a book on the theme of women, its title and basic content closely tied to Simone de Beauvoir: *The Church and the Second Sex.* For Daly, too, one does not arrive in the world as a woman, but one becomes a woman.[4] In view of the theory of evolution, we can no longer speak of an "essence" of man or of woman or, likewise, of an immutable God who grounds immutable orders of things.[5] Hence, there are no longer any creation-imposed presuppositions to serve as standards for transformation of society and the Church, but only the ideal of "equality".

In her 1973 critique, Daly has been inspired once again by Simone de Beauvoir, who had pointed out the contrast between the ancient goddesses and Mary as early as 1949; whereas the goddesses commanded autonomous power and utilized men for their own purposes, Mary is wholly the servant of God: " 'I am the handmaid of the Lord.' For the first time in the history of mankind, a mother kneels before her son and acknowledges, of her own free will, her inferiority. The supreme victory of masculinity is consummated in Mariolatry: it signifies the rehabilitation of woman through the completeness of her defeat."[6]

Daly now sharpens this critique and puts it in a wider systematic context: Mary is "a remnant of the ancient image of the Mother Goddess, enchained and subordinated in Christianity, as the 'Mother of God' ".[7] To this attempt to "domesticate" the mother goddess, Daly opposes a striving to bring together the divine and the feminine.[8]

In the later work *Gyn/Ecology* (1978), Daly abandons the ideal of "androgyny" that she had previously still advo-

---

spective du féminisme américain" [Mary in the perspective of American feminism], *Études mariales* 44/45 (1989): 84. Cf. above, 81.

[4] Daly, *Church,* 71–72.

[5] Ibid., 148, 180–82, and passim.

[6] Beauvoir, 182.

[7] Daly, *Father,* 83; cf. 82.

[8] Ibid., 81–82.

cated and becomes the most important representative of gynocentric "goddess feminism". Mary is "a pale derivative symbol disguising the conquered Goddess", a "flaunting of the tamed Goddess".[9] Her role as servant in the Incarnation of God amounts to nothing other than a "rape".[10] For Daly, the subordination of man to God is something negative, especially when this state of affairs is expressed in a feminine symbol—such as Mary.

Mary as a "domesticated goddess"—this basic notion of Daly's is not something original to feminism. The same objection can be found, from another perspective and primarily since the nineteenth century, in liberal polemics against the Catholic teaching on Mary. Particularly the title "Mother of God" is often "explained" in terms of the common people's need to worship a goddess. It seems unnecessary to discuss this "unsellable" item from anti-Church polemics further here.[11] Whereas, however, the anti-Catholic literature of earlier generations found it important to stress that Mary is no "goddess", the feminists emphasize Mary's "place-holding" function: Mary discloses the female attributes of God that have heretofore been suppressed. The title of a book by Protestant theologian Christa Mulack provides a characteristic example here: *Maria. Die Geheime Göttin im Christentum* [Mary: The secret goddess in Christianity]. From this perspective, Mary is not an independent personality but something more like a projection screen for archetypical urges that—the author stresses—really need to be directed toward the image of God.

---

[9] Daly, *Gyn/Ecology,* 84, 88.
[10] Ibid., 84.
[11] On this, cf. G. L. Müller, "Gottesmutter" [Mother of God], ML 2 (1989): 690–92.

2.2 The Reinterpretation of Dogmas about Mary

Mary Daly has not only given currency to the thesis that Mary is a "domesticated goddess" but also offered a feminist interpretation of dogmas about Mary that must be briefly reviewed here.

The basic principle behind Daly's interpretation is that of establishing independent status for the figure of Mary, who needs to be freed from her relation to Christ. Mary's *virginity* then becomes a paraphrase for female autonomy: woman is independent and not defined solely through her relationship to man.[12] This interpretation of Mary's virginity has gained almost universal acceptance in feminist circles. A literal understanding of the virginal birth is not, however, part of this. Christa Mulack refers to the assumption of biological virginity as "materialistic",[13] and Catharina Halkes, probably the best-known Catholic feminist in Europe, holds that virginity is an attitude, not an abstinence.[14]

On Mary's being the *Mother of God* — which is, after all, central to the whole of Mariology — Daly simply refrains from making any definite commentary, even about its function as an isolated symbolic image. The reason for this is understandable: "being a mother" always implies an inherent relation to a child. That, however, is obviously not compatible with Daly's feminist ideal of autonomy.

The title "Mother of God" is also largely blurred over, or at least not raised for discussion, by feminists after Daly.[15] An exception here is Mulack, who reinterprets the Mother of God title so as to imply an incarnation of the divine in the body of every individual woman. Just as matriarchy precedes patriarchy, and the collective uncon-

---

[12] Daly, *Father,* 84–87.
[13] Mulack, *Göttin,* 36.
[14] Halkes, Wb, 274, passim.
[15] Cf. Burggraf (1986), 19; Beinert (1989), 129.

scious precedes individual consciousness, so the new male element originates from woman.[16] Regarding representations of Mary with the child Jesus, Mulack applauds the fact "that the male is always depicted here as smaller than the female", for love can only find expression "where the female powers are preponderant". What is essential is not the procreator but the birth-giver.[17]

As distinct from the Mother of God aspect, Daly finds Mary's *Immaculate Conception* to be something, once again, worth reinterpreting: divested of dogma, what is involved here is a negation of female evil and a rejection of patriarchy. Woman has no need of being redeemed by a male.[18] "Immaculate Conception" is a "metaphor" that evokes parthenogenetic powers and represents the "process of a woman creating herself", free of fathers and chains.[19]

Otherwise, the Immaculata dogma is a source of irritation to feminists, including Daly: Mary is placed on an unreachably high pedestal and cannot serve as a genuine model for all real women. The image of woman is split into two halves: the evil Eve, with whom all real women are equated, and the impossible ideal of a virginal Mother of God, who is free of all sin.[20]

In opposition to Mary, the serpent-trampler, Daly posits the ideal of the serpent-goddess.[21] Following C. G. Jung—for whom evil, too, has to be positively "integrated" and the devil included in the image of God[22]—some female theologians, beginning with Daly,[23] call for an overturning of the merely good and holy in Mary. Christa Mulack regards the archetypical Mary as a reincarnation of the

---

[16] Mulack, *Göttin,* 92–160, esp. 122, 159; cf. above, 64.
[17] Mulack (1984), 162.
[18] Daly, *Father,* 87.
[19] Daly, *Lust,* 102–16, here 113–14.
[20] Daly, *Father,* 81–82.
[21] Daly, *Lust,* 391.
[22] Keintzel, 80f., 102–4.
[23] Daly, *Father,* 89.

serpent, in which all oppositions are cancelled out, including that between good and evil. Thus, even the behavior of Eve is to be viewed as positive, since she had obeyed herself, that is, the serpent, and stood up to the jealous Yahweh.[24] Mulack is quite aware that she is adopting Gnostic positions here.[25]

Along with the Immaculata dogma, the *Assumpta dogma* is also given a new interpretation by Daly. That Christ actively "ascended" (*ascendit*) into heaven, whereas Mary "was taken up" (*assumptus est*), she considers a reinforcement of patriarchalism. As a symbol in itself, however, the *"assumptio"* signifies the ascendance of woman into the divine sphere, which C. G. Jung has expressed in his talk of a quaternity.[26]

3. Basic Currents in Feminist Mariology since Daly

3.1 Rejection of the Figure of Mary

Mary Daly's position represents a beginning that decisively set the course of later feminist Mariology. From it, some female theologians have inferred the need to abandon the figure of Mary altogether. According to Kari Børresen, a Catholic theologian from Norway, veneration of Mary is a reaction to the masculine image of God and, therefore, superfluous.[27] Mary's role within feminist theology strikes her as "utterly contradictory, because this figure is anchored in an androcentric typology". The "linkage of femininity and subordination"

---

[24] Mulack, *Göttin,* 171, 179f., 192.

[25] Ibid., 172f., passim; "Gnosis".

[26] Daly, *Father,* 89; on Jung, cf. Unterste, 139ff.

[27] K. E. Børresen, "Männlich-Weiblich: eine Theologiekritik" [Masculine-feminine: A critique of theology], *Una sancta* 35 (1980): 333.

remains "fundamental in both ecclesiology and Mariology".[28]

Elisabeth Moltmann-Wendel makes a similarly sceptical
judgment: the three female witnesses to Jesus' Resurrection,
and especially Mary Magdalen, are much "closer to life"
for modern women than is Mary of Nazareth, even if, as
our "sister", she is not to be completely rejected.[29] By
contrast with the Mother of Jesus, Mary Magdalen, as
Jesus' friend, is not tied to any notions of order. Hence, for
women who are becoming more independent, the model is
not Mary but Mary Magdalen.[30]

3.2 The School Oriented toward Psychoanalysis

Either a rejection of Mary or a cautious scepticism about
her would probably predominate in the attitudes of feminists
as a whole. Along with this, however, there are attempts to
redefine Mariology and, thus, to overthrow Mary's traditional image. Basically, two main currents can be found in
feminist discourse about Mary: one tending more toward
psychoanalysis, and the other more toward sociology and
liberation theology. In the German-speaking realm, the
main representatives of the psychoanalytic stream are the
Protestant theologian Christa Mulack and, on the Catholic
side, Maria Kassel, who for some years headed the research
unit for "Feminist Theology" in the Catholic Theological
Faculty of the University of Münster. A definitive role has
been played here by the theories of C. G. Jung and his
student Erich Neumann, who assumes that human history
began with a primal matriarchate. The development from
the matriarchy to patriarchy, the phylogenesis, is formally

---

[28] Børresen, "Maria", 83f.

[29] Moltmann-Wendel, *Milch,* 202.

[30] Elisabeth Moltmann-Wendel, "Maria oder Magdalena—Mutterschaft
oder Freundschaft?" [Mary or Magdalen—motherhood or friendship?],
in Moltmann-Wendel, Küng, and Moltmann (1988), 55f.

reflected in the ontogenesis of the individual: a development from the maternal, transpersonal unconscious to consciousness.[31] Because of the higher value placed on the feminine in this conception, female Jungians tend toward gynocentric feminism and worship of a goddess.[32]

Also traceable back to C. G. Jung is the talk about ostensibly timeless archetypes[33] that was first heard from Andrew Greeley[34] and then taken up, with particular logical consistency, by Eugen Drewermann.[35] Greeley and Drewermann, too, are frequently cited by feminists.[36]

Another frequent source of reference, especially for "psychoanalytically" oriented feminists, is the comprehensive work of the English writer Marina Warner, who also regards Mary as a myth, but a myth that, because of its negative consequences, will vanish into the realm of legend like the ancient goddesses. In contrast to Jung, Warner emphasizes the historical rootedness of the figure of Mary, which is why she rejects the archetype interpretation. Mary is not a naturally arising archetype but an instrument of ecclesiastical oppression.[37] Nevertheless, assiduous use is made of Warner by Christa Mulack, who thinks in terms of "timeless archetypes".[38]

---

[31] Cf. above, 64.

[32] Cf. Brockmann.

[33] Keintzel, 89–97.

[34] Andrew Greeley, *The Mary Myth—On the Femininity of God* (New York, 1977); on this, see Hauke, *Women in the Priesthood?*, 309–12.

[35] Eugen Drewermann, "Die Frage nach Maria im religionswissenschaftlichen Horizont" [The question of Mary in the context of religious studies], *Zeitschrift für Religions- und Missionswissenschaft* 66 (1982): 96–117; *Tiefenpsychologie und Exegese* 1 [Psychoanalysis and exegesis 1] (Olten, 1984), 194, 309, 503f.

[36] Greeley: Halkes, *Söhne,* 117; "Maria, die Frau", in Schöpsdau, 67; Drewermann: Mulack, *Göttin,* 23f., 48; Halkes, *Suchen,* 95f.

[37] Warner, xxiv–xxv, 337–38.

[38] Mulack, *Göttin,* passim.

3.3 The Movement Based on Liberation Theology

Goddess feminism has been subjected, even within feminist theology, to sometimes severe criticism.[39] In academic theological circles, a higher standing is enjoyed by feminist schools that have a stronger orientation toward liberation theology. The main representatives of that direction (in relation to Mariology) are the American Rosemary Ruether and Catharina Halkes from Holland. The relevant biblical watchword comes from the Magnificat: "God throws down the rulers from their thrones, but lifts up the lowly" (Lk 1:52). Rosemary Ruether interprets this scriptural passage— as do the Latin American liberation theologists—as a call for revolutionary overthrow.[40] Everything connected with "hierarchy", with superordination and subordination, has to disappear. Mariology, according to Ruether, "becomes a liberating symbol for women only when it is seen as a radical symbol of a new humanity freed from hierarchical power relations, including that of God and humanity".[41]

Ruether recognizes quite clearly that, in the Catholic symbolism around Mary, the Church and man's soul before God are seen, as it were, in the same perspective. The common analogical link is receptivity, or readiness to receive.[42] Yet Ruether passionately rejects this symbolization: when the Letter to the Ephesians characterizes Christ as a "bridegroom" and the Church as a "bride", that is the result of "intellectual confusion",[43] creating, in fact, a sado-masochistic model[44] that strengthens the social

---

[39] Cf. Heine, *Göttinnen;* Wacker; Maeckelberghe, 31f.

[40] Ruether, *Sexism,* 152-53; on the liberation-theological interpretation of Mary, see J. G. Piepke, "Befreiungstheologie" [Liberation theology], ML 1 (1988): 400f.; Horst Goldstein, *Kleines Lexikon zur Theologie der Befreiung* [Concise lexicon on liberation theology] (Düsseldorf, 1991), 143–46.

[41] Ruether, *New Woman,* 58.

[42] Ruether, *Sexism,* 139, 145, 149.

[43] Ibid., 141.

[44] Ruether, *New Woman,* 57.

subordination of women. In conformity with the democratic worldview, it is not only subordination between human
beings that is rejected, but also — as in the case of Daly —
the subordination of man in relation to God.[45]

Catharina Halkes adopts a somewhat more cautious
position. To be sure, like Ruether, she regards the Magnificat as "dynamite" that ought to explode traditional
Mariology.[46] It is characteristic of Halkes, however, to
want to "swing" between "Magnificat" and "fiat", that is,
between revolt against injustice and assent to the divine.
She concedes that Mary's affirmative response has a positive quality as an expression of creaturely receptivity.[47]
But Halkes, too, vigorously rejects any attempt to establish
a link between (1) Mary's privilege of being allowed to give
free, active consent to the Incarnation and (2) being a
woman. To put any emphasis on Jesus' maleness and Mary's
femaleness is a threat to women.[48] Receptivity is not a
trait for which women have more aptitude than men.[49]

3.4 The Emancipatory Interpretation of Mariology

That Mary's being a woman has no exemplary function
specifically related to women is also the view of Elisabeth
Gössmann, probably the most "moderate" of those feminists who have written on the subject of Mariology in
German. Any remythologizing of the figure of Mary (as
advocated by Mulack), as well as any sweeping mistrust of
Church tradition, are both rejected by Gössmann.[50] But a
central element in feminism is also characteristic of her,

---

[45] See above, 142–51; on Ruether's Mariology, cf. Maeckelberghe, 14–18.
[46] Halkes, "Maria, die Frau", 64; "Maria/Mariologie", 318.
[47] Halkes, "Maria, die Frau", 65; Wb, 273.
[48] Halkes, "Maria, die Frau", 59f.
[49] Halkes, in Wb, 273.
[50] Gössmann, *Schwestern,* 99–104; "Maria und die Frauen"; Gössmann
and Bauer, 63–85, 168–79; Wb, 279–83.

namely, a tendency to disregard the complementarity of the sexes.[51]

Elisabeth Gössmann is the main representative of a feminist Mariology that could be characterized as "emancipatory".[52] Mary is seen as a prototype of human activity by virtue of her collaboration in redemption: Mary is "no 'goddess', but ... a strong human being, with faith and decisiveness, who has the authority to represent the whole of mankind and to accept God's redemptive offer in an effective way. For that is tradition's interpretation of the 'fiat', and not a submissive maidenliness."[53]

Franz Courth sees in Gössmann's position the "danger of an activistic narrowness" that "could end in a Pelagian image of man".[54] Mary's receptivity, which is not simply human in general but also has a typically womanly coloring, is blurred over. The fact that her virginity is not appraised in its concrete physicalness, but is reduced to a sexually neutral "relation to transcendence", is also unsettling.[55] This is all the more puzzling since Gössmann takes a positive view of Mary's physical assumption into heaven: the belief that she retains her female nature in her state of eternal glory disburdens the Church of the charge of hostility to the body.[56]

In Gössmann's Mariology, too, scepticism about the existence of predetermined essences of man and woman leads to a denial that Mary has any special exemplary

---

[51] See above, 95.

[52] Courth (1991), 252, 262, speaks of a "historico-critical" approach of feminist Mariology.

[53] Gössmann, *Schwestern,* 104.

[54] Courth (1991), 262.

[55] Gössmann and Bauer, 81: "Mariology is not gynecology. Mary's virginity is understood in recent theology as an expression of man's relation to transcendence. Mary's motherhood of the Messiah is bound up with this relation to transcendence of all, is a theologomenon, a theological statement, in that sense, no matter what may be hidden behind it"; cf. Wb, 279f., 282.

[56] Gössmann, in Wb, 441; cf. Gössmann and Bauer, 84; Lucchetti Bingemer, 516f.

significance for women. Statements to the contrary by the Pope, in his apostolic letter *Mulieris dignitatem*,[57] are rejected by her. She cannot understand how John Paul II can emphasize a receptivity in woman "that is characteristic of their femininity".[58] According to Gössmann, women by no means have a greater capacity for attentiveness to the concrete individual than do men. She is critical of the complementary view of the sexes that is presupposed by the Pope.[59]

3.5 Rejection of Complementarity of the Sexes as a Common Bond among Feminist Mariologists

The result so far, then, is that the feminist denial of the complementarity of the sexes extends all the way up to the figures of Jesus and Mary. The symbolic significance of maleness and femaleness for the order of redemption is not given due recognition by those feminists who wish to remain in the framework of Christianity, such as Halkes and Gössmann; and if its determinative structure is recognized, then Christianity is either discarded as a whole (as by Daly) or reinterpreted in a hominizing sense (with particular crassness by Ruether).

---

[57] *Mulieris dignitatem,* nos. 16–19, 25f., 30f.

[58] Ibid., no. 16.

[59] *Die Zeit der Frau. Apostolisches Schreiben "Mulieris dignitatem"* [The era of woman: The apostolic letter *Mulieris dignitatem*] with an introduction by Joseph Cardinal Ratzinger and commentary by Elisabeth Gössmann (Freiburg, 1988), 142, 149. Quite similar in tone are the remarks by Beinert (1989), who judges the complementarity of the sexes to be an outmoded theory of the Romantics (117, 150, 162, 171).

4. The Relation between Feminist Statements and Christology[60]

For Daly, God's Incarnation as a male human being is the decisive reason for rejecting Christianity. "Christ-worship", Daly says, "is idol-worship."[61] It has already been shown that most of the "moderate" representatives of feminist theology also reject Jesus' eternal divine Sonship. The denial of Jesus' divinity automatically entails the collapse of the unique significance of Mary. When the "new Adam" is levelled down and integrated into human history, the "new Eve" also loses her profile. When one can no longer appreciate the human significance of the Mother of God, who surpasses every other creature in her worth, then one must either turn Mary into a "secret goddess" or see her special role as being to reveal the feminine attributes of God.

To conclude this chapter (in a somewhat abridged style), the main relevant points may be reviewed under three broad headings: (1) positive elements of truth in feminist Mariology; (2) reasons for rejecting feminism as a total position; and (3) tasks awaiting resolution in future Mariology.

5. Positive Elements of Truth in Feminist Mariology

1. The determinative significance of the symbolism of the sexes

Sexually stamped religious symbolism is no merely peripheral factor but a reality that enters most intimately into the shaping of our life and actions as Christians. The fact that Scripture and tradition characterize God largely in terms of masculine images and man's position before God largely in terms of feminine ones must be taken seriously and studied theologically.[62] Insofar as feminist theology calls

---

[60] Cf. above, 161ff.
[61] Daly, "Sprung", 110.
[62] Cf. Hauke, *Women in the Priesthood?*, 121–94, 216–325; see also the

attention to the significance of symbolism with a masculine or feminine stamp, it is fundamentally correct, even if evaluation of this factor must lead to other kinds of conclusion.

2. The importance of Jesus' maleness and Mary's femaleness

If the "sexual" coloring in religious symbolism is significant, then that applies especially to those two persons who hold the greatest significance within Christianity: Jesus Christ, the Son of God become man; and Mary, the prototype of the Church and of redeemed man. Precisely the irate rejection of this differentiation makes one sensitive to its positive significance.

3. Mary as revelatory of the "feminine" attributes of God

Mary is not merely emblematic of the human being who opens himself to God and collaborates in the redemptive process but also revelatory of the "feminine" or "maternal" attributes of God. This observation is not something new,[63] despite being heavily stressed by feminists. It must be noted, however, that Mary does not directly represent the "maternity" of *God* but is the Mother of God and thus embodies *creaturely* worth at its supreme level.

4. Mary as receptive of human longings

Even though Mary is no "secret goddess", she still serves to attract the positive psychological forces in man that were directed, in paganism, toward goddesses. From that viewpoint, there is a certain justification in the approach taken to the figure of Mary by comparative religion. At the same time, however, the case of Mary suggests the need for a refinement and fundamental correction here: Mary is not

---

Bibliography in the German edition: *Die Problematik um das Frauenpriestertum vor dem Hintergrund der Schöpfungs- und Erlösungsordnung,* 3d ed. (Paderborn, 1991), 500–503; above, 118ff.

[63] Cf. the references in Hauke, *Women in the Priesthood?,* 307.

simultaneously sinful and holy, not simultaneously whore and virgin, but the totally holy woman, who does not provide mankind with a kind of self-confirmation but, rather, draws man "higher upward". In so doing, Mary is not an exchangeable projection screen for human needs[64] but the historical Virgin and Mother of God, who gives a firm historical anchoring to mankind's strivings. The fact that the feminine religious symbolism is removed from the divine sphere here, and tied to human collaboration, should not be interpreted negatively: the worth of created beings, including the worth of woman in particular, is increased by this.

5. The human nearness of Mary, our "sister" in faith

When reflecting on Mary's exemplary role, one must take into account not only her wealth of graces but also her human nearness. In order to help emphasize this point, Christian feminists like to recommend referring to Mary as "sister",[65] a title that is quite traditional.[66] But here, too, it is necessary to remain within proper bounds. The term "sister" cannot express what is centrally characteristic in Mary's position.

6. The "emancipatory" significance of Mary

To equate virginity with "autonomy" is to overlook that aspect of the virginal life that refers beyond itself, that is not sufficient to itself, but, in its own individually appropriate way, enters into the larger order of Christ and the

---

[64] As, for example, Mulack, *Göttin,* 23f., 122.

[65] For example, Halkes; in Wb, 274; Moltmann-Wendel, *Milch,* 202; Herlinde Pissarek-Hudelist, "Maria—Schwester oder Mutter im Glauben?" [Mary—sister or mother in faith?], in Gössmann and Bauer (1989), 146–67, esp. 157, 167; Schneider-Böklen and Vorländer, 107f.; cf. Beinert (1989), 167f., who maintains: "Not hierarchical but familial relations provide the pattern for reciprocal behavior and action" (168); does Beinert understand "family" "anarchically"?

[66] Valentino Macca, "Sorella", in Stefano de Fiores and Salvatore Meo, eds., *Nuovo dizionario di Mariologia,* 2d ed. (Milan, 1986), 1323–27.

Church.[67] Nevertheless, Mary's active collaboration also has, so to speak, an "emancipatory" significance,[68] which Pope Paul VI has identified in "*Marialis cultus*": "The modern woman, anxious to participate with decision-making power in the affairs of the community, will contemplate with intimate joy Mary, who, taken into dialogue with God, gives her active and responsible consent."[69]

Here, one might also recall an important thought of Gertrud von le Fort: The virgin who is consecrated to God "does not have her place within generation, but she marks an end to generation.... From that position, she is an invocation to belief in an ultimate worth of the person as such ... ; the virgin naturally symbolizes the religious emphasis on, and affirmation of, the worth of the person in its ultimate, immediate relation to God alone."[70]

6. Opposing Negative Factors

1. The failure of feminism as a total conception

Reflecting on the elements of truth in feminism can create a feeling for the important concerns of women today. Feminist Mariology, however, has nothing new to offer that would not already be accessible to Catholic teaching through its own existing sources. Above all, it must not be forgotten when evaluating feminist theology that its basic anthropological starting point, which influences its stand on all more specific issues, is irreconcilable with Christian faith. God did not create humans as androgynous, or the male as an imperfect satellite-being to the female, but as man and woman, equal in value but not in kind. Here, Barbara

---

[67] Cf. Manfred Hauke, "Maria als Vorbild der Jungfrauen" [Mary as a model for virgins], ML 3 (1991): 484–87.

[68] As in Gössmann (1988), 56; Courth, "Feministische Theologie", 461.

[69] "Marialis cultis", no. 37.

[70] Le Fort, 38.

Albrecht deserves approval when she clearly stresses that "feminist theology as a whole should . . . be rejected."[71] The task of Catholic Mariology is not to "fertilize"[72] feminist theology but to lead its representatives (female and male) to change their ways.

2. The basic ecclesiological significance of feminine symbolism

In critically evaluating theological feminism, it is quite permissible to point to the so-called "quarrel among sisters", to their disagreements with each other. The difference between the sexes, which is found throughout all cultures and whose impress is profoundly significant, is emphasized by the gynocentric feminists but blurred over by those pursuing equality. Here, the androgynous direction has what is probably, in the long run, the weaker position. It seems paradoxical that precisely the gynocentric feminists, who recognize that being a woman means having a certain predetermined essential nature, are also, because of their worship of the "goddess", the most far-removed from Christianity. Serious regard for the difference between the sexes leads either to decisive affirmation of the biblical symbolism of the sexes, and thus to rejection of feminism,[73] or to an indignant abandonment of Christianity.

All feminists are particularly offended by the fact that, in the biblical symbolism of the sexes, the female role is subordinate to the male, most notably in the parallel drawn

---

[71] Albrecht (1983), 56; Burggraf (1986), 13; Feminism is "a high point of the modern anti-Christian revolution"; Schlichting, 12; cf. Simonis (1986), 483: Feminism is absolutely unusable for working out a very necessary theology of female being. Numerous other supporting voices could be cited here. This runs contrary to Beinert (1989), for whom feminism is "an irreversible phenomenon" (as was once claimed of National Socialism and Marxism by other theologians), which has "its ultimate roots" in the gospel; feminist Mariology represents "no real break with the traditional Marian doctrine" (1988), 9; (1989), 124.

[72] Courth, "Feministische Theologie", 461.

[73] Cf., for instance, the works of Burggraf and Schlichting.

between the relations of Christ to the Church and the Bridegroom to the Bride. References to Mary as the "self-effacing handmaid" make them positively livid.[74] At the same time, they repress the fact that the female symbolism here is also authoritative for males. Man's position before God requires certain attitudes whose symbolic structures are more strongly "feminine" than "masculine": receptivity, but also active cooperation. Here, the female symbolizes a reality with which she is herself identical. In the case of masculine symbolism, the situation is quite different: when, for instance, the male partner in marriage is compared to the Bridegroom Christ, it is fully clear that the husband is not Christ but only representative of his loving devotion. Regarding the relationship to God, even males must take the female, "Marian" attitude as their standard. The Church *as* Church, in her receiving from Christ and cooperating with him, is—as Hans Urs von Balthasar rightly stresses—primarily "feminine" and not "masculine".[75]

3. Jesus' maleness as a bridge
to the emancipatory concern

The fact that Jesus was not a woman but a man can, moreover, be quite reasonably accounted for precisely from a "feminist", or emancipatory, perspective. Susanne Heine stresses: Men are much more strongly tempted to misuse their power. But in Jesus Christ a man has exemplified the attitude of service.[76]

---

[74] Mulack (1984), 152: "Most frequent is the offense we find being caused by the notion of the 'obedient handmaid of the Lord'. . . . "

[75] H. U. von Balthasar, "Epilog: Die marianische Prägung der Kirche" [Epilogue: The Marian impress of the Church], in Wolfgang Beinert, ed., *Maria heute ehren* [Devotion to Mary today], 2d ed. (Freiburg, 1977), 276; H. U. von Balthasar and Joseph Ratzinger, *Joseph, Maria—Kirche im Ursprung* [Joseph and Mary—the origin of the Church] (Freiburg, 1980). It should be remembered that Balthasar is the only modern theologian quoted at length in *Mulieris dignitatem* (no. 27, n. 55): "Women Priests?", in his *New Elucidations* (San Francisco, 1979), 187–98.

[76] See above, 177.

4. Mary as a prototype of the Church and of redeemed man

The decisive significance of Mary consists, not in revealing the "feminine" attributes of God, but in embodying the way that man collaborates in the redemptive process. That such religious symbolism is treated by feminists as bearing exclusively on the image of God, but not on the collaborative role of man and the Church, seems connected with Protestant assumptions that give stress, in the redemptive process, to the "*solus Deus*".[77] This probably also explains the fact that feminist theology has been much more successful in the Protestant sphere than in the Catholic; among Protestants, feminine religious symbolism, especially in the form of Mariology, has been much attenuated for centuries. Protestantism is therefore subject to vehement criticism from the feminist viewpoint.[78] But even the manifesto of the conservative Confessing Communities stresses: "An uncompleted task still facing Protestant theology is that of inquiry into the meaning of the testimony of Holy Scripture to Mary as the exemplary model of both the believing woman and the believing communion."[79]

5. The exemplary character of Mary

Mary does not set an "impossible example". In her, of course, virginity and motherhood are combined in a unique, inimitable way. This serves to demonstrate precisely the unexchangeable self-containedness of Mary, which cannot be resolved into either Christology or ecclesiology. But

---

[77] On this see Hauke, *Women in the Priesthood?*, 311f.

[78] For example, Daly, *Father*, 82-85; Ruether, *Maria*, 70-75; Halkes, *Söhne*, 106; Krattiger, 48, 56f.; Wb, 239; Mulack, *Göttin*, 9: "After just five hundred years . . . we find the soul suffering from religious and emotional deprivation. The iconoclasts did a very thorough job, leaving nothing remaining of the emotional warmth that Mary continued to radiate, in word and image, in the Catholic sphere."

[79] Beyerhaus, *Aufstand*, 56f.

precisely this aspect of relative "self-containedness" is overlooked by feminists, who otherwise like to object that Mary is regarded merely as a being "in relationship".[80]

Yet Mary's privileges are transferable, in an analogical way, to every Christian, in which connection the prototypical function of the Mother of God has a specially pronounced relevance for women. Reference may be made here to what is said in *Mulieris dignitatem* about the exemplary character of virginity and motherhood. There, the Pope speaks of the "two particular dimensions of the fulfillment of the female personality".[81] By preserving virginity for the sake of the heavenly Kingdom, a woman confirms herself in her being as a person, having been created for her own sake, and realizes her calling to love through devotion to Christ. This fundamental "bridal" attitude of Christian love is also reflected in marriage and extends outward, through spiritual motherhood, to all people, who are embraced by the love of Christ.[82]

The Eve-Mary parallel[83] yields no grounds for complete dismissal of Eve. In any case, Church tradition—contrary to Tatian—presupposes that the progenitors of the species repented of their sin and were redeemed by Christ.[84] In patristic theology, the paradisal Eve is definitely a kind of prefiguration of Mary, and Dante's *Divina Commedia* depicts Eve as seated at the feet of Mary.[85]

---

[80] For example, Halkes, *Söhne,* 105; "Maria/Mariologie", 316.

[81] *Mulieris dignitatem,* chap. 6, here no. 17.

[82] Ibid., nos. 20f.

[83] On this, see Georg Söll, "Eva-Maria-Parallele" [Eve-Mary parallels], ML 2 (1989): 420f.; Manfred Hauke, *Heils verlust in Adam. Stationen griechischer Erbsündenlehre: Irenäus—Origenes—Kappadozier* [The loss of salvation in Adam: Stages in the Greek doctrine of original sin: Irenaeus—Origen—the Cappadocians] (Paderborn, 1993), index.

[84] Hauke, *Heilsverlust,* 124, 228f.

[85] Cf. the references in Gössmann, *Schwestern,* 102f.; the discussion in Wb, 95–97 ("Eva"), goes significantly beyond this justified point (for example, in praising a depiction of Eve holding a dragon), as did already Gössmann and Bauer, 177, where a "fusion" of Eve with Mary is suggested. Moltmann-Wendel, cited as reference by Gössmann (Wb, 97), thinks that:

Eve and the "concrete woman" are no more dismissed than Adam and the "concrete man" but are represented as capable of being converted and saved.

An exemplary model leads to nothing, of course, if it does not "lead further" the one who observes it. An exemplary model that is not "revered" does not deserve the name.[86] To take as one's model a "mixture" of Eve and Mary, or even a Jungian "blend" of Holy Virgin and cruel witch, would by no means further, but rather hinder, man's progress toward God.

7. Tasks for Mariological Research

1. The relationship of Mariology to the image of woman

It is recurrently objected in feminist Mariology that Mary is an impossible model for women. Rosemary Ruether even maintains that the more Mary has been venerated, the more living women have been devalued.[87] Elisabeth Gössmann is much more cautious here: suppositions about the negative effect of Mariology in past centuries have "not yet been verified".[88] Something in Mary that is quite positive for women, for example, is being an "archetype of the mystical experience of the birth of God in the human

---

"The dragon with the apple in its jaws, which she is so lovingly intertwined with, is the world of wisdom, knowledge, and sensual lust, to which she gives herself—voluntarily, sovereignly, without archaic constraints" (*Milch*, 119). For a critical view on this, cf. Josef Sudbrack, "Feministische Theologie. Fragen um ein aktuelles Thema" [Feminist theology: Questions about a current topic], *Geist und Leben* 59 (1986), 302.

[86] I find incomprehensible the claims of Beinert (1989), who describes the "traditional" image of Mary as follows: "Mary, to be sure, is regarded as second only to Christ in human perfection; but that is precisely why she is irrelevant to the question of women. The more her sanctity was praised, the more lastingly her force as an example abated" (103; cf. 26). What, then, would be the implications of this sort of reasoning for the exemplary force of the Son of God who became man?

[87] Ruether, *Mary*, 64.

[88] Gössmann, *Schwestern*, 103.

soul", but also being representative of humanity when giving her word of assent.[89] An important research task would be to examine women's contribution to Mariology and its links to the image of woman.[90]

One may certainly feel able to endorse that suggestion, although with the added qualification that it is not just in relation to the work of female authors that the links between Mariology and the image of woman merit further study. The fact that veneration of Mary can produce in men, too, a heightened esteem for concrete women is occasionally acknowledged even by a feminist as extreme as Christa Mulack.[91] But the links between Mariology and the image of woman do warrant further elucidation.[92]

2. The Holy Spirit and Mary

A topic already dealt with many times in German Mariology is that of the links between the Holy Spirit and Mary.[93] Although that relationship cannot be seen as one of exclusivity—after all, Christ, and not Mary, is the supreme "bearer of the Spirit"—it does introduce some interesting viewpoints. This area of research, too, still seems capable of further development.[94] It might then emerge more clearly that, on the one hand, Mary's receptivity and relational nature have a certain analogical grounding in the divine sphere, while, on the other hand, the main bearing of feminine religious symbolism is on man's position before God.

---

[89] Gössmann and Bauer, 66, 69.

[90] Ibid., 80; Wb, 282.

[91] Mulack, *Göttin,* 129.

[92] As also in Courth (1988), 148.

[93] Cf., most recently, Anton Ziegenaus, ed., *Maria und der Heilige Geist* [Mary and the Holy Spirit], Mariol. Studien 8 (Regensburg, 1991).

[94] Cf. Hauke, *Women in the Priesthood?,* 277-96, 316f.; Pneumatologie.

8. Final Observations: Our Lady of Guadalupe and Mary's Humanity

Mary—Mother of God or domesticated goddess? This alternative can, in conclusion, be illumined quite well through an example from Latin America. The image of the Mother of God in Guadalupe shows Mary with facial features similar to those of Mexicans.[95] The place where she appeared is not far from the destroyed temple of the mother goddess Tonantzin. The appearance of the Mother of God in Guadalupe led to the greatest mass conversion in the history of the Church. In the wake of liberation theology, even feminist theologians, regardless of confession, praise the image of the Mother of God at Guadalupe as a benefactor of the oppressed.[96] Yet a certain old misunderstanding not infrequently arises in this context, as, for instance, in Christa Mulack's claim that Mary is a "reincarnation of the ancient Mexican earth mother".[97] Again, for Eugen Drewermann—whom feminists are fond of citing—the Church has simply "renamed" a goddess here.[98]

And in fact, the picture of Mary that arose miraculously on the visionary's cloak does contain motifs pertaining to the world of the Aztec gods: sun, moon, stars, and serpent. However, through the way that those symbols are arranged, paganism is turned completely upside down. Mary stands

---

[95] Francis Johnston, *So hat Er keinem Volk getan. Das Wunder von Guadalupe* [He has done nothing like this for any people. The miracle of Guadalupe] (Stein am Rhein, 1986), 66f. Cf. also Richard Nebel and Horst Rzepkowski, "Guadalupe", ML 3 (1991): 38-42.

[96] For example, Halkes, *Suchen,* 88f.; Wb, 274; Mulack, *Göttin,* 74; Carr, 242; Schneider-Böklen and Vorländer, 109. A different view is taken by Arnold, 26, who is disturbed by Mary's folded hands, as she thinks this expresses the subjection of the Aztecs to rule by the Spaniards.

[97] Mulack, *Göttin,* 7.

[98] Drewermann, *Tiefenpsychologie* 2:318; the unscientific nature of Drewermann's method is exposed in this example; Harald Grochtmann, *Unerklärliche Ereignisse, überprüfte Wunder und juristische Tatsachenfestellung* [Inexplicable happenings, researched miracles, and juristic establishment of facts] (Langen, 1989), 221-25.

before the sun and is thus more powerful than the feared
sun god. She has one foot placed on the half-moon, a
symbol of the feared serpent god, to whom thousands upon
thousands of humans were sacrificed and whose machina-
tions she has overcome. She is more powerful than all
goddesses and gods, than the stars. And yet Mary is no
goddess, for she folds her hands together in prayer and
bows her head before one who is greater than she. She
wears no mask in order to conceal her godly nature—as do
the Aztec gods—but quite openly displays her human
status.[99]

What we see here is a process of simultaneous interlinkage
and contradiction: the heritage and longings of humanity
(in this case, of the Central American Indians) are acknowledged yet simultaneously transformed and directed toward
God. Should the same thing be impossible in relation to
modern feminism?

Veneration of Mary signifies the end of the idolization
of creaturely values and certainly the day of judgment for
any sort of pantheistic self-idolization. Mary points human
beings toward Christ. Could the experience of Guadalupe
also serve to inspire feminists? At any rate, a Spanish Jesuit
observed several centuries ago: "From this image, as from
a refracting prism, stream forth many intimations of glory
. . . , of light and splendor. May all women learn from it."[100]
To which might be added, also all men.

---

[99] Johnston, 110f. Quite misdirected is a syncretistic interpretation by
one author, according to which the image of Mary effects an adding of the
female aspect to the male God, a "new religion" arises from the mutual
complementarity of paganism and Christianity, and the Virgin is adorned
with the quality of omnipotence: Virgil Elizondo, "Maria und die Armen.
Ein Modell eines evangelisierenden Ökumenismus" [Mary and the poor:
A model of evangelizing ecumenism], in Moltmann-Wendel, Küng, and
Moltmann (1988), 131–41.

[100] Johnston, 67.

X. THE IMAGE OF THE CHURCH

1. Descriptive Account

Feminist theology's furious protests are sparked by the reality of the Church, which they regard as primarily an institutional power structure. Offense is caused, in particular, by the sacramental priesthood, which grounds the Catholic Church as instituted by Christ.[1] Not just the fact that women are not granted ordination as priests but also the sacramental office as such come under attack. A so-called "Women-Church", made up of female advocates (particularly from a Catholic background) of the ordination of women, was formed in the USA in 1983.[2] To a certain extent, this was modelled on the liberation-theological "base" communities of Latin America. In order to be better able to combat "patriarchalism", the "Women-Church" leads its own liturgical life, from which males are excluded. Among the definitive figures in this movement, two authors are cited again and again: Elisabeth Schüssler Fiorenza and Rosemary Radford Ruether.[3]

Since the 1970s, *Schüssler Fiorenza* has propounded the theory that the first Christian communities had an "egalitarian" structure: a "succession-based community of equals".[4]

---

[1] CCC, nos. 858–62; 874f.

[2] Cf. R. R. Ruether, "Frauenkirche. Neuentstehende feministische liturgische Gemeinschafter" [Women-church: Recently arising feminist liturgical associations], *Concilium* 22 (1986): 275–80; *Women-Church,* 11–95; Prüller, 62–91.

[3] Cf. above, 63, 87–88.

[4] Schüssler Fiorenza, *In Memory of Her,* 138–40.

Jesus had rejected any sort of ruling structure.[5] He had denied that "any father and any patriarchy" had the right to exist. Paternal authority was reserved for God alone.[6] Only in later times (after Paul and Peter) did the Church adapt herself to her patriarchal surroundings.[7] The Letters to the Colossians and the Ephesians, the Pastoral Epistles, and the First Letter of Peter, which are hostile to women, were the product of this adaptation strategy. Previously, however, there had been female apostles, in particular, Junia,[8] and community leaders, such as Phoebe.[9]

Accordingly, the will of Jesus had already been betrayed in the New Testament. The selection of biblical writings regarded as authoritative for Christians, the biblical canon, is a document of the historical victors, who had thereby prevailed, especially over Gnosticism.[10] The ability to comprehend these points depends, however, on "an intellectual conversion that cannot be logically deduced but is rooted in a change of patriarchal-social relationships".[11]

Schüssler Fiorenza asks herself why she bothers to concern herself with the Church at all, in which, according to her theory, patriarchalism has prevailed over an original egalitarianism. Her answer rests less on religious than on pragmatic grounds: since Western culture has, in fact, been

---

[5] Ibid., 148–49.

[6] Ibid., 151.

[7] Ibid., 334.

[8] Ibid., 47, 171–72; on this subject, see Hauke, *Women in the Priesthood?*, 358–59; Norbert Baumert, *Frau und Mann bei Paulus* [Woman and man in Paul] (Würzburg, 1992), 187f. Whether the accusative "Kounian" in Romans 16:7 is derived from the woman's name Junia or from an abbreviated form of the man's name Junianos (= Junias) remains open exegetically. Nor is it ever clear whether Andronikos and Junia(s) are to be classed—as most suppose—among the "apostles" or were merely esteemed by them. Even if one supposes a "Junia" and ascribes the notion of apostle to her, the breadth of the notion of apostle in the New Testament must be considered as well as the prohibition of official teaching in the divine service by women (1 Cor 14:33b–38; 1 Tim 2:12).

[9] Schüssler Fiorenza, *In Memory of Her*, 47, 169–71.

[10] Ibid., xv, 55–56.

[11] Ibid., xxi.

basically stamped by Christian influences, it is necessary to wrest history from the patriarchal Church, to make visible what has become invisible, and to rewrite the Bible.[12]

The ideal image of the Church that Schüssler Fiorenza has in view is strongly influenced by the democratic ideal of equality, which she reads back into the New Testament: "Ecclesia—the term for church in the New Testament—is not so much a religious as a civil-political concept. It means the actual assembly of free citizens gathering for deciding their own spiritual-political affairs."[13]

Whereas Schüssler Fiorenza wants to establish the "Women-Church" on a historical basis, the feminist communities' most important systematic reflections, both theoretical and practical, stem from Rosemary Radford Ruether. She adopts Schüssler Fiorenza's basic historical approach (opposition between the Church and the "Jesus movement"), but places it in a more comprehensive context. No such thing as an ordained office whose purpose consists in the mediation of sacramental grace can possibly exist, according to Ruether, for the simple reason that she denies the distinction between created nature and the grace bestowed by God in Christ.[14] A "sacrament" thus confers nothing new on a person but is "the symbol of our . . . mutual empowerment", in which we recognize our "authentic human life"—something "upon which we stand naturally".[15] Accordingly, the so-called "functions of church" serve the purpose of furthering our reciprocal confirmation of each other in her (the Church).[16] Ministry involves no element of divine authorization but is "simply the self-articulation

---

[12] Ibid., xix, 36.

[13] Ibid., 344.

[14] Ruether, *Women-Church,* 86: "Women-Church is rooted in what has been defined recently as 'creation-based spirituality'. This means that the grace of redemptive life is not beyond nature, but grace or divine gift is the ground of being of nature. Creation is itself the original grace or blessing."

[15] Ibid., 87.

[16] Ibid., 87–88.

of the community's life together".[17] The aim here is a transformation of "leadership from power over others to empowerment of others".[18]

This view is perfectly compatible with the pantheistic notion of God, which posits an identity of God and world[19] in which there can be no personal intervention by God ("grace"). Concern for eternal salvation is thus not an issue for the "Women-Church"; rather, it is concerned solely with the inner-worldly struggle against the social primacy of males. The "Women-Church" is a "community of liberation from patriarchy",[20] which appropriates Israel's exodus from slavery in Egypt as its "foundational myth"[21] and looks ahead to the domination-free "New Age".[22]

Ruether herself knows that her conceptions no longer have anything to do with Church dogma. She even admits that those lines of biblical tradition that feminism claims as its own have "never really been developed".[23] Her understanding that "redemption" consists essentially in knowledge of one's self is similar to the basic principle of ancient Gnosticism, for which she expressly acknowledges sympathy.[24]

The groundwork for the feminist theories was first prepared by "progressive" Catholic theologians like Küng and Schillebeeckx, for whom spiritual office represents a mere function but does not rest on any authorization affecting one's personal being through sacramental consecration.[25]

---

[17] Ruether, *New Woman*, 81; cf. *Sexism*, 209–10.

[18] Ruether, *Sexism*, 207.

[19] Cf. above, 146.

[20] Ruether, *Women-Church*, 57.

[21] Ibid., 41.

[22] Ibid., 42, 64.

[23] Ibid., 37.

[24] Ibid., 47–48.

[25] Cf. for example Carr, 26–27; Ruether, *Women-Church*, 89–90; on Küng and Schillebeeckx, see Gisbert Greshake, *Priestersein* [To be a priest], 5th ed. (Freiburg, 1991), 24–29, 193–96.

This functionalistic understanding of office is, however, not an original, modern idea, but can be found, in principle, already in Martin Luther.[26] The democratic ideal of equality in the feminist image of the Church cannot be understood apart from Reformation theology (and its influence on postconciliar Catholicism), which effectively prepared the way for it. A familiar image from "progressive" theology often also appears in feminist works: to the "pyramid of power" is opposed the "circle of equals".[27]

In order to break down the influence of the Church, there are three basic strategies:[28] departure from the Church in favor of the "cosmic sisterhood" of the "Antichurch";[29] establishment of a subculture ("Women-Church"); and, finally, calculated subversion from within. The last two of these strategies usually go hand in hand. Rosemary Ruether, for example, observes: "It is my view that the feminist option will be able to develop much more powerfully at the present time if it secures footholds in existing Christian churches."[30]

Feminists of Catholic background do not normally feel a need to be integrated into the established priesthood. As Ruether puts it: "The call to ministry is not a call to become the passive supporter of the public order or the toady of the powerful in the church or society."[31] Nevertheless, many female theologians continue striving to change the office of priest from within.[32] The words of Luise Rinser are typical here: "One can quite well remain in the Church and at the

---

[26] On this, see Holsten Fagerberg, "Amt/Ämter/Amtsverständnis VI. Reformationszeit" [Office/offices/understanding of office: VI. Reformation period], TRE 2 (1978): 557–61.

[27] Cf., for example, Halkes, *Söhne,* 84, 90; *Suchen,* 44, 71; see also Hauke, *Women in the Priesthood?,* 67.

[28] Cf. Gerber, *Eroberung,* 152–54.

[29] Daly, *Father,* 138ff., 155.

[30] Ruether, *Women-Church,* 39; cf. 62.

[31] Ruether, *Sexism,* 207.

[32] Cf. for example Halkes, *Söhne,* 45f.; Carr, 55; Raming in Wb, 330.

same time overcome her."[33] The criticism of authority structures is also directed at the Protestant Church. Ruether writes that women in ministry "find themselves in a double bind", which commits women to a "masculinity game" while at the same time demanding femininity of them. Moreover, the female pastors would not constitute a serious threat to the monopoly of male power anyway.[34]

2. Critical Evaluation

The critique made by feminist theology contains an element of truth, namely, the fact that, by virtue of baptism, all members of the Church enjoy a fundamental equality ("priesthood of the faithful").[35] This equality is grounded in their common directedness toward Christ, who confers the gifts of the Holy Spirit on those belonging to him. In decisive situations, however, Christ acts by means of human mediators. The apostles, as their very name implies, were already "emissaries" and representatives of Christ: "Whoever listens to you listens to me" (Lk 10:16). In the New Testament, we hear of office-bearers whose activity stems from their having been sent by the apostles.[36] The apostolic succession grounds the hierarchic structure of the Church, a continuous personal chain of sending and being sent, which ultimately goes back to Jesus Christ's knowing himself to be sent by the Father.

---

[33] Luise Rinser, "Ich möchte den weiblichen Geist einbringen" [I would like to bring in the feminine spirit], in Sommer (1985), 37.

[34] Ruether, *Sexism,* 201. These remarks are quite reflective of a kind of criticism made repeatedly by Protestant female theologians, e.g., Erika Reichle, *Die Theologin in Würtemberg. Geschichte—Bild—Wirklichkeit eines neuen Frauenberufes* [The female theologian in Würtemberg: History—image—reality of a new calling for women] (Bern and Frankfurt, 1975), 310; Friederike Rupprecht, "Frauen im Pfarrant" [Women in ministry], *Theologia practica* 22 (1987): 113–21; Knie.

[35] Cf. *Lumen gentium,* no. 32; CCC, nos. 871–73.

[36] Especially Acts 6:1–6; 14:23; 1 Tim 4:14; 2 Tim 1:6.

Among other documents, the often overlooked First Letter of Clement is important for understanding the historical foundations of ordained office. This writing is addressed to the community at Corinth—which Schüssler Fiorenza sees as providing the original, ideal example of merely functional office and of an egalitarian community.[37] The First Letter of Clement bears the name of Clement I, the third successor of St. Peter, and was written around 96 A.D., which means roughly forty years after the founding of the Corinthian community by Paul. Now, the Corinthians had removed some presbyters from office; and the intervention from Rome was aimed at opposing this, notably on the basis that the office of presbyter[38] goes back to something instituted by Jesus. Any arbitrary dismissal from office is therefore out of the question:

> The apostles received the gospel for us from the Lord, Jesus Christ; Jesus, the Christ, was sent by God. Christ thus comes from God, and the apostles come from Christ; both these things took place, therefore, in a well-ordered way according to God's will. They consequently received their commissions, were filled with conviction by the Resurrection of our Lord, Jesus Christ, and were confirmed in fidelity by the Word of God. . . . So they preached in the towns and in the country and appointed their firstfruits, after prior testing in the Spirit, to serve as bishops and deacons for future believers.[39]

The apostles, "given that they had received precise instructions in advance, [appointed] those mentioned above, directing at the same time that, if they were to die, other tested men should take over their duties."[40]

---

[37] Schüssler Fiorenza, *In Memory of Her,* 291-93.

[38] Who, in 1 Clement, are still regarded as equal to the episcopes (bishops).

[39] 1 Clement 42:1-4: J. A. Fischer, *Die Apostolischen Väter* [The apostolic fathers], 7th ed. (Darmstadt, 1976), 77, 79.

[40] 1 Clement 44:2: Fischer, 81.

These comments correspond to what is also stated in those Pauline letters whose authorship is uncontested by even the most liberal interpreters of Paul. In the oldest Pauline letter, the First Letter to the Thessalonians, office-bearers are already mentioned (1 Th 5:12). The opening part of the Letter to the Philippians mentions bishops and deacons (Phil 1:1). The mention of "firstfruits" in the First Letter of Clement, who were preferentially entrusted with official duties, has a striking parallel in 1 Corinthians 16:15. If the Corinthians had originally formed an egalitarian "base" community, the letter from Rome would hardly have met with success. However, the Corinthians felt themselves so honored by the First Letter of Clement that they were still reading it aloud regularly at divine service decades later. In other words, they had accepted the letter and its reasoning.[41]

The testimony of the First Letter of Clement has been brought in here solely to illustrate the problems that result, on the purely historical level alone, from a feminist interpretation of the early Church.[42] For a more detailed account of the development of ecclesiastical office, further relevant literature might be consulted.[43]

---

[41] Cf. Fischer, 16f.

[42] Against this, Ruether (*Women-Church,* 289, n. 5) claims that the doctrine of the apostolic succession has existed only since the second century, as Irenaeus (!) and others would serve to prove.... In order to preserve her hypotheses in this area, Schüssler Fiorenza (*In Memory of Her,* 291–92) is forced to portray the things stated in 1 Clement as "innovations" and to argue against even the findings of a Protestant historian.

[43] Ludwig Ott, *Das Weihesakrament* [Priestly ordination], Handbuch der Dogmengeschichte IV, 5 (Freiburg, 1969), 1–18; Robert Zollitsch, *Amt und Funktion des Priesters. Eine Untersuchung zum Ursprung und zur Gestalt des Presbyterats in den ersten zwei Jahrhunderten* [Office and function of the priest: An inquiry into the origin and structure of the presbyterate in the first two centuries], FThSt 96 (Freiburg, 1974); Ernst Nellessen, "Die Einsetzung von Presbytern durch Barnabas und Paulus (Apg 14,23)" [The appointment of presbyters by Barnabas and Paul (Acts 14:23)], in J. Zmijewski and E. Nellessen, eds., *Begegnung mit dem Wort.*

In the struggle against sacramental office, the feminists are aware of their strong reliance on the notion of "base" democracy, which is applied, in an unexamined way, to the Church. Behind this democratism ("Church from below") is an ultimate failure to recognize that the religious community is not the work of man but stems from Christ. The "apostolic succession" derives its meaning from the fact that Christ, as head of the Church, wishes to maintain his symbolic presence until the world reaches its end. Implicit in the term "hierarchy" is the fact that the "sacred Origin", Jesus Christ himself, is continuously handed on by men (and not merely by impersonal "functions"). Vatican II, to which feminists occasionally make sloganistic references (usually without any concrete documentation),[44] quite clearly upholds the christological nature of ordained office.[45]

Divine authority does not exclude that of men but includes it. No doubt the authority of office is also to be understood as a serving. It is from an awareness of this that Augustine can make the striking observation: "For you, I am a bishop; with you, I am a Christian."[46] The apostolically grounded authority expressed in the ordained hierarchy of bishop/priest/deacon is at the service of the people of God; precisely through it the fundamental equality of all members of the Church is first created. Ordained office fittingly embodies the authority of Christ, which, in that form, does not represent a fading memory but is capable of being concretely experienced in word, sacrament, and eucharistic offering. Here, even the office-bearer is subordinate to the prior action of Christ, for which he renders

---

FS H. Zimmermann (Bonn, 1980), 175–93; Johann Auer, *Die Kirche— Das allgemeine Heilssakrament* [The Church—the universal holy sacrament], KKD 8 (Regensburg, 1983), 169–284.

[44] For example, Carr, 24.

[45] *Lumen gentium,* nos. 18–29; *Presbyterorum ordinis,* esp. no. 2.

[46] Sermo 340:1 (PL 38, 1483); cf. *Lumen gentium,* no. 32.

himself a servant and upon which, like all other Christians, he remains dependent.[47]

The system of apostolic office makes possible a communion extending far beyond any small circle of the like-minded. The universal Church aims to include all men of all times and cultures. Such an all-embracing ("catholic") communion is grounded in a mission that goes much deeper than any grouping of people based merely on shared sympathies. Will the often contradictory feminist circles, with their group-centered orientations, be able to measure up to that?

As regards effective power in the Church and the inner relationship with God, the crucial thing is not one's possession of ordained office but the depth of one's influence by the Holy Spirit. "The greatest of those in the kingdom of heaven are not the office-bearers but the saints." With that sentence, the Sacred Congregation (in 1976) put right the feminist perception that women are inferior if they are not called to hierarchic office.[48] For Paul, too, all the members of the Church have their own specific functions, which can no more be played off against each other than can a hand complain of "discrimination" because it is not a foot (1 Cor 12). Hence, statements like Anne Carr's, according to which ordination to the priesthood is a sacrament required for full affirmation of the personhood of all individuals,[49] are completely unfounded. Would this mean that only clergymen (or clergywomen) are fully affirmed persons in the Church? Carr's reasoning reveals a clericalistic image of the Church that should really be regarded, after Vatican II, as no longer possible.

In the matter of appointment to the office of priest, no

---

[47] Leo Scheffczyk, *Aspekte der Kirche in der Krise. Um die Entscheidung für das authentische Konzil* [Aspects of the Church in crisis: About the decision for the authentic Council] (Sieburg, 1993), 84–102.

[48] *Erklärung,* no. 6, 20.

[49] Carr, 22–23, 36, 42.

abstract deliberations about equal rights can be determinative but only reference back to the will of Jesus Christ, which is conveyed to us in Holy Scripture and in Church tradition. In almost two thousand years, the Church has not seen herself as authorized to institute priesthood for women, even though, already in antiquity, some sects (Gnostics, Montanists) had ordained women, and even when such a step would by no means have been opposed by the spirit of the times. The justification for rejection of women in the priesthood—regarding which further relevant literature might be consulted[50]—does not consist in any inferiority of women. Pope Innocent III wrote to a Spanish abbess in the Middle Ages, who had presumed to undertake priestly duties: "Even though the most blessed Virgin Mary may stand higher, and even though she may be more illustrious, than all the apostles taken together, the Lord has still not entrusted her, but rather them, with the key to the kingdom of heaven."[51]

The example of Mary[52] demonstrates, to an outstanding degree, how the activity of holy women influences the Church at all levels. Further examples are so obvious that it would be superfluous to list them. The grace-inspired influence of an individual who transcends the dimension of the visible is by no means tied to the office of priest.

---

[50] Hauke, *Women in the Priesthood?*; see extensive Bibliography in the German edition: *Die Problematik um das Frauenpriestertum vor dem Hintergrund der Schöpfungs- und Erlösungsordnung,* 3d ed. (Paderborn, 1991). Cf. also my two essays: "Das Weihesakrament für Frauen—eine Forderung der Zeit?" [Ordination of women—a demand of our times?], FKTh 3 (1987): 119–34; "Überlegungen zum Weihediakonat der Frau" [Reflections on ordaining women as deacons], *Theologie und Glaube* 77 (1987): 108–27. In a more popular vein: "'Die Kirche is doch echt frauenfeindlich!' Emanzipation und kirchliches Frauenbild" ["But the Church is genuinely hostile to women!" Emancipation and the Church's image of woman], in Michael Müller, ed., *Plädoyer für die Kirche,* 4th ed. (Aachen, 1992), 203–5, 209–12.

[51] 10, X, de poenitentiis, v. 35: ed. Friedberg, 2, 886.

[52] Cf. above, 193–204.

XI. FEMINIST LITURGY

1. Rituals of the "Women-Church"

From its very inception, the "Women-Church" in the USA has been associated with its own appropriate rituals. The best-known work on this was written by Rosemary Ruether: *Women-Church: Theology and Practice of Feminist Liturgical Communities.* A mere initial glance at its table of contents reveals the prominence of elements reminiscent of a nature religion, which are based on certain "nodal points" in the life of feminist women and in the seasonal cycle. One finds, for example, headings like the following: "Menstrual and New Moon Rituals", "Fall Festivals and Remembrances", "Winter Solstice", "Summer Solstice Party", "Covenant Celebration for a Lesbian Couple", "Menopause Liturgy".... Even some of those who support liturgical feminism criticize the neo-pagan cast of these practices and deplore their syncretistic mixing of various religions.[1]

Christian elements, insofar as they are still present, undergo a reinterpretation. "Baptism", for example, no longer has anything to do with an event of grace that allows man to receive participation in Divine Life: "The transcendence of grace is not beyond the human nature given to us at biological birth. Rather, it is beyond cultural consciousness and the systems of unjust power that have shaped us."[2]

The purpose of "baptism" is liberation from "patriarchy",

---

[1] As in Teresa Berger, "Kult", in FLex, 600.
[2] Ruether, *Women-Church,* 126; cf. 77, 86.

with appropriate "exorcisms" playing a central role. For the "communion ceremony" that follows the "act of baptism", milk, honey, and sweet cakes are provided.[3]

The "rituals of atonement" involve no acknowledgment of one's own sins but consist of incensed accusations against "patriarchy" and the Church, for example, "Ash Wednesday Liturgy: Repentance for the Sins of the Church".[4] Ethical standards, insofar as they pertain to sexuality and the child in the womb, are watered down. Abortions are lamented as tragic but are justified in principle.[5]

2. Influence of the *Inclusive Language Lectionary*

The "liturgies" devised by the "Women-Church" have so far been the exotic playthings of marginal groups comprising only a few thousand persons. Similar attempts are undertaken, of course, by numerous other special groups (particularly women's associations or students' organizations),[6] and these not infrequently show admixtures of neo-pagan influence (notably, in certain Protestant academies).[7] In North America, even witches who practice exorcism (like "Starhawk") have collaborated in relevant courses at a "Catholic" university.[8]

---

[3] Ibid., 128-30.

[4] Ibid., 241-51.

[5] Ibid., 161.

[6] Cf., for instance, Christine Hojenski, et al., eds., *Meine Seele sieht das Land der Freiheit. Feministische Liturgien—Modelle für die Praxis* [My soul sees the land of freedom: Feminist liturgies—practical models] (Münster, 1990). Hojenski has meanwhile become Diözesanreferentin in the Department for Pastoral Care of Women in the General Episcopal Curacy of Münster: *Deutsche Tagespost,* January 16, 1993, 4.

[7] Cf., for instance, the activity of the "goddess feminist" Heide Göttner-Abendroth, who, as the "Nature-goddess Astarte", staged a Walpurgis Night, including 150 "witches", in the "Protestant Academy Hofgeismar": *Deutsches Allgemeines Sonntagsblatt,* May 22, 1983; cf. Padberg (1985), 227, n. 245.

[8] Cf. Ferreira (1987), 10; (1989), 8.

More consequential than these limited activities, however, has been the introduction of the earlier-noted *Inclusive Language Lectionary*.[9] This lectionary, which aims to free the text of the Bible from "sexism", plays a large role in Anglo-Saxon Protestantism, especially in the USA.

In Germany as well, Protestant initiatives for creating a "language that does justice to women" were given a decisive impetus by this.[10] Meanwhile, in the Catholic sphere, close contacts have arisen between feminist-oriented women's associations and liturgical scholars. Although the resultant expressions of opinion are not uniform, they tend, as a whole, to support alteration of liturgical texts, with some even calling for a new reform of the liturgy.[11]

The guidelines on "inclusive language" issued in 1990 by bishops in the USA express opposition to attempts to make changes in christological, ecclesiological, and trinitarian symbolism. Faithfulness to the revealed word of God is

---

[9] Cf. above, 126.

[10] Hildburg Wegener, " 'Siehe, das ist meine Beauftragte'. Frauengerechte Sprache in der Übersetzung der Bibel" ["Behold, that is my female delegate": Language that does justice to women in the translation of the Bible], in Hildburg Wegener, Hanne Köhler, and Cordelia Kopsch, eds., *Frauen fordern eine gerechte Sprache* (Gütersloh, 1990), 84.

[11] Cf. the diverse essays in Teresa Berger and Albert Gerhards, eds., *Liturgie und Frauenfrage* [Liturgy and the women's issue] (St. Ottilien, 1990); Teresa Berger, "Auf dem Weg zu einer 'frauen-gerechten' Liturgie" [Toward a liturgy appropriate to the needs of women], *Gottesdienst* 22 (1988): 132; " 'Wie eine Mutter ihre Kinder zärtlich um sich schart . . . ' Zu Versuchen mit neuen 'Frauen-gerechten' Eucharistiegebeten in den Kirchen" ["As a mother tenderly gathers her children around her . . . " On experiments in the Church with new forms of eucharistic prayer more agreeable to women], BThZ 10 (1993): 2–14; Albert Gerhards, " ' . . . Der uns zu seinen Söhnen zählt'? Zum Stand der Bemühungen um eine frauengerechte Liturgie" [" . . . Who counts us among his sons"? The current state of attempts to achieve a liturgy acceptable to women], *Stimmen der Zeit* 117 (1992): 115–24; " 'Einschließende Sprache' im Gottesdienst—eine übertriebene Forderung oder Gebot der Stunde?" ["Inclusive language" in divine service—an exaggerated demand or the need of the moment?], LJ 42 (1992): 239–48. See also the statement by the directorship of the Arbeitsgemeinschaft Frauenseelsorge [Working Group on Pastoral Care of Women]: *Gottesdienst* 26 (1992): 117.

obligatory. At the same time, however, with a view to church services, a limited linguistic adaptation of the scriptural text is recommended. In particular, it is advised to avoid any references, even when occurring in the biblical text itself, to the entire congregation as "brethren", "sons", and so forth, because these generic terms, while fully inclusive as such, are often misunderstood as applying only to males.[12]

3. Feminist Linguistics and Its Problems

From outside the Church, these liturgical endeavors are bolstered by feminist linguistics, which has gained considerable influence in the political sphere.[13] Here, too, decisive impulses came from the USA. Probably the best-known German authoress (along with Senta Trömel-Plötz)[14] observes, for example: "I owe my most important insights into the structure of patriarchalism to the radical thinker Mary Daly, and I therefore admire and respect her more than any other present-day woman thinker."[15]

In order to characterize the basic concern of "linguistic feminism", its adherents (female and male) use the earlier-noted slogan "inclusive language": women should be "included", integrated, in the sense of being (at least) no less visibly reflected in the language than men. The underlying problem is especially evident in the case of terms applying to persons [and more so in German, where use of a feminine suffix, like the "-ess" in "authoress", is standard]: in

---

[12] U.S. Bishops' Meeting, "Inclusive Language in Liturgy: Scriptural Texts", *Origins* 20 (1990): 405–8.

[13] Cf. Wegener, Köhler, and Kopsch, 153–57.

[14] Whose concern is concisely outlined in Senta Trömel-Plötz, "Sprachkritik, feministische" [Language critique, feminist], in FLex (1988): 1067–74.

[15] L. F. Pusch, *Alle Menschen werden Schwestern. Feministische Sprachkritik* [All men will be sisters: Feminist critique of language] (Frankfurt, 1990), 104.

many instances, a masculine substantive serves as the classificatory term, in which both men and women are included, for instance, [the German words for] "citizen", "taxpayer", "customer". In this use of language, according to the feminists, a typical androcentrism is manifest: the linguistic standard is based on the male, and females are only "also included". In order to change this social androcentrism, one must also restructure the language.[16]

The feminist arguments have made their mark in various ways. No [German] politician now risks beginning a speech with the words "My good citizens"; rather, it must be "My good citizenesses and citizens". This sort of usage, however, is far from consistent; so far, there is as little talk of a "citizeness' and citizen's rights" as of a "driveress' and driver's license". Luise Pusch would like to combat androcentrism by "feminizing" the classificatory term.[17] A set of regulations governing diploma-level examinations in Bielefeld was prepared in accordance with these criteria and consistently makes use of the terms "professoresses" and "studentesses" to cover individuals of both sexes.[18] More widespread, in written German, is use of the slant-line device (student/ess), which is of course not applicable to spoken language. Since use of neutral forms ("the member", and so on) is not always possible, it is usually urged that there should be a consistent "splitting", that is, mentioning both the feminine and the masculine forms together.

---

[16] A summary of these concerns from a feminist viewpoint is given (among others) by Hildburg Wegener, "Von Kindergärtnern, Amtsfrauen und Ratsdamen. Sprachkritik und Sprachpolitik in feministischem Interesse" [On male kindergarten-teachers, female officials, council ladies: Linguistic criticism and linguistic politics in the feminist interest], in Wegener, Köhler, and Kopsch (1990), 9–24; Gisela Schoenthal, "Geschlecht und Sprache" [Sex and language], in Deutsche Akademie für Sprache und Dichtung, *Jahrbuch 1991* (Darmstadt, 1992), 90–105 (with bibliog.).

[17] Pusch, *Schwestern,* 85–101.

[18] Johannes Rogalla von Bieberstein, "Frauen-Quotierung als feministisch-soziale Politik" [Quotas for women as feminist-social politics], *Criticón* 118 (March/April 1990): 84.

As an illustration of discriminatory use of language, a short passage has been used from a constitutional draft for Lower Saxony: "The prime minister installs the ministers. He appoints his deputy." Transforming this passage in a way "congenial to women" would result in something roughly like this: "The prime minister or the prime ministress installs the ministers or ministresses. He appoints his deputy or deputy-ess, or she her deputy or deputy-ess".[19]

In order to combat the linguistic monstrosities that have issued from many official chambers as a result of "splitting", some recommend (along with use of the generic feminine) that new, neutral forms be created for German nouns otherwise having both masculine and feminine forms, for instance, in place of *der Lehrer* (male teacher) and *die Lehrerin* (female teacher), a neutral word, *das Lehrer,* should be created.[20]

Linguistic feminism has encountered vehement opposition.[21] Above all, the difference is pointed out between gender ("grammatical sex", which in German includes masculine, feminine, and neuter) and sex ("natural sex",

---

[19] Cf. Gerhard Stickel, "Beantragte staatliche Regelungen zur 'sprachlichen Gleichbehandlung'. Darstellung und Kritik" [Proposed state regulations for "equal linguistic treatment": Summary and critique], *Zeitschrift für germanistische Linguistik* 16 (1988): 349.

[20] As, for example, in L. F. Pusch, *Das Deutsche als Männersprache* [German as a men's language] (Frankfurt, 1984), 63; Wegener, "Sprachkritik", 21.

[21] Cf., for instance, Gerhard Doerfer, "Das Korana und die Linguistinik" *Sprachwissenschaft* 10 (1985): 132-52; Joachim Dyck, "Männerherrschaft als Sprachherrschaft? Eine Kritik der feministischen Linguistik" [Domination by males as domination of language? A critique of feminist linguistics], *Jahrbuch Rhetorik* 8 (1989): 95-104; Stickel; Miorita Ulrich, " 'Neutrale' Männer—'markierte' Frauen. Feminismus und Sprachwissenschaft" ["Neutral" men—"indicated" women: Feminism and linguistics], *Sprachwissenschaft* 13 (1988): 383-99; Wilhelm Zauner, "Brüderlichkeit und Geschwisterlichkeit" [Brotherliness and brothersisterliness], ThPQ 137 (1989): 228-37; D. E. Zimmer, *Redens Arten. Über Trends und Tollheiten im neudeutschen Sprachgebrauch* [Speaking's ways: On trends and follies in recent German use of language] (Zurich, 1988), 65-79.

which is male or female). This is evident, for instance, in the fact that German feminine substantives can serve as classificatory concepts (*die Schwalbe:* a swallow; *die Menschheit:* humanity; *die Kirche:* the Church), and that the grammatical sex of words can be used in ways that run counter to the natural sex of the referents (*der Backfisch:* masculine for "teenage girl"; *die Drohne:* feminine for "drone"; *die Wache:* feminine for "watchman"). Again, if one were to adopt the recommendations of "linguistic feminism",[22] would it not also be necessary to demand that masculine counterparts be provided for feminine classificatory concepts, such as *der Person, der Fachkraft,* and *der Leiche* (masculine modifications of normally feminine German substantives)? And if the title *(der) Bürger* (masculine for "citizen") is offensive, why not also *der Mensch* (masculine for "human being")? Are we now to say *die Mensch* (feminine modification)? Or are we to speak "more inclusively" of "masculine and feminine human beings"?

Also questioned here is the assumption of an intrinsic structural correspondence between society and language. In Turkish, for example, there is no gender at all, which certainly does not serve to prove that females have equal rights in that society;[23] again, the Hottentot language corresponds in a virtually exemplary way to feminist wishes for an "inclusive way of speaking", yet patriarchal conditions among the Hottentots far exceed anything imaginable by Europeans.[24] The fact that the masculine form of substantives designating persons is normally used as the classificatory concept in German is not just linked to "male dominance". The more important reason is that the masculine forms "are usually simpler than the feminine

---

[22] Stickel, 331.
[23] Ulrich, 386.
[24] Doerfer, 148f.

and thus better suited to the purposes of sex-neutral usage".[25]

Another argument is based on linguistic simplicity. The often prodigious convolutions of "fem-speak" give rise to much joking and bewildered head-shaking. Considerations of linguistic economy cannot just be trampled underfoot. In the end, if feminist wishes were acceded to, the sexual aspect would have to be expressed even when the important thing were precisely not one's maleness or femaleness but, rather, one's applicable kind of function.[26]

On the other hand, the feminists seem to have observed correctly that linguistic usage does reflect structures of social order that "are lagging behind" any development measured strictly in terms of the equality postulate: "Symmetry, in the sense of equal linguistic treatment of males and females, is hardly achievable in any language that incorporates grammatical gender. We can perceive, or paint, woman and man simultaneously and on an equal footing—in space. But language unfolds in time, which requires succession, an order of before and after, and this appears as superordination and subordination."[27] For just such reasons, some prominent feminists are led to demand that the feminine gender be used as the classificatory term for all attractive sorts of personal designation. The asymmetrical aspect, as such, is then retained, but also reversed: "All men shall be sisters. . . . "[28]

Now, there is certainly such a thing as justified change in both society and linguistic usage. If the entry of women into public life represents a "sign of the times", then it also implies, in principle, an increased "visibility" of women in

[25] Stickel, 341.

[26] Ibid., 350; Doerfer, 143.

[27] Wegener, "Sprachkritik", 11.

[28] Pusch (1990).

the linguistic sphere. From that viewpoint, the concern for "inclusive language" is not without justification. The question is only whether complete symmetry can be attained or is desirable. At the social level, there is a certain "asymmetry" insofar as males are more strongly represented in leadership positions. This structure of order is also reflected in the linguistic sphere, for instance, in the stock enumerative phrase "father, mother, and child". If this were to be any different, then it would be necessary to give primacy to the feminine concept, which cannot be acceptable to logically consistent advocates of equal rights. But how far must this notion of "equal rights" be taken?

An anthropology based on the Bible can advert here to those scriptural passages in which the husband is characterized as "head" of the wife. The "head" represents the whole (just as the father represents the family). Through this "asymmetry", the unity and stability of social groups (especially the family) is guaranteed to a greater extent than would be possible through a distinctionless aggregation of equals. A similar asymmetry renders language, too, "more economical" than a chaotic "splitting". It was shown earlier here[29] that, from the Christian viewpoint, the "cephalic" structuring of the relations between the sexes does not imply a lesser valuing of women as opposed to men. Still unclear is just how, in concrete detail, an increased "visibility" of women in the linguistic sphere—which definitely seems desirable—might be achieved despite a certain persisting element of asymmetry. In this connection, one may suppose that organic evolution of the language would be healthier and more effective than acts of linguistic violence.

---

[29] Cf. above, 110–14.

4. Liturgical Language

4.1 The Interhuman Sphere

The linguistic theme (which has to be left to linguistic scholars to debate fully) must still be considered here with a view to liturgical language. This means that the problem presents itself in a new way: what is involved is no longer just the relationships between humans but also the relationship between God and man. These two dimensions need to be treated in methodologically distinct ways.[30]

"Don't call us brethren!" This title[31] is suitably indicative of the concern that applies on the interhuman level. As a form of address in the New Testament, "brethren" does not exclude women but (normally) includes them. In contrast to German [and English], in which the words "brothers" and "sisters" have different roots, these concepts differ in Greek only minimally (*adelphoí/adelphaí*). Moreover, in the New Testament, using the same designation for men and women is a mark of the equal worth of the sexes: before God there is no difference between male and female (Gal 3:28). Hence, the biblical form of address "brethren" by no means implies any devaluation of women.[32]

In German-speaking countries, addressing the whole congregation as "brethren" is not usual in the Catholic Church; also, prior to the French Revolution, the expression "fraternity" was not current in German, although it later acquired a certain emotiveness, especially as a result

---

[30] This is also emphasized by Louis Roy, "Inclusive Language Regarding God", *Worship* 65 (1991): 207-15.

[31] Norbert Sommer, ed., *Nennt uns nicht Brüder! Frauen in der Kirche durchbrechen das Schweigen* [Don't call us brethren! Women in the Church break the silence] (Stuttgart, 1985).

[32] On the biblical findings, cf. O. B. Knoch, " 'Nennt uns nicht Brüder! Überlegungen zu einer 'Entmännlichung' liturgischer Texte" ["Don't call us brethren!" Reflections on a "demasculinizing" of liturgical texts], *Klerusblatt* 67 (1987): 134f.; Zauner, 231-34.

of the Freemason movement (which even today normally includes only males).[33] One reason for this reluctance to use the term "brethren" is probably the above-noted fact that, in the German language (as opposed to Greek), the words "brothers" and "sisters" have different roots. After the Council, when the liturgical texts were issued in the vernacular, the Latin "fratres" (for example, in the confiteor) was rendered as "brothers and sisters" in at least the German missal of 1975. All the more surprising, then, was the introduction in 1982—by no means necessary on the basis of the Roman guidelines—of the term "brethren", which precedes many New Testament readings, in the new lectionaries.[34] This step was highly problematic and could only provoke counterreactions. It seems that the term "brethren", and some particularly criticized passages in the hymnbook,[35] reflect not so much normal Catholic linguistic usage as the peculiar linguistic milieu—described by a critical observer as one of "fraternity euphoria"[36]—of the youth movement whose formative liturgical experience occurred prior to the Second World War.

In order to eliminate the offensiveness of the term "brethren" in liturgical readings, the following suggestions were made:

(1) To let the liturgical texts stand and to explain the term "brethren" in its New Testament context.

(2) To change the form of address preceding the readings to "brothers and sisters".[37]

---

[33] On this see Zauner, 228, 231f., 235.

[34] On this, see Balthasar Fischer, "Zur Anrede bei den Lesungen in der Meßfeier" [On the form of address for readings used in the celebration of the Mass], *Klerusblatt* 68 (1988): 141.

[35] Esp. no. 637: "Let us praise, brethren, praise. . . . "

[36] Gerhards, "Frauengerechte Liturgie", 116; cf. Theodor Maas-Ewerd, "Frauen sprachlich nicht ausgrenzen. Zu einer Empfehlung der Liturgie-kommission der Diözese Aachen" [No linguistic exclusion of women: Comments on a recommendation by the liturgical commission of the diocese of Aachen], *Klerusblatt* 72 (1992): 234.

[37] Knoch; Balthasar Fischer, " 'Inklusive Sprache' im Gottesdienst.

(3) To use "sisters and brothers" as the form of address preceding the readings.[38]

(4) To use the form of address "brothers and sisters" for passages read out by a woman, and "sisters and brothers" for passages read out by a man.[39]

(5) To revise the biblical readings themselves on the model of suggestion number 2, 3, or 4 above.

(6) To do away altogether with the opening form of address, which does not properly belong to the biblical text anyway.[40]

German professional theologians, quite rightly, were almost unanimous in criticizing the fifth of these solutions. It would require tampering with the biblical text, which would then lead to further instances of such willfulness. A Protestant theologian has observed: "The apparent harmlessness of this step, when taken in itself, would be matched by the extent of its consequences. Were the liturgy to use a biblical text differing from that used for the exegesis and the sermon based upon it, Christian divine service would lose that common basis that can always be clearly verified even by the congregation."[41]

Eine berechtigte Forderung?" ["Inclusive language" in divine service — a justified demand?], in Berger and Gerhards (1990), 361f.

[38] Albrecht Greule, "Frauengottesdienste, feministische Liturgien und integrative Sprache" [Women's religious services, feminist liturgies, and integrative language], in Berger and Gerhards (1990), 633; Diözesansynode Augsburg 1990, *Die Seelsorge in der Pfarrgemeinde* [Ministry in the parish] (Donauwörth, 1991), 86f. Opposed to this, Fischer (1990): "Since the one speaking these words of address . . . is not the lector but the apostle, it seems inappropriate to attribute modern forms of politeness to him. . . . If one were to look into the historical background of the "ladies first" custom (*sexus fragilis*), significant discrepancy with the present-day image of woman would no doubt emerge."

[39] Maas-Ewerd, in line with a suggestion made by a diocesan liturgical commission.

[40] Lectionaries prior to 1982.

[41] H.-M. Müller, "Feministische Theologie und kirchliche Praxis" [Feminist theology and Church practice], *Theol. Beiträge* 22 (1991): 149; Peter Stuhlmacher, "Feministische Theologie und Auslegung des Neuen Testaments" [Feminist theology and interpretation of the New Testa-

Full debate about the remaining suggestions here must be left to liturgical scholars. In my own view, solutions no. 1 and no. 6 seem the most workable.

In this whole discussion, one should not forget that the controversial term of address that introduces the readings pertains, not to the difference between male and female, but to the common quality of being a Christian (cf. Gal 3:28). Precisely here, a "sexualization" (read: "splitting") of the language would be problematical. (It is presumably not a widespread feminist dream, for example, to give the "Ave Maria" an "inclusive" formulation: "Pray for us sinneresses and sinners.")

The situation differs in the case of attributions that are "sexually" colored because of their function in some specific symbolic context. This characteristic ought not to be obscured. An example here would be those scriptural texts in which the baptized are described as "sons" who participate in the life of the "Son" of God. Here, the "sonship" serves to emphasize a kind of equivalence in nature with Christ,[42] and women are obviously meant by the term as well. This role of "being meant as well" also falls, in other contexts, to males, as when the images of the "bride", the "virgin", and the "mother" are used to designate the Church.[43] The latter point is often forgotten when the cry for "inclusive language" goes up.

---

ment], *Theol. Beiträge* 22 (1991): 138; Fischer (1988); Greule, 633; Knoch, 135; Maas-Ewerd, 233; Diözesansynode Augsburg, 86f., n. 108: "The scriptural and liturgical texts used in divine service in the Church are not to be altered."

[42] Diözesansynode Augsburg, 86f., n. 108.

[43] Cf. above, 154.

4.2 The Relationship between God and Man

Much more fraught with difficulty than alterations in descriptive terminology at the interhuman level are any changes in symbolism that bear on the relationship between God and man. Since this topic was covered at length in the preceding chapters, a few brief points will suffice here. A new, "sex-neutral" version of the Our Father, which so-called "experts" had suggested to the American bishops, was rightly met with vigorous resistance.[44] Even one of the main protagonists of "inclusive language"—the Lutheran Gail Ramshaw-Smith—submitted the following point for reflection: " 'Naming God' is a privilege that belongs to God. It is only God who reveals the name of God. When men attempt to name God as they themselves see fit, the temptation of idolatry is not far away."[45] The title of "father", which is central to both divine revelation and the human sphere, cannot be treated like a mass of arbitrarily moldable clay.

Further, to address the first Divine Person as "Mother and Father" can create the misconception that the prayer is directed at a divine couple[46] or a divine family.[47] It must also be remembered that the title "Mother" is already held by Mary.[48] Neutral descriptions of God, on the other hand, obscure the fact that God is a person and thus has a kind of being that is tied linguistically to the convention of

---

[44] *Deutsche Tagespost,* November 5, 1991, 5 (KNA).

[45] Gail Ramshaw-Smith, "Lutheran Liturgical Prayer and God as Mother", *Worship* 52 (1978): 517–42; as reviewed in Teresa Berger, "Auf der Suche nach einer 'integrativen Liturgie' " [The search for an "integrative liturgy"], LJ 37 (1987): 53. This did not, however, prevent Ramshaw-Smith from including the addressing of God as "Mother"—supposedly not to be used as a name for God—in her liturgical prayer-text proposals: Berger, 54.

[46] Fischer (1990), 364.

[47] H.-M. Müller, 148.

[48] Geoffrey Wainwright, "An Inclusive Language Lectionary: Systematic Liturgical Observations", BTB 14 (1984): 29.

"grammatical gender".[49] Again, to recommend that the "Father" title be used more sparingly is no solution,[50] as that would serve only to obscure the existing situation.

In the end, the accentuation expressed in the biblical symbolism of the sexes is so deeply anchored in the Christian faith, and, at the same time, so anthropologically central, that any "egalitarianizing" of the liturgical language would also produce a change in content and lead in the direction of an apersonal pantheism.[51] Even in the liturgy, man and woman are not "interchangeable".

5. Justified Concerns

The feminists have a justified concern (beyond the others mentioned earlier here) when they call attention to the importance of symbols, which have an effect on the whole person in divine service. An over-intellectualized, merely verbal liturgy (of which especially Protestantism is often accused) is also incapable of doing justice to the incarnational structure of Christianity: God did not become "word" but, rather, "flesh". And, in a certain way, what was perceptible and tangible in Christ is perpetuated in the sacraments of the Church. The charges that the liturgy is too intellectualized do not, then, apply to "classic" Catholic liturgy but (in addition to constricted Protestant forms) to the fruits of a (misunderstood) liturgical reform, under which man was regarded almost exclusively as a "hearer of the word". In many places, the phobia about ecclesiastic "triumphalism" has led to a withering of popular religious customs, as well as to a reduction in traditional features of the liturgy, which, with its incense, candles, colors, and so

---

[49] H.-M. Müller, 148.

[50] As in Fischer (1990), 365f.

[51] Roy, 209–13; A. F. Kimel, "The Holy Trinity Meets Ashtoreth: A Critique of the Episcopal 'Inclusive' Liturgies", *Anglican Theological Review* 71 (1989): 41f.; cf. above, 114–15.

forth, draws the entire person into the praise of God. Here, limits are nevertheless set to human "creativity" insofar as the core aspects of the liturgy (the sacraments) are anchored in the foundational will of Jesus and transcend all human caprice. In the Eucharist, for example, bread and wine cannot be replaced by milk, honey, and sweet cakes. It should not be forgotten, of course, that there is much scope for formative human activity in the area of the sacramentals, where specifically feminine concerns can also be integrated.[52]

More important than questions about details of liturgical language and the structure of divine service, of course, is the significance that the liturgy has for life in general. Do the Church's liturgical ceremonies really contribute to enabling people to join wholeheartedly in the praise of the triune God? To their being taken up, by virtue of the sacred mysteries, into the Divine Life? To their drawing strength for everyday existence? Only in view of these core questions does the striving to work out a feminine contribution to the liturgy appear in its proper framework. It is not tense disputes about liturgical "quota regulations" that will make people joyous in their faith but their own self-commitment to the performance of the divine service — the measure of which is the love in their heart (and not their position before or behind the altar).

---

[52] For example, the blessings of the mother before and after the birth: *Benediktionale. Studienausgabe für die katholischen Bistümer des deutschen Sprachgebietes* [Benedictional: Text-edition for Catholic dioceses in German-speaking world] (Einsiedeln, 1981), 89–95.

XII. THEOLOGICAL "ECO-FEMINISM"

1. The Relevant Concern

Destruction of the environment is one of the greatest menaces of our time. Preservation of creation is therefore an important concern that finds (at least in theory) broad support. In order to explain this destructive behavior toward nature, some critics place the blame on Christianity: God's directive that men should have dominion over the earth (Gen 1:26) — the so-called "mandate to till the earth" — is the most fundamental cause of the devastation of the environment in the modern age. For it elevates man above the realm of nature around him and simultaneously sunders him from the harmony of the cosmos. This anthropocentrism needs to be replaced by a cosmocentrism.[1]

The critique of the "mandate to till the earth" in Genesis is taken up by feminist theology, namely, in theological "eco-feminism".[2] Mary Daly had already denounced patriarchalism as the cause of the exploitation of nature, whose roots go back ultimately to the male image of God: men's domination over women is perpetuated in rapacious exploi-

---

[1] For arguments along these lines, see: K. M. Meyer-Abich, *Wege zum Frieden mit der Natur. Praktische Naturphilosophie für die Umweltpolitik* [Ways toward peace with nature: A practical philosophy of nature for politics of the environment] (Munich, 1984); Eugen Drewermann, *Der tödliche Fortschritt. Von der Zerstörung der Erde und des Menschen im Erbe des Christentums* [Fatal progress: On the destruction of the earth and of man as the heritage of Christianity], Herder/Spektrum 4032 (Freiburg, 1991).

[2] Cf. the survey by Ina Praetorius, Luise Schottroff, and Helen Schüngel-Straumann, "Schöpfung/Ökologie" [Creation/ecology], in Wb, 354-60.

tation of the forces of nature.[3] But the earth is there "*with* us, not *for* us".[4]

Feminism and ecology are linked with particular logical consistency in the work of Rosemary Ruether.[5] The account of creation in Genesis 1 subordinates the earth to man. Through this subordination, the earth is made to appear "bad".[6] But it is also reprehensible that nature is subordinated to God, since this reflects a male worldview. Inasmuch as God issues his word and thereby creates something new outside himself, God is depicted on a masculine model. For on that model of the procreative act, the seed comes, not from the body of the woman, but from outside. Nature, then, is "no longer the maternal womb in which gods and men are engendered".[7] By contrast, Ruether shows an enthusiasm for "actual solidarity with . . . our mother, the earth, which is the actual ground of our being". In this sense of wholeness, she even glimpses a substitute for personal immortality: "The whole, not the individual, . . . is that 'infinite' out of whose womb we arise at birth and into whose womb we are content to return at death."[8]

In this conception, the divine is equated with the realities of nature, which amounts to pantheism.[9] Man's subordination to a personal God who existed prior to the world must be overthrown. Only then can the mind's domination of the body be broken and, with that, the destructive exploitation of nature by humans and of women by men.[10]

---

[3] Daly, *Father,* 174-78; *Gyn/Ecology.*

[4] Daly, *Father,* 178.

[5] Ruether, *New Woman; Sexism,* 72-92.

[6] Ruether, *New Woman,* 187; cf. *Sexism,* 72-73.

[7] Ruether, *Sexism,* 77.

[8] Ruether, *New Woman,* 211.

[9] Cf. above, 146-56.

[10] Ruether, *Sexism,* 19-20, 85.

Elisabeth Moltmann-Wendel[11] and Catharina Halkes[12] take the same direction as Ruether. Halkes stresses that the "earth" has always been regarded, symbolically, as feminine.[13] Alluded to here is the notion of a common destiny shared by women and the earth, which is much more strongly emphasized in gynocentric goddess feminism.[14] Unlike Ruether, the Dutch theologian refrains from criticizing the biblical accounts of creation, tending to aim her attacks at the modern period (Bacon, Descartes): only through the rise of the modern natural sciences was victory achieved for the mechanistic worldview, in accordance with which organic interconnections were reduced to the quantitatively measurable and technically controllable.[15]

Halkes wishes to avoid pantheism, which equates God and the world, just as much as deism, which separates God from the world. However, her "middle way", panentheism, is only slightly different from the pantheistic interfusion of God and world: creation appears as "God's body", in which God himself is vulnerable. As opposed to the Christian doctrine of a creation out of nothing[16] that was achieved through divine omnipotence, Halkes characterizes "creation" as a working "with that . . . which was already present".[17] Like Ruether, Halkes objects to both hierarchic thinking and linear thinking "in terms of cause and effect".[18]

---

[11] Every sort of hierarchy (including that between God and man) is to be dismantled; the "element of condescending love" is then "transformed into reciprocal love . . . ": Moltmann-Wendel, *Frauentexte*, 69; cf. *Milch*, 164.

[12] Halkes, *Söhne*, 82f.; *Antlitz;* on Ruether: *Antlitz*, 133f.

[13] Halkes, *Antlitz*, 29.

[14] For example, Carol Christ, "Vom Vatergott zur Muttergöttin" [From father-god to mother-goddess], in Sommer (1985), 285–87.

[15] Halkes, *Antlitz*, 29, 37–54.

[16] Cf. already 2 Macc 7:28.

[17] Halkes, *Antlitz*, 183; cf. above, 119–21.

[18] Ibid., 137.

2. Critical Evaluation

Feminist theology rightly emphasizes man's intimate connectedness with all the other realities of creation. Previously,
the Church Fathers often combined this idea with another
idea stemming from Greek philosophy (Aristotle): man is a
world in miniature, a "microcosmos", in which the various
dimensions of sensible reality can all be found along with
the reality of the spirit.[19] According to the second biblical
account of creation, man has been formed out of "the clay
of the ground" (Gen 2:7); his relationship with the whole
of material creation is thus clearly stressed.

Things become problematic, however, when feminist
theology denies, or detracts from, man's special nature as
"created in God's image" and the "mandate to till the
earth" that follows from this (Gen 1:26-28). Inherent in
man's spiritual soul is the capacity not only to respond
consciously and freely to God's creative call but also to
assume responsibility for the subhuman dimensions of
creation. The instruction to have dominion over the earth
by no means implies the exploitation and destruction of
creation. Precisely the disastrous abuses of the "mandate
to till the earth" underscore the significance that attaches
to man's exerting a *responsible* influence. Paradise is
described in the Bible as a "garden", which man has to
cultivate and care for (Gen 2:15). To place man on the
same level as wellsprings, plants, and animals would deprive
him of his personal responsibility.

All created realities have their own kind of being, which,
in the way unique to each, is directed toward the glory of
God; at the same time, however, the biblical worldview
contains a hierarchic order, within which all subhuman
realities are inherently referred to man, and thus also to

---

[19] Cf. M. Gatzemeier and H. Holzhey, "Makrokosmos/Mikrokosmos",
HWP 5 (1980): 640f.; see also Günter Lanczkowski et al., "Makrokosmos/
Mikrokosmos" [Macrocosm/microcosm], TRE 21 (1991): 745-54.

Jesus Christ, in whom the eternal Son of God became man (cf. Col 1:16). By contrast, a large part of the feminist-theology movement can obviously imagine order only as a ribbon-like succession or "bonding" of equals. This sort of democratic worldview fails to do justice to the christocentric structure of creation. It is also questionable whether feminist theology could ever realize its own aims on that kind of conceptual basis. Does it not itself appeal to man's overall responsibility precisely when denouncing his past mistakes?

Pointedly expressed, the "bonded" ecological approach replaces "ego" (the self) by "eco"(-logy). Halkes, for example, dreams "of an *oiko*-theology instead of an ego-theology".[20] On the other hand, feminist theology emphasizes most strongly the "autonomy" of the individual, to the point of an assumed "bodily autonomy" relevant to abortion.[21] These two perspectives, "bonding" and individualism, can be reconciled only with great difficulty. On the one hand, the autonomy of woman is played off against the complementarity of the sexes; and, on the other, the inherent uniqueness of mankind is reduced to a sameness with the apersonal world.

A true note is struck by those criticisms that are directed against an aggressive, hyper-masculine desire to dominate, which finds one outlet in destruction of the environment. There are also real links here to the oppression of women. But even feminists, such as Halkes, must admit that this mentality is a product of the modern age, which has thereby broken with the ancient and medieval view of creation.

Not only the "mandate to till the earth" is criticized by feminist ecology but also the ontological distinction, grounded in the creation out of nothing, between God and man. Here it should be noted that distinction does not

---

[20] Halkes, *Antlitz*, 184.
[21] Cf. Ina Praetorius, "Autonomie/Emanzipation", in Wb, 36–38; Halkes, *Söhne*, 20–23 ("Befreiung zur Autonomie" [Being freed for autonomy]); above, p. 98.

mean separation: God is present in his creation and, in the well-known formulation of Augustine, more deeply so in us than our own deepest self.[22] The ontological distinction sets man free, however, to respond in love to God's benevolent love (or to withhold himself from God). The relationship of love is unthinkable apart from the distinctness of the loving participants. And the subhuman level of creation also has its own relative independence, so that it is left essentially open to the responsibility of man (which would be problematic if it had a formally divine stamp).

Relationship is more than self-identity (as of a person with his body) and implies an attachment that grows along with personal commitment. Man is called, not to universal coalescence with the cosmos, but to personal, eternally enduring communion with the triune God after the new creation at the end of time. Christian hope thus breaks through one's absorption in transient life, throws open the perspective of eternity, and, from that perspective, sets one free for concrete action to preserve creation.

A pantheistic (or panentheistic) worldview cannot impart that kind of hope. Halkes laments the disintegration of the world.[23] She regards the world as "God's body"—does God, then, also suffer from inner disintegration? In any case, Halkes has certainly maintained that God is "vulnerable" and bereft of his omnipotence.[24] To assume a disintegration of God would, of course, be little more than a recycling of ancient Manichaeism: the divine as a tragically divided principle in which good and evil do battle with each other.[25] Here, evil and the disintegration of the world are posited as primordial, indeed, as divinely accepted. This fatalistic view is the logical result to which a pan(en)theistic conception ultimately leads. That such a view might

[22] *Confessions,* III, 6:11.
[23] Halkes, *Antlitz,* 182.
[24] Ibid., 182, 185.
[25] Cf. Rudolph, 352–79.

encourage active commitment to the preservation of creation can reasonably be doubted.

Along with the Manichaean threat in feminist theology, there is a reversion to pagan idolatry through the elevation of "Mother Earth" to an object of divine homage. This occurs in "goddess feminism" but also in so-called "moderate" circles. Catharina Halkes warns about a religion of earth and moon, such as had led, precisely in Germany, to unhappy consequences once before.[26] And Ingeborg Hauschildt, a committed Protestant Christian, reports: "In 1981, when the liturgy being performed for Women's World Prayer Day reached the point of formally invoking Mother Earth, one of our women in Neumünster suddenly cried out, 'But that sounds just like Hitler's "blood and soil"!' Some members of the congregation do not want to go through all that again. What must be proclaimed here is quite simply the First Commandment."[27]

Feminist theology's contribution in the area of ecology comes down largely to restoration of a nature-idolizing paganism that remains enmeshed in worldly immanence. The woman theologians who are typically active here lack belief in a personal God who created the world and whose plan incorporates human responsibility for creation. Not least importantly, they also discount the idea that God will ultimately perfect the world in the "new heaven and new earth". They lack the deep breath of hope that liberates creation.[28]

---

[26] Cf. Gerber (1984), 582.

[27] Hauschildt, "Feministische Theologie", 21; cf. Beyerhaus, *Aufstand,* 41.

[28] The topic of ecology could only be touched on briefly in this chapter. A helpful view of it is available in Anton Ziegenaus, "Die Umweltproblematik in schöpfungstheologischer Sicht" [The environmental problem from the creation-theological perspective], FKTh 8 (1992): 81–98.

XIII. FEMINIST ESCHATOLOGY, OR
THE LOST HOPE OF ETERNAL LIFE

1. Descriptive Account

At the center of feminist theology is a struggle for power in this world. The idea of a hope for the future that includes the individual person's living on after death is normally denied and spurned as a piece of patriarchal ideology.[1] Mary Daly's phasing out of individual immortality is obviously connected with her application of A. N. Whitehead's process philosophy, according to which being consists only of dynamic processes but not of realities with an enduringly self-identical nature (such as a personal God or the human spiritual soul).[2] The adherents of goddess feminism affirm the eternal cycle of life and death, which they think they find reflected in matriarchal cults. Elga Sorge, for example, holds that "an 'eternal life' in which there is no death seems, from the viewpoint of goddess feminism, a fatal misunderstanding."[3] Christa Mulack definitely excludes any resurrection of the body but not a reincarnation.[4] "Immortality" consists in mothers being born again in their daughters, in the cyclic process of nature.[5] Whether, along with this, there is also personal survival of death is

---

[1] On the following, cf. also the surveys by Luzia Sutter Rehmann, "Eschatologie", in Wb, 86–89; Gerber, *Eroberung,* 162–78.

[2] Daly, *Father,* 188–89; cf. above, 82.

[3] Sorge, 69.

[4] Mulack, *Jesus,* 270–77.

[5] Mulack, *Weiblichkeit,* 315f.; *Jesus,* 268f.

not really made clear.[6] Only a minority of authors seem, like Hildegunde Wöller,[7] to assume that human consciousness lives on after death.

Among the "moderate" authors, the subject of eschatology is treated most extensively by Rosemary Ruether,[8] whose ideas are taken up by numerous other writers.[9] A new creation and a bodily resurrection, both of which exceed the limits of inner-worldly powers, and a continued personal existence after physical death are rejected by Ruether, although with the "agnostic" qualification that "we should not pretend to know what we do not know."[10] The "modern revolutionary hope cannot promise the resurrection of the dead; it can promise only that someday our descendents will see a better day."[11] The hope for personal immortality attests to a masculine "egotism" that only distracts us from the problems of our bodily and social nature.[12] The visionary goal is "a 'new humanity' appropriate to a 'new earth' ", a world in which there is neither ruler nor ruled.[13]

In Ruether's case, something of the Marxist position probably shows through, according to which hope in immortality is a deceptive consolation that only diverts attention from the political struggle.[14] The same sort of background

---

[6] Cf. Mulack, *Jesus*, 272: "possibility that physical death can be spiritually survived" (as held by the Gnostics, with whom this theologian sympathizes) with 282: "Jesus lives on in the preaching of the gospel . . . as in the hearts of women and men."

[7] Hildegunde Wöller, "Glaube an den dreieinigen Gott. Versuch einer Neuinterpretation" [Belief in the triune God: Attempt at a new interpretation], *Frauen. Anstöße* 28, no. 3 (1981), 106; cited in Gerber, *Eroberung*, 174.

[8] Cf. especially Ruether, *Sexism*, 253–58.

[9] On the significance of Ruether, cf. Gerber, *Eroberung*, 162; Gössmann, "Zukunft" [Future], in Wb, 440.

[10] Ruether, *Sexism*, 257.

[11] Ibid., 243.

[12] Ibid., 236, 258.

[13] Ruether, *New Woman*, 229; *Sexism*, 3; cf. 5, 120.

[14] On the Marxist influence in Ruether, cf. above, 50.

is evident in Dorothee Sölle, who, together with Luise Schottroff, stresses: "From the feminist viewpoint, the notion of an immortal soul is regarded as fundamentally inimical to the body and to women, because it implies dualism of body and soul and a devaluation of the body."[15] "Resurrection", for Sölle, is only a symbol-like expression for "'rising up' and 'rebelling' against injustice";[16] it is necessary (as Bultmann similarly holds) to work out a "demythologized, nonmiraculous formulation of resurrection".[17]

Along with this political reinterpretation of "resurrection", we also find in "moderate" feminists the idea—related in particular to goddess feminism—that bodily resurrection on the Last Day reflects a temporally "linear", masculine way of thinking. Contrasted with this is the natural, "feminine" cycle of life and death.[18] For Maria Kassel, then, "resurrection" means, "empathizing with the rhythm of death and life as life's own tidal flux".[19] She therefore expresses her sympathy (as do numerous other women theologians) with the cult of Astarte in ancient Canaan, a typical religion based on the cycles of nature.[20]

Halkes and Moltmann-Wendel, by contrast, remain more strongly oriented toward the political sphere. To illustrate "eschatological hope", Halkes cites the biblical image of "the lion with the lamb". This is, to be sure, only a utopia, "but . . . one that has real effects". The goal is the psychological wholeness of every person but also a reconciliation

---

[15] Schottroff and Sölle, "Auferstehung", in Wb, 35f. Cf. Sutter Rehmann, "Eschatologie", in Wb, 87f.

[16] Schottroff and Sölle, "Auferstehung", 35.

[17] Sölle, "Kreuz", in Wb, 236; cf. also the Sölle quotes in Gerber, *Eroberung,* 172f.

[18] For example, in Sutter Rehmann, "Eschatologie", in Wb, 88f.; Ingrid Riedel, "Leben/Tod" [Life/death], in Wb, 240.

[19] Maria Kassel, "Tod und Auferstehung", in her *Feministische Theologie* (1988), 221. Maria Kassel was for several years head of the "Feminist Theology Work and Research Establishment" at the Catholic Theological Faculty of the University of Münster.

[20] Ibid., 218.

of man with the cosmos. This hope will be "realized, not apart from us, but also not through us alone".[21] Particularly Galatians 3:28, according to which there is neither male nor female, appears as a "hopeful vision".[22] Success in strivings of this sort would be equivalent to "resurrection" or "liberation from slavery".[23] In that sense, "resurrection" occurs "anew at every moment".[24] Nowhere is it made clear here that there is a hope of bodily resurrection.

The "dream of a world of cosmic peace" is embodied for Moltmann-Wendel in the biblical phrase "a land flowing with milk and honey".[25] Milk, in the ancient Orient, was a symbol of "biological life and also immortality".[26] However, the idea of immortality and a hope reaching beyond this world does not feature in her elucidation of the current relevance of this symbol. "Milk and honey" mean quite simply "living space for all" and the transition to "a society in which domination has been abolished". The ancient biblical "theme of wandering, with its closeness to the earth", can "accompany" us on the way to this utopia.[27]

Within feminist theology, there is almost never any criticism of the abandonment and denial of personal immortality. One exception here is Elisabeth Gössmann: "In my opinion, feminist theology has hitherto concerned itself far too little with eschatology or has treated it in an excessively one-sided way."[28] Her own understanding of the immortality of the soul is not made very clear.[29] But she no doubt welcomes the fact that the "Greater Church", in opposi-

---

[21] Halkes, *Suchen,* 20.
[22] Ibid., 111; cf. 121; *Söhne,* 34.
[23] Halkes, *Suchen,* 48.
[24] Halkes, *Antlitz,* 180.
[25] Moltmann-Wendel, *Milch,* 120, 10.
[26] Ibid., 10.
[27] Ibid., 15, 66, 205.
[28] Gössmann, "Zukunft", in Wb, 440.
[29] Immortality through divine grace? Entry of the individual spirit into the universal spirit, as in Latin Averroism? Ibid., 440f.

tion to Gnostic and Manichaean currents, has upheld the doctrine that men and women retain their sexual character after resurrection. With that, the Church is disburdened of the charge of being hostile to the body. "It is no progressive step to depict 'the eschatological doctrine of the disappearance of the difference between the sexes' as a special interest of women."[30]

2. Critical Evaluation

Elisabeth Gössmann's criticism of the eschatology of most of her comrades-in-arms opens a festering wound: the lost hope of eternal life. Here, according to Gössmann, the Catholic Church is more well-disposed toward women than are the feminists. Consternation about the denial of resurrection is also expressed by the Protestant theologians Schneider-Böklen and Vorländer, who themselves advocate feminist approaches.[31] Eschatology is perhaps the area that is most inherently suited to giving feminists cause for reassessing their position. This is because the desire for personal immortality (which is present in the heart of every person) can find fulfillment only in partnership with the God who, in his omnipotence and goodness, has called the world into being from nothingness and, through the Resurrection of Jesus, effected the historical beginning of the transfiguration of the entire cosmos. Here, the symbolically more "masculine" features in the image of God (powerful intervention in history, creation "from outside" . . .) could take on new radiance in their vital significance for women and men. But it must also be remembered that, according to the Catholic faith, redemption has been fully actualized only in a woman, in Mary, to the point of an

---

[30] Ibid., 441. Here, Gössmann is opposed to Ilona Riedel-Spangenberger, "Christentum" [Christianity], in FLex, 150.

[31] Cf. above, 171–72.

already accomplished transfiguration of the female body. Mary thus lights the way, as an emblem of hope, for the people of God on their pilgrimage.[32]

Feminist theology transfers the eschatological hope to the this-worldly sphere. "Resurrection" becomes a "rising up", and the new creation is reduced to the earthly ideal of a "domination-free society". This reinterpretation is not, however, without a certain tragic aspect—the object of its aspiration, as its proponents themselves admit, is a "utopia" that can never be achieved.

Christian hope, by contrast, relies on personal immortality and resurrection, with the divinely effected transformation of the whole of creation into the "new heaven and the new earth" (Rev 21). This hope reaches beyond the worldly here-and-now yet, precisely because of that, generates the strongest impulses even in the temporal-earthly realm. The prospect of the new creation, to be brought about by God alone, confers a great inner calmness and strength for selfless service even when inner-worldly certainties begin to falter. "This world" is the proving ground for "the beyond", for eternal communion with God. The depersonalization of God in feminist theology, on the other hand, also ultimately depersonalizes man: the eternal significance of love is abandoned in favor of annihilation and destruction. And that dream of "wholeness"—does it not then burst like a bubble?

---

[32] Vatican II, *Lumen gentium*, 68.

XIV. FEMINIST THEOLOGY—OPPORTUNITY OR DANGER? SUMMARY EVALUATION AND FUTURE PROSPECTS

The foregoing reflections on the topic of eschatology may serve to bring to a close the expository survey of the individual thematic aspects of feminist theology. To conclude this study, there remains the task of providing a summary evaluation of the significance of feminist theology and attempting to offer some viewpoints on that theology's future.

The substantial interconnectedness of the various subareas treated in theological feminism is rooted in the area of anthropology, whose structure enters determinatively into all the others. Fundamentally, the intent is to apply either the "androgynous" or the "gynocentric" ideal to all aspects of life, and not least to the image of God. Common to all forms of feminism is the struggle against males having the more strongly defined responsibility for leadership tasks in the family, society, and the Church. The notion that men and women should complement each other is rejected.

At the formal level, a common link between feminist theologies is discernible in their use of female "experience" as an evaluative criterion, which, given the strongly subjective cast of that criterion, is at least difficult to reconcile with the scholarly character of theology. In any case, feminists themselves understand their enterprise as relieving them of any need to measure it against the standard of divine revelation. The only elements retained from Scripture and tradition are those that accord with the feminist perspective.

From the viewpoint of the history of ideas, the Marxist influence has been, from the very start, the most effective; linked to this is the "role-oriented thinking" that dominates feminism in the Church but also the rejection of superordination and subordination in the social sphere ("domination"). As well, there is an understanding of freedom that shows the influence of existentialism (Simone de Beauvoir) and, in "equality feminism", leads to regarding the female body, not as an opportunity, but a hindrance. Forms of feminist theology characterized by a more strongly political thrust exist alongside approaches deriving from the psychoanalysis of C. G. Jung, which have influenced mainly the gynocentric direction. The "androgynous ideal" in equality feminism can be traced back (partly via intermediary forms) to ancient Gnosticism, which is sometimes also directly reverted to. The influence of pagan nature-religions and occultism, especially on "goddess feminism", must also be taken into account.

Regarding the image of God, both androgynous and gynocentric feminism show an overwhelming tendency to pantheism: God and the world are blended together, with the result that the personal natures of God and man recede from view. This result is particularly clear in the area of eschatology, where the idea of personal immortality is repudiated as patriarchal ideology.

Feminist theology is not a unified phenomenon. Reference has often been made here to the "quarrel among sisters". Many of the individual positions cancel each other out, especially in the area of anthropology. Also, to discover something specifically "feminine" in the feminist ideas is a problem of its own. The basic elements of the ideologies go back to males (Marx, Engels, Jung, Sartre, Tillich . . .). Cornelia Ferreira thus observes—in a very committed and pointed way—that she is forced to acknowledge a paradox: precisely those women who wish to free themselves from slavery to males have fallen into a slavery to paganism that results from manipulation by wicked men.[1]

In a certain way, feminist theology presents opportunities for the Church; but it also poses a preeminent danger, which pertains to the substance of being human and of Christian belief. This theology presents an opportunity insofar as it quite vigorously calls attention to the fact that man exists only in a "dual version", as male and as female. The sexual stamp that is intrinsic to being human needs to be reflected on more deeply. Precisely the exaggerations and attacks of feminism can sharpen our sense for some basic truths that have hitherto been grasped in a rather intuitive and unthematic way but must now be consciously examined and deepened. Feminist theology also sharpens our sense for the disadvantaging and suppressing of women, both of which, as consequences of sin, are to be combatted by every Christian.[2] Men and women have an equal value and an equal dignity.

This positive concern is brought into discredit, however, by extreme sorts of approach. The equality of value is often confused with an abstract notion of equal rights that fails to do justice to the complementarity of the sexes. Equality feminism, in particular, forgets that greater "rights" accrue to women in some areas of life and to men in others. Feminist theology as a whole makes the serious error of condemning the—by no means exclusive, but more strongly defined—leadership role of men as the epitome of evil. That women should have opportunities for greater responsibility in positions of leadership, even within the Church, is certainly sensible. But the strident demand for a fifty-fifty (or, for Mulack, a seventy-thirty) "quota

---

[1] Ferreira (1991), 433: "The irony is that women who have striven hard for 'liberation' from men have descended into *slavery*—the slavery of paganism from which Christ freed us—by being manipulated by wicked men."

[2] *Mulieris dignitatem,* nos. 8-10.

arrangement"[3] could, in the longer term, provoke male counterreactions not likely to help the female cause.

Muddled and extremist though the feminist positions may often be, they constitute an urgent challenge to reflect more deeply on the Christian image of God and man. Here, in opposition to that equality feminism and its sociologistic "role-oriented thinking" that predominates in the Church, it must be stressed that the male and female natures, as grounded in creation, are no mere "functions" but point beyond pure inner-worldly connections to the love between God and man. This simultaneously symbolic and redemptive relationship is expressed in the sacrament of marriage, in which the mutual submission of bridegroom and bride refers symbolically to Christ and the Church. It is also manifest, however, in the relationship between the special and the general priesthood, regarding which a distinction is to be made between the "apostolic-Petrine dimension"—or the representation of Christ as the head of the Church—and the "Marian" dimension. Pope John Paul II refers insistently to this in *Mulieris dignitatem*. [4] It is solely from this symbolic-sacramental worldview—now largely lost to a mentality based on rationalistic calculus of the practicable[5]—that those decisive answers can come which show feminist theology to be a false path.

At bottom, such reflective activity merely gives verbal form to something that the Church has long since recognized in her life: our relation to God, who became man in Jesus Christ, and to Mary, the bridal prototype of the Church. Especially the Marian aspect is highly important

---

[3] Cf. above, 21, 41.

[4] *Mulieris dignitatem*, nos. 22–29; cf. above, 210–15.

[5] On this, see Anton Ziegenaus, " 'Als Mann und Frau erschuf er sie' (Gen 1,27). Zum sakramentalen Verständnis der geschlechtlichen Differenzierung des Menschen" ["Male and female he created them" (Gen 1:27): On the sacramental understanding of man's sexual differentiatedness], MThZ 31 (1980): 210–22.

here, for it is Mary who both concentrates the greatest mysteries of faith in herself and radiates them into the world,[6] which is why the Church, drawing on the experience of the Church Fathers, has characterized her since the eighth century as the "vanquisher of all heresies".[7] Veneration of Mary, with its relevance to life, confers a feeling for the specific calling and dignity of women. Is it just coincidence that feminist theology finds scarcely any support in the Orthodox Church or in Catholic countries having more vital Marian traditions?

To what extent can feminist theology be integrated into existing theological scholarship? Enthusiasm for feminist theology is so great in some circles that institutes and academic chairs devoted to it are being established.[8] Behind such steps, of course, is the assumption that, not just particular aspects, but the fundamental approach of these feminist theologies can be accepted. Within academic theology, gynocentric "goddess feminism" is fairly generally rejected, while "androgynous" varieties find comparatively wide acceptance. The present study clearly shows, however, the extent to which, precisely among "moderate" women theologians, the ideal of a polarity-nullifying androgyny is reflected in all the specific formulations. The dissolution of the specific identities of male and female that is pursued by "church-oriented" feminist theology is diametrically opposed to the Christian image of man. Attractive-sounding notions like "wholeness" and "freedom from domination" serve to conceal an ideology that shatters both the human personality and cooperative social order.

This affirmation of "androgyny" and rejection of the complementarity of the sexes militates not only against the

---

[6] *Lumen gentium,* no. 65.
[7] Anton Ziegenaus, "Häresie" [Heresy], ML 3 (1991): 67–69; cf. also Ratzinger, *Report,* 104–6.
[8] Cf. above, p. 58.

establishment of feminist academic chairs and institutes. Also to be refused is the demand that feminist theology—like ecumenical theology—must be represented in all the individual theological disciplines.[9] To be sure, the concern for more research on the position of women, as an integral part of working out a comprehensive theological anthropology of the sexes, is justified.[10] Such an undertaking must not, however, focus exclusively on women but must take both sexes into account to the same degree. The complementarity of the sexes, and not some late-Marxist ideal of equality, should serve as the basis for this necessary task.

On the other hand, just the basic androgynous idea (but also the gynocentric) is, of itself, alien to Christian belief. That there is an unmistakable pull away from Christianity among women who become involved with feminist theology can therefore come as no surprise. A Dutch woman who is herself an adherent of feminist theology observes that, "for many women", promoting the feminist critique of religion is "not uncommonly the ultimate purpose . . . of the alliance between feminism and theology".[11] According to the Protestant theologian Martie Dieperink, the anti-Christian wine is merely diluted with "Christian" feminism but still remains the same wine.[12] Or, to adopt Elisabeth Motschmann's formulation, feminist theology leaves in its wake a theological and human "rubble-heap".[13]

Another indicative factor here is the drift of many women theologians to the consciously neo-pagan "goddess" move-

---

[9] Gössmann, *Schwestern,* 19f.; Meyer-Wilmes, 13f. Similarly, Schneider-Böklen and Vorländer, 140.

[10] This is also the view of Simonis (1986), 83f.; Gerl (1988), 76.

[11] Schaumberger and Maassen, 101; cf. Gössmann, *Schwestern,* 32.

[12] Dieperink, *Feministische Theologie,* 26. Here, Dieperink adverts in an exemplary way to the relation between Mary Daly and Catharina Halkes.

[13] Cf. Motschmann (1985), 291.

ment.[14] Goddess feminism is an important current within the so-called "New Religiosity" ("New Age")—a new version of paganism accommodated to present-day conditions, which aims at anything but a revitalization of Christianity.[15] What is beginning to appear here has many parallels with ancient Gnosticism, which the Church previously engaged (mainly in the second century) in a life-and-death struggle. Androgyny was, and is, a basic Gnostic idea, which, so to speak, recurrently erupted from the underground: from Jewish Gnosticism, the Cabbala, all the way to Jakob Boehme, Franz von Baader, and C. G. Jung.[16] The Gnostic scholar Gilles Quispel characterizes ancient Gnosticism as a "mythic projection of (human) self-experience".[17] According to Hans Jonas, Gnosticism wrongly elevates man to the level of "an inner-worldly god", who "puts" the Creator "in his place".[18]

Regarding the way that Christians should deal with feminist theology, it would be a pity if the old saying were to apply: Whoever remains ignorant of history is condemned to repeat it. The Church cannot do justice to the challenge of feminist theology by demonstrating a naive "openness" and allowing—with well-meaning forbearance—all the aberrations of this theology to infiltrate the Church's educational work and the universities.

It is, however, a sensible aim to make "feminine" per-

---

[14] Distressing examples are provided by the personal histories of Ursa Krattiger (originally Protestant) and Lucie Stapenhorst (initially Catholic): Krattiger, e.g., 106f.; Lucie Stapenhorst, *Als Tochter der Göttin von Zwängen befreit* [As a daughter of the goddess, freed of constraints] (Olten, 1992).

[15] Cf. above, 44–48.

[16] Cf. Sill; Hauke, *Women in the Priesthood?*, 158–65 (Gnosticism); 168–75 (Cabala); 268–70, 294 (influence of Boehme); 132 (C. G. Jung and Gnosticism).

[17] Quispel, 17.

[18] Hans Jonas, *Gnosis und spätantiker Geist* 1 [Gnosticism and the spirit of late antiquity 1], FRLANT 51, 2d ed. (Göttingen, 1957), 383.

spectives more fruitful in the area of theology as well as others.[19] This applies to feminine contexts of experience as well as to the more characteristically feminine capacities for concrete relatedness to life and a holistic participation of understanding and feeling. To preclude malicious misunderstandings here, it might be expressly stressed that this does not imply denial of a capacity for abstract thought to women. Women hold an exceedingly strong position in the history of mysticism (which currently plays no particular role in German academic theology); the significance of a St. Teresa of Avila, for example, could not easily be rivalled by any man. From a St. Hildegard and a St. Catherine of Siena come writings that testify to a fascinating, visionary insight into the truths of faith. The "feminine" theology of holy women could serve as an important corrective to a modern pursuit of science that not infrequently loses its way in "masculine" rationalistic abstractions. An intuitive sense, anchored in the Church and inclusive of feeling, ought to be combined more closely with precise reflective thought not only in every individual Christian but also in theology. Neither a doubling of the masculine nature in females nor an irascible feminism can contribute to furtherance of this concern; what can, however, are women theologians who are happy to be women and set about making their faith fruitful for the Church without any inferiority complexes.[20]

Here, it is not necessary to begin from nothing. Interesting female examples can be found even in antiquity and the Middle Ages. Not least importantly, there are highly cultured women in the twentieth century who, from a Catholic perspective, have made outstanding contributions,

---

[19] On this, cf. Albrecht (1983), 49–52.
[20] A multifaceted collective work by forty-seven women provides a refreshing example of faithful commitment (and not only for women theologians): Ursula Zöller et al., *Deine Dich liebende... Briefe an Mutter Kirche* [Your loving... Letter to Mother Church] (Aschaffenburg, 1993).

and precisely to the question of women: the writers Gertrud von le Fort, Sigrid Unset, and Ida Friederike Görres; the philosopher Edith Stein; the catechist Oda Schneider, the theologian Barbara Albrecht; and many others. Feminist theology is blind to testimonies like these.

Apart from theology, many more examples could be found of areas in which a "wholeness" that integrates both mind and heart—a harmonious unity not to be confused with androgynous uniformity—is not properly valued. Here, it is precisely women who possess a decisive and irreplaceable significance. Pope John Paul II deplores the darker sides of material progress, which has brought with it a "loss of sensitivity to man, to what is truly human". "In that sense, our times are particularly anxious for the 'genius' of women to show itself, which preserves that sensitivity to man under all circumstances, simply because he is man, and thus testifies that 'the greatest thing is love' (cf. 1 Cor 13:13)."[21]

The preceding remarks have already opened several positive perspectives that seem to bear importantly on the situation of women in the Church. Some further relevant thoughts may be added (although without any claim to exhaustiveness).

In and through the tasks allotted to women, the nature of the priesthood of the faithful is made apparent with particular clarity. The position of women in the Church is something like an "acid test" of the sort of worth accorded the laity. The general and the special priesthoods are to be seen as related but are not to be played off against one another.

Regarding recent developments in the Church, there is often talk of a twofold danger: a temptation, on the one hand, to laicize the clergy and, on the other, to clericize the laity. The significance of the layman derives, not from

---

[21] *Mulieris dignitatem,* no. 30.

any assumption of clerical tasks or approximation to this, but is grounded in baptism and confirmation. On that basis, the central task, as the Council states, is to knead the leaven of the gospel into every area of life.[22] It is the clergyman's job to instill confidence for this great task as well as to communicate God's word and the power of the sacraments.

Assisting in the conduct of organized groups within the female congregation is surely one of the important duties of a parish priest. There is a certain tension here between (1) the ranks of the female functionaries, who often tend to be critical of the Church (as evident in the publications of these organizations, like the German KFD's *Frau und mutter* [Wife and mother]) and (2) the so-called "base", whose members, by virtue of their own experience of family and Church, tend to think more realistically and feel comfortable in the concrete congregation. In this connection, the results (as summarized by Bishop Lehmann) of an important survey carried out by the Allensbach Institute on "Women and the Church" seem worth noting: Having a comparatively high constancy of involvement in an actual congregation leads to a more positive experience of the Church than would be indicated by "the semi-official image of the Church as reflected in public opinion". "The percentage of those who take a special interest in having the offices of deacon and (especially) priest opened to women is relatively quite small and largely coincides with the important group of active opinion-makers."[23]

Not a few Catholic women tend to regard the activities

---

[22] *Lumen gentium,* 31.

[23] Karl Lehmann, "Einführung" [Introduction], *Frauen und Kirche. Eine Repräsentativbefragung von Katholikinnen im Auftrage des Sekretariats der Deutschen Bischofskonferenz durchgeführt vom Institut für Demoskopie Allensbach* [Women and the Church: A representative poll of Catholic women commissioned by the office of the German Bishops' Conference and carried out by the Allensbach Institute for Opinion Research], Arbeitshilfen 108 (Bonn, 1993), 8.

of the large women's organizations with a critical
the feminist wing is continually increasing in
especially in the KFD, the founding of a counterorganizat.
could well be on the way, which would not set women
against the Church but, rather, encourage them out of
their sheltered faith and into a concretely committed stance.
Along these lines, meanwhile, the *Marianische Frauen- und
Müttergemeinschaft* (MFM) [Marian Women's and Mothers'
Association] has been founded in Switzerland. According
to its statutes, the members of this association "subscribe
to the Church's image of woman as defined by Catholic
doctrine. As women and child-raisers, we understand ourselves to have a mission to transmit the teachings of the
faith. In these areas, we see ourselves as carrying out, in
our families and occupations, the concrete priesthood of
the faithful, which means that we clearly dissociate ourselves from that theology of woman which does not con-
form to the Catholic faith and teaching."[25] Without a
doubt, if an inner renewal could take place, especially
within the KFD, a renewal dissociating itself from feminism,
this would be welcomed as a new foundation.

A major problem today is that many women find joyful
affirmation of their female nature to be difficult. A depress-
ing example is provided by the Catholic writer Anita Röper,
who observed in an interview with Karl Rahner: "As long
as human beings are not produced in test tubes, but have
to be brought into the world by women, women will remain,
from the very start, disadvantaged in comparison to men."[26]
The responsibility for a view like this lies with a mentality
oriented toward the technologically possible and an image
of man modelled more or less on the male nature. To

---

[24] A universal sentence should not be passed herewith, and especially
not on the other associations that are combined with the KFD in the
"Union of Catholic Women's Associations and Groups". Necessary and
fruitful work is carried out here.

[25] *Herder-Korrespondenz* 47 (1993): 358.

[26] Röper, 51.

counter this, an important task is that of encouragement:
the male and female natures are both God's good creations.
Every person is entrusted by God with talents that no one
else shares in exactly the same way. Precisely women have
been granted powerful gifts that are not similarly given to
men.

Along with all the concern for the role of women in the
Church, we should not forget, of course, that spiritual care
aimed specifically at men also deserves our attention. One
need only recall here the oft-quoted reference to the
"fatherless society" (A. Mitscherlich). At the world synod
of bishops on the laity in 1987, after the topic of women
had been extensively illumined, Thomas Forrest—one of the
leading personalities in the charismatic revival movement—
spoke up, warning of the dangers of exclusive obsession
with women's issues. Women often played so large a role in
the congregations that priests no longer knew how to approach pastoral dialogue with men.[27] "The major churches
—at least in the Federal Republic of Germany—are, with
80 percent of their participating members being women,
virtually 'women's institutions'."[28] Alongside the stock critique of the Catholic Church as a "male Church", the view
is almost equally held, among committed female members
of the congregation, that the Catholic Church is "more a
women's Church".[29] It is necessary, then, to avoid one-
sided focus on the topic of women. The kind of responsibility specific to men is also important, especially that of a
head of family, in which self-confident authority is combined with devoted solicitude.[30] Neither a "feminization"

---

[27] *Herder-Korrespondenz* 41 (1987): 525; see also L. J. Podles, "The
Alienation of Men from Christianity", HPR 89 (1988): 56–63.

[28] Schneider-Böklen and Vorländer, 15.

[29] *Frauen und Kirche,* 103 (38 to 36 percent).

[30] Cf. here Hermann Wesseln, "Der Vater in der Erziehung" [The
father's role in child-raising], in Manfred Balkenohl and Hermann Wesseln,
eds., *Erziehung in Verantwortung* (Hamm, 1982), 142–52; St. E. Müller,
*Personal-soziale Entfaltung des Gewissens im Jugendalter. Eine moral-
anthropologische Studie* [The personal-social development of conscience

nor a "masculinization" is the need of the moment but, rather, the distinctively contoured natures of both man and woman in mutual support.

Modern industrial society has led to a great transformation in the roles of women but also to a dangerous crisis. Within the Church's endeavors today, a central emphasis should be placed on strengthening the family. The role of women is certainly not to be limited to the family alone; but family demands, especially when there are several children, fall more heavily upon the mother than the father. What a child needs as reference persons is not two androgynous role-bearers but a father and a mother. That the average German family has only 1.5 children is understandable for several reasons but unhealthy in human terms. Only children, now so numerous, have a much harder time in their social development than those with the experience of brothers and sisters.[31] In short, fewer children in our country means more problems. Today, a housewife and mother with several children is looked upon in many circles as inferior and anti-social. This mentality needs to be changed, and inside the Church as well. We should provide encouragement for families with more than 1.5 children, and encouragement to the pursuit of responsible fatherhood and motherhood.[32] And legislators, too, are challenged to create circumstances favorable to this.

---

in adolescence: A moral-anthropological study] (Mainz, 1984), 88–93, 156–65, 245–63; the meditation by Christa Meves, *Ein neues Vaterbild. Zwei Frauen unserer Zeit entdecken Josef von Nazaret* [A new father-image: Two women of our time discover Joseph of Nazareth] (Stein am Rhein, 1989).

[31] Cf. on this Paul Nikolajczyk, "Das Geschwistererleben im Lebensraum der Familie" [Experiencing brothers and sisters in the life-context of the family], in Manfred Balkenohl and Hermann Wesseln, eds., *Erziehung und Seelsorge im Dienste des Menschen,* (Paderborn, 1991), 181–97.

[32] On this, cf. P. C. Düren, *Elternschaft verantwortet leben. Moral-theologische und methodische Aspekte* [Realizing responsible parenthood: Moral-theological and methodical aspects], 2d ed. (Leutesdorf, 1993).

Along with strengthening the family, there is certainly a plethora of other tasks that can only be hinted at here. Among them is creating employment conditions compatible with the needs of women and amplifying the significance of honorary positions, as well as renewing the conditions of monastic life and deploying the resources of religious communities. Particular attention needs to be given to full-time service by women in the Church, in both the charitable and pastoral spheres. Barbara Albrecht rightly stresses that spiritual care is

> not a matter for priests alone. Spiritual care must become the vital concern of mothers who are well-versed in the faith but also of women theologians and women pastoral and community advisers who have grasped the seriousness of the situation and become involved in . . . [the] currently pressing areas of pastoral need—and have done so with appropriate competence, on the basis of baptism and confirmation, and with an affirmative attitude toward the concrete Church. Such women would have to be accepted by Church authority, and regarded as coworkers in the area of spiritual care, responsible coworkers! . . . Whenever collaboration between bishops and women theologians can successfully occur, this is a true enrichment.[33]

There is a virtual superabundance of tasks for women in the Church, tasks that require a large and varied wealth of talents and charisms. A few years ago, I was invited to address a religious organization whose members were from quite differing social groups and backgrounds. When I then asked what was generally typical of the membership, one of the officers gave the following significant reply:

---

[33] Barbara Albrecht, "Vom Dienst der Frau in der Kirche" [On women's service in the Church], in Franz Breid, ed., *Der Dienst von Priester und Laie. Wegweisung für das gemeinsame und hierarchische Priestertum an der Wende zum dritten Jahrtausend* [The service of priest and layman: A guide to the general and hierarchical priesthood at the turn of the millennium] (Steyr, 1991), 47f.

"That's hard to say—we are not so much a casserole as a full-course meal."

Not a casserole but a full-course meal. That surely applies as well to the whole Church, in which differing kinds of gifts are to be brought together through the power of the Holy Spirit. The decisive thing here is not whether one holds hierarchical office but what position one holds before God. The greatest of those in the Church are not the office-bearers but the saints.[34] The best example of this is Mary, who is praised in the Litany of Loreto as "Queen of the Apostles", although she was not herself an apostle. Tatiana Goritcheva, the famous Russian civil-rights campaigner and Orthodox Christian, initiated a women's movement in Soviet Russia that called itself "Mary". Regarding this, Goritcheva writes: "It was in the Church, through the Mother of God, that I discovered the worth of woman, her identity and her dignity."[35]

As well, the apostolic letter *Mulieris dignitatem*[36] exhibits a wholly Marian approach. Beyond the merely biological level, receptivity and motherliness are indicative of spiritual attitudes that are concentrated in Mary. The Pope thus discloses a perspective that far transcends any shortsighted "role-oriented" view while, at the same time, offering guidelines for practical life.

A similar position was expressed, in 1987, by the world synod of bishops on the laity: "You, our women, are rightly struggling for full recognition of your dignity and your rights. This initiative ought to lead to a world of dialogue and mutual support, as was originally intended by the Creator, and whose continuance was entrusted to man and woman. In the Church, through the Virgin Mary, he effectively restored woman to us, renewed in her dignity and

---

[34] Cf. *Erklärung,* no. 6.
[35] *Deutsche Tagespost,* October 15, 1987, 5.
[36] Cf. above, 200.

grace." "Mary . . . is an archetype of feminine dignity and an incomparable example of the meaning of participation in God's redemptive work."[37]

What is required today is not to run breathlessly after the banners of androgynous or gynocentric feminism. The real need is a new self-assurance on the part of women, which should take its direction from Mary. According to Vatican II, Mary concentrates "the greatest mysteries of the faith in herself and radiates them out again".[38] There are also stimuli here for the issue of "women in the Church" that do not have a destructive effect but contribute to the building of the religious community.

---

[37] *Deutsche Tagespost,* November 3, 1987, 5 (concluding message of the World Synod of Bishops).

[38] *Lumen gentium,* no. 65.

ABBREVIATIONS

BTB	*Biblical Theology Bulletin*
BThZ	*Berliner Theologische Zeitschrift*
CCC	*Catechism of the Catholic Church*
CChr.SL	*Corpus Christianorum. Series latina*
DS	Heinrich Denzinger. *Kompendium der Glaubensbekenntnisse und kirchlichen Lehrentscheidungen.* Latin-German. Ed. Peter v. Hünermann. Freiburg, 1991
EK	*Evangelische Kommentare*
EKD	Evangelische Kirche in Deutschland
ELTG	*Evangelisches Lexikon für Theologie und Gemeinde.* Wuppertal and Zurich, 1992–
EvTh	*Evangelische Theologie*
EZW	*Evangelische Zentrale für Weltanschauungsfragen*
FAZ	*Frankfurter Allgemeine Zeitung*
FKTh	*Forum Katholische Theologie*
FLex	*Frauenlexikon* (see Bibliog.)
FRLANT	*Forschungen zur Religion und Literatur des Alten und Neuen Testaments*
FS	Festschrift
FThSt	*Freiburger Theologische Studien*
HPR	*Homiletic and Pastoral Review*
HWP	*Historisches Wörterbuch der Philosophie*

KFD	Katholische Frauengemeinschaft Deutschlands
KKD	*Kleine Katholische Dogmatik*
LJ	*Liturgisches Jahrbuch*
LThK	*Lexikon für Theologie und Kirche*
ML	*Marienlexikon.* Ed. Remigius Bäumer and Leo Scheffczyk. St. Ottilien, 1988–
MThZ	*Münchener Theologische Zeitschrift*
PL	*Patrologia latina*
QD	*Quaestiones disputatae*
StZ	*Stimmen der Zeit*
ThGl	*Theologie und Glaube*
ThLZ	*Theologische Literaturzeitung*
ThPQ	*Theologisch-praktische Quartalschrift*
TRE	*Theologische Realenzyklopädie*
Wb	*Wörterbuch der Feministischen Theologie* (see Bibliog.)
WdF	*Wege der Forschung*
ZKTh	*Zeitschrift für Katholische Theologie*

BIBLIOGRAPHY

Adnes, Pierre. "Mariage spirituel", *Dictionnaire de spiritualité* 10 (1980): 388–408.

Ahl, Ruth. *Eure Töchter werden Prophetinnen sein: Kleine Einführung in die Feministische Theologie* [Your daughters will be prophets: A short introduction to feminist theology]. Freiburg, 1990.

Albrecht, Barbara. *Jesus—Frau—Kirche* [Jesus—woman—Church]. Vallendar and Schönstatt, 1983.

——. *Vom Dienst der Frau in der Kirche* [On women's service in the Church]. Vallendar and Schönstatt, 1980.

——. "Vom Dienst der Frau in der Kirche" [On women's service in the Church]. In *Der Dienst von Priester und Laie. Wegweisung für das gemeinsame und hierarchische Priestertum an der Wende zum dritten Jahrtausend* [The service of priest and layman: A guide to the general and hierarchical priesthood at the turn of the millennium], edited by Franz Breid, 33–64. Steyr, 1991.

Alliata, Vittoria. *Harem. Die Freiheit hinter dem Schleier* [Harem: The freedom behind the veil]. Munich and Gütersloh, 1981.

Ammicht-Quinn, Regina. "Ehe" [Marriage]. In Wb, 67–73.

Arnold, Joan. "Maria—Gottesmutterschaft und Frau" [Mary—Mother of God and a woman]. *Concilium* 12 (1976): 24–29.

Auer, Johann. *Die Kirche—Das allgemeine Heilssakrament*

[The Church—the universal holy sacrament]. KKD 8. Regensburg, 1983.

——. Jesus Christus—Gottes und Mariä "Sohn" [Jesus Christ—Son of God and Mary]. KKD, vol. 4, no. 1. Regensburg, 1986.

Auer Falk, N. E. "Feminine Sacrality". In *The Encyclopedia of Religion,* vol. 5, edited by Mircea Eliade, 302-12. New York and London, 1987.

Axmacher, Elke. "Feministisch von Gott reden? Eine Anseinandersetzung mit Rosemary Radford Ruethers Buch 'Sexismus und die Rede von Gott' " [Feminist talk with God? A quarrel with Rosemary Radford Ruether's book *Sexism and God-talk*]. *Zeitschrift für Evangelische Ethik* 35 (1991): 5-20.

Badinter, Elisabeth. *Ich bin Du. Die neue Beziehung zwischen Mann und Frau oder Die androgyne Revolution* [I am you: The new relationship between man and woman, or the androgynous revolution]. Munich, 1987.

Balthasar, Hans Urs von. "Epilog: Die marianische Prägung der Kirche" [Epilogue: The Marian impress of the Church]. In *Maria heute ehren* [Devotion to Mary today], edited by Wolfgang Beinert, 263-79. 2d ed. Freiburg, 1977.

——. "Women Priests?". In *New Elucidations,* 187-98. San Francisco, 1986.

Balthasar, Hans Urs von, and Joseph Ratzinger. *Joseph, Maria—Kirche im Ursprung* [Joseph and Mary—the origin of the Church]. Freiburg, 1980.

Balz-Cochois, Helgard. "Gomer oder die Macht der Astarte. Versuch einer feministischen Interpretation von Hos 1-4" [Gomer, or the power of Astarte: An attempted feminist interpretation of Hos 1-4]. EvTh 42 (1982): 37-65.

Barz, Helmut. *Männersache: kritischer Beifall für den Feminismus* [Male business: Critical applause for feminism]. Zurich, 1984.

Barz, Monika, Herta Leistner, and Ute Wild, eds. *Hättest du gedacht, daß wir so viele sind? Lesbische Frauen in der Kirche* [Would you ever have thought there were so many of us? Lesbian women in the Church]. Zurich, 1987.

Bauer, Angela. "Sexismus" [Sexism]. In Wb, 367–70.

Bäumer, U. *Wir wollen nur deine Seele* [We only want your soul]. 2d ed. Wuppertal, 1985.

Baumert, Norbert. *Frau und Mann bei Paulus* [Woman and man in Paul]. Würzburg, 1992.

Baumgardt, Ursula. "Anima/Animus". In FLex, 52–54.

Baus, Magdalena. "Emanzipation". In FLex, 212–21.

Beauvoir, Simone de. *Das andere Geschlecht. Sitte und Sexus der Frau* [The second sex: Morality and sexuality of women]. Reinbek, 1968.

Beinert, Wolfgang, ed. *Frauenbefreiung und Kirche* [Women's liberation and the Church]. Regensburg, 1987.

———. *Maria in der Feministischen Theologie. Wege und Abwege feministischer Theologie* [Mary in feminist theology: Directions and aberrations in feminist theology]. Kevelaer, 1988. (Cf. his "Maria in der Feministischen Theologie". *Catholica* 42 [1988]: 1–27.)

———. *Unsere Liebe Frau und die Frauen* [Our Lady and women]. Freiburg, 1989.

Bellenzier, M. T. "Donna". In *Nuovo Dizionario di Mariologia,* edited by Stefano De Fiores and Salvatore Meo, 499–510. 2d ed. Milan, 1986.

Benediktionale. Studienausgabe für die katholischen Bis-

tümer des deutschen Sprachgebietes [Benedictional: Text-edition for Catholic dioceses in German-speaking world]. Einsiedeln, 1981.

Bereschit Rabba, Der Midrasch. Bibliotheca rabbinica 1. First translated into German by August Wünsche. Leipzig, 1881; reprint, Hildesheim, 1967.

Berg, Werner. "Die Mütterlichkeit Gottes im Alten Testament" [God's motherliness in the Old Testament]. In *Ausgewählte Themen der Theologie des ATs I. Gott im AT* [Selected themes in the theology of the Old Testament I: God in the Old Testament], by Josef Scharbert, 185-97. Skripten des Lehrstuhls für Theologie des ATs, no. 5. Munich, 1982.

Berger, Teresa. "Auf der Suche nach einer 'integrativen Liturgie'" [The search for an "integrative liturgy"]. LJ 37 (1987): 42-58.

———. "Kult". In FLex (1988), 597-601.

———. "Auf dem Weg zu einer 'frauen-gerechten' Liturgie" [Toward a liturgy appropriate to the needs of women]. *Gottesdienst* 22 (1988): 129-32.

———. "Women and Worship: a Bibliography". *Studia liturgica* 19 (1989): 96-110.

———. *Liturgie und Frauenseele. Die Liturgische Bewegung aus der Sicht der Frauenforschung* [Liturgy and the female soul: The liturgical movement from the perspective of women's studies]. Stuttgart, 1993.

———. "'Wie eine Mutter ihre Kinder zärtlich um sich schart...' Zu Versuchen mit neuen 'Frauen-gerechten' Eucharistiegebeten in den Kirchen" ["As a mother tenderly gathers her children around her..." On experiments in the Church with new forms of eucharistic prayer more agreeable to women]. BThZ 10 (1993): 2-14.

Berger, Teresa, and Albert Gerhards, eds. *Liturgie und Frauenfrage* [Liturgy and the women's issue]. St. Ottilien, 1990.

Beyerhaus, Peter, ed. *Frauen im theologischen Aufstand. Eine Orientierungshilfe zur "Feministischen Theologie"* [Women in theological revolt: A guidebook to "feminist theology"]. Wort und Wissen 14. Neuhausen and Stuttgart, 1983. (*Aufstand*)

——. "Die Feministische Theologie in religionswissenschaft licher und missions theologischer Sicht" [Feminist theology from the perspective of religious thought and the theology of the missions]. *Theologische Beiträge* 22 (1991): 149–53.

Blaasvaer, E. M., ed. *Bibliography on Feminist Theology.* Geneva, 1986.

Blechschmidt, Erich. *Wie beginnt das menschliche Leben?* [How does human life begin?]. 2d ed. Stein am Rhein, 1984.

Bleibtreu-Ehrenberg, Gisela. "Matriarchat/Patriarchat". In FLex, 710–18.

——. "Eheformen" [Forms of marriage]. In FLex, 177–81.

Bloesch, D. G. *Battle for the Trinity: The Debate over Inclusive Language.* Ann Arbor, 1985.

Böhme, Karen. *Zum Selbstverständnis der Frau. Philosophische Aspekte der Frauenemanzipation* [On female self-understanding: Philosophical aspects of the emancipation of women]. Meisenheim am Glan, 1973.

Bogerts, Hildegard. *Bildung und berufliches Selbstverständnis lehrender Frauen in der Zeit von 1885 bis 1920* [Formation and professional self-image of women teachers in the period 1885 to 1920]. Frankfurt, 1977.

Bornemann, Ernest. *Das Patriarchat. Ursprung und Zukunft*

unseres Gesellschaftssystems [Patriarchy: On the origin and future of our social system]. Frankfurt, 1975.

Børresen, K. E. "Männlich-Weiblich: eine Theologiekritik" [Masculine-feminine: A critique of theology]. *Una sancta* 35 (1980): 325-34.

——. "Maria in der katholischen Theologie" [Mary in Catholic theology]. In Moltmann-Wendel, Küng, and Moltmann (1988), 72-87. ("Maria")

Brockhusen, Gerda von. "Brautsymbolik" [Bridal symbolism]. In *Praktisches Lexikon der Spiritualität* [Practical lexicon of spirituality], edited by Christian Schütz, 172-74. Freiburg, 1988.

Brockmann, Doris. *Ganze Menschen—Ganze Götter. C. G. Jung in der feministischen Theologie* [Whole humans—whole gods: C. G. Jung in feminist theology]. Paderborn, 1990.

Brooten, Bernadette. " 'Junia . . . hervorragend unter den Aposteln' (Rom 16,7)" ["Junia . . . prominent among the apostles" (Rom 16:7)]. In Moltmann-Wendel (1978), 148-51.

——. "Liebe unter Frauen" [Love between women]. In Sommer (1985), 351-57.

Brox, Norbert. *Offenbarung, Gnosis und gnostischer Mythos bei Irenäus von Lyon* [Revelation, gnosis, and gnostic myth in Irenaeus of Lyons]. Salzburg, 1966.

Brugger, Walter. *Summe einer philosophischen Gotteslehre* [*Summa* of a philosophical theology]. Munich, 1979. (*Gotteslehre*)

Buckley, G. A. "Mary, the Alternative to Feminism". HPR 91 (1991): 11-16.

Bührig, Marga. *Die unsichtbare Frau und der Gott der Väter. Eine Einführung in die feministische Theologie*

[The invisible woman and the God of the Fathers: An introduction to feminist theology]. Stuttgart, 1987.

——. *Spät habe ich gelernt, gerne Frau zu sein. Eine feministische Autobiographie* [Late have I learned to like being a woman: A feminist autobiography]. 3d ed. Stuttgart, 1988.

Burggraf, Jutta. "Die Mutter der Kirche und die Frau in der Kirche. Korrektur der Irrwege feministischer Theologie" [The Mother of the Church and women in the Church: Correcting the aberrations of feminist theology]. *Offerten-Zeitung ("Theologisches")* 38 (1985): 6445–53, 6507–13.

——. *Die Mutter der Kirche und die Frau in der Kirche. Ein kritischer Beitrag zum Thema "feministische Theologie"* [The Mother of the Church and women in the Church: A critical essay on "feminist theology"]. Kleine Schriften des Internationalen Mariologischen Arbeitskreises. Kevelaer, 1986.

——. "Frauenlexikon" [Women's lexicon]. FKTh 5 (1989): 285–90.

——. "Maria als Vorbild für die Frau. Das Marienbild bei Gertrud von Le Fort" [Mary as a model for women: The image of Mary in Gertrud von Le Fort]. In Pontificia Academia Mariana Internationalis, *De cultu mariano saeculis XIX–XX . . . ,* 7:125–45. Rome, 1991.

——. "Bemerkungen zum Feminismus" [Observations on feminism]. *Die Neue Ordnung* 47 (1993): 14–20.

Capra, Fritjof. *Wendezeit. Bausteine für ein neues Weltbild* [Pivotal times: Building blocks for a new cosmology]. 10th ed. Bern, 1985.

Carr, Anne E. *Transforming Grace: Christian Tradition and Women's Experience.* San Francisco, 1988.

Carroll, E. A. "La figura de María y los movimientos feministas" (to appear in English in the Acts of the World Mariological Congress in Huelva 1992: Pontificia Academia, Via Merulana, 124, I-00185 Roma).

Catechism of the Catholic Church. Vatican, 1994. English edition.

Christ, Carol. "Vom Vatergott zur Muttergöttin" [From father-god to mother-goddess]. In Sommer (1985), 282–87.

Clark, S. B. *Man and Woman in Christ: An Examination of the Roles of Men and Women in Light of Scripture and the Social Sciences.* Ann Arbor, 1980.

Congar, Yves. *Der Heilige Geist* [The Holy Spirit]. Freiburg, 1982.

Congregation for the Doctrine of the Faith. *Declaration on the Admission of Women to the Ministerial Priesthood.* In Vatican Council II: *More Postconciliar Documents,* edited by A. Flannery, O.P. Boston, 1982.

Congregation for the Doctrine of the Faith. "Instruction on Certain Aspects of the 'Theology of Liberation' ". Boston, 1984.

Courth, Franz. "Zum Gottes- und Menschenbild der Feministischen Theologie" [On the images of God and man in feminist theology]. *Kath. Bildung* 87 (1986): 669–75.

——. "Mariologie im Umfeld von Ökumene und Feminismus. Akzente neuerer mariologischer Literatur" [Mariology in the context of ecumenicism and feminism: Emphases in recent mariological literature]. ThPQ 136 (1988): 140–49.

———. "Feministische Theology". ML 2 (1989): 459–61. ("Feministische Theologie")

———. "La Mère de Dieu, une déesse chrétienne? Marie dans la théologie féministe de langue allemande". *Études Mariales* 45 (1989): 61–79.

———. *Mariologie (Texte zur Theologie)* [Mariology (texts on theology)]. Graz, 1991.

———. *Der Gott der dreifaltigen Liebe* [The God of trinitarian love]. Paderborn, 1993.

Cramon-Daiber, Birgit et al. *Schwesternstreit. Von den heimlichen und unheimlichen Auseinandersetzungen zwischen Frauen* [Dispute among sisters: On the secret and uncanny disagreements among women]. Reinbek, 1990.

Crawford, Janet. "The Community of Women and Men in the Church: Where are we now?". *Ecumenical Review* 40 (1988): 37–47.

Cumbey, Constance. *Die sanfte Verschwörung. Hintergrund und Gefahren der New-Age-Bewegung* [The gentle conspiracy: Background and dangers of the New Age movement]. 5th ed. Asslar, 1987.

Daly, Mary. *The Church and the Second Sex.* New York, 1968. (*Church*)

———. *Beyond God the Father: Toward a Philosophy of Women's Liberation.* Boston, 1973. German ed.: *Jenseits von Gottvater Sohn & Co. Aufbruch zu einer Philosophie der Frauenbefreiung.* Munich, 1980. (*Father*)

―――. *Gyn/Ecology: The Metaethics of Radical Feminism.* Boston, 1978. German ed.: *Gyn/Ökologie—eine Meta-Ethik des radikalen Feminismus.* Munich, 1980. (*Gyn/Ecology*)

―――. "Der qualitative Sprung über die patriarchale Religion" [The qualitative leap beyond patriarchal religion]. In Moltmann-Wendel (1983), 110–23. ("Sprung")

―――. *Pure Lust: Elemental Feminist Philosophy.* Boston, 1984. German ed.: *Reine Lust. Elemental-feministische philosophie.* Munich, 1986. (*Lust*)

Daly, Mary, and Jane Caputi. *Websters' First New Intergalactic Wickedary of the English Language.* Boston, 1987.

Degenhardt, Johannes J. *Marienfrömmigkeit* [Marian piety]. Paderborn, 1987. 50–60.

Diekamp, Franz, and Klaudius Jüssen. *Katholische Dogmatik nach den Grundsätzen des hl. Thomas* 1 [Catholic dogmatics based on the principles of St. Thomas 1]. 12/13th ed. Münster, 1958.

Dieperink, Martie. *New Age en christelijk geloof. Over de invloed van New Age op de Kerk.* 3d ed. Kampen, 1990. (*New Age*)

―――. *Vrouwen op zoek naar God. Wat is er gaande in de feministische theologie?* 2d ed. The Hague, 1988. (*Feministische Theologie*)

―――. *God roept de vrouw. Over de plaats en taak van de christenvrouw.* Kampen, 1990.

Dijk, Denise. "The Goddess-Movement in the U.S.A. A Religion for Women Only". *Archiv für Religionspsychologie* 18 (1988): 258–66.

Dion, Michel. "Mary Daly, théologienne et philosophe féministe". *Études théologiques et religieuses* 61 (1987): 515–34.

Diözesansynode Augsburg 1990. *Die Seelsorge in der Pfarrgemeinde* [Ministry in the parish]. Donauwörth, 1991.

Dirks, Marianne. "Maria" [Mary]. In FLex, 704–10.

Doerfer, Gerhard. "Das Korana und die Linguistinik". *Sprachwissenschaft* 10 (1985): 132–52.

Dokumentation "Jenseits der Grenzen legitimer Theologie. Stellungnahme der nordelbischen Bischöfe zum Thema Feministische Theologie" (1.7.85) [Beyond the bounds of legitimate theology: Statement by the bishops of the northern Elb region on the subject of feminist theology (July 1, 1985)]. *Materialdienst der EZW* 50 (1987): 104f.

Drewermann, Eugen. "Die Frage nach Maria im religionswissenschaftlichen Horizont" [The question of Mary in the context of religious studies]. *Zeitschrift für Religions- und Missionswissenschaft* 66 (1982): 96–117.

———. *Tiefenpsychologie und Exegese* 1/2 [Psychoanalysis and exegesis 1/2]. Olten, 1984/1985. (*Tiefenpsychologie*)

———. *Der tödliche Fortschritt. Von der Zerstörung der Erde und des Menschen im Erbe des Christentums* [Fatal progress: On the destruction of the earth and of man as the heritage of Christianity]. Herder/Spektrum 4032. Freiburg, 1991.

Duden 1. 19th ed. Mannheim, 1986.

Düren, Peter C. *Elternschaft verantwort leben. Moral theologische und methodische Aspekte* [Realizing responsible parenthood: Moral-theological and methodical aspects]. 2d ed. Leutesdorf, 1993.

Durwell, F. X. Der Geist des Herrn. Tiefe Gottes—schöpferische Weite [The Spirit of the Lord: Depth of God—breadth of creation]. Salzburg, 1986.

Dux, Günter. *Die Spur der Macht im Verhältnis der Geschlechter. Über den Ursprung der Ungleich heit zwischen Mann und Frau* [The position of power in the relationship of the sexes: On the source of the dissimilarity between man and woman]. Frankfurt, 1992.

Dyck, Joachim. "Männerherrschaft als Sprachherrschaft? Eine Kritik der feministischen Linguistik" [Domination by males as domination of language? A critique of feminist linguistics]. *Jahrbuch Rhetorik* 8 (1989): 95–104.

EKD-Frauenzentrum. idea-Dokumentation 10/93. Wetzlar, 1993.

Elizondo, Virgil. "Maria und die Armen. Ein Modell eines evangelisierenden Ökumenismus" [Mary and the poor: A model of evangelizing ecumenism]. In Moltmann-Wendel, Küng, and Moltmann (1988), 131–41.

Emmerich, Marilone. "Schwestern, seid nüchtern und wachsam!" [Sisters, be prudent and watchful!]. *Kath. Bildung* 89 (1988): 1–8.

Engels, Friedrich. *Der Ursprung der Familie, des Privateigentums und des Staates* [The origin of the family, private property, and the state]. 17th ed. Stuttgart, 1919.

Erler, Ursula. *Zerstörung und Selbstzerstörung der Frau. Emanzipationskampf der Geschlechter auf Kosten des Kindes* [Destruction and self-destruction of women: The emancipatory struggle between the sexes at the expense of the child]. Stuttgart, 1977.

Fagerberg, Holsten. "Amt/Ämter/Amtsverständnis VI. Reformationszeit" [Office/offices/understanding of office: VI. Reformation period]. TRE 2 (1978): 552–77.

Fander, Monika. "Reinheit/Unreinheit" [Cleanliness/uncleanliness]. In Wb, 349–51.

Fernet-Betancourt, Raúl. "Marxismus". In H. Goldstein (1991), 146–50.

Ferreira, Cornelia. *The Feminist Agenda within the Catholic Church.* Toronto, 1987.

——. "The Emerging Feminist Religion". HPR 89 (1989): 10–21.

——. "The Destructive Forces behind Religious Feminism". *Christian Order* (1991), 426–33.

Fiores, Stefano de. *Maria nella teologia contemporanea.* Serie pastorale di studio 6. 2d ed. Rome, 1987.

Firestone, Shulamith. *Frauenbefreiung und sexuelle Revolution.* Frankfurt, 1975. English ed.: *The Dialectic of Sex: The Case for Feminist Revolution.* New York, 1970.

Fischer, Balthasar. "Zur Anrede bei den Lesungen in der Meßfeier" [On the form of address for readings used in the celebration of the Mass]. *Klerusblatt* 68 (1988): 141.

——. " 'Inklusive Sprache' im Gottesdienst. Eine berechtigte Forderung?" ["Inclusive language" in divine service—a justified demand?]. In Berger and Gerhards (1990), 359–67.

Fischer, J. A. *Die Apostolischen Väter* [The apostolic fathers]. 7th ed. Darmstadt, 1976.

Frauen und Kirche. Eine Repräsentativbefragung von Katholikinnen im Auftrage des Sekretariats der Deutschen Bischofskonferenz durchgeführt vom Institut für Demoskopie Allensbach [Women and the Church: A representative poll of Catholic women commissioned by the office of the German Bishops' Conference and carried out by the Allensbach Institute for Opinion Research]. Arbeitshilfen 108. Bonn, 1993.

Frauenlexikon [Lexicon on women]. Edited by Anneliese Lissner, Rita Süssmuth, and Karin Walter. Freiburg, 1988. (FLex)

Friedan, Betty. *The Feminine Mystique.* New York, 1963.

——. *It Changed My Life: Writings on the Women's Movement.* New York, 1963, 1967.

——. *The Second Stage.* New York, 1981.

Gadamer, Hans Georg. *Wahrheit und Methode* [Truth and method]. 2d ed. Tübingen, 1965.

Galot, Jean. "Marie, modèle de la femme dans la théologie catholique". *Studia missionalia* 40 (1991): 95–114.

Gaspari, Christof. *Eins und Eins ist Eins—Leitbilder für Mann und Frau* [One and one make one—models for man and woman]. Vienna, 1985.

Gatzemeier, M., and H. Holzhey. "Makrokosmos/Mikrokosmos". HWP 5 (1980): 640–49.

Gerber, Uwe. "Feministische Theologie. Selbstverständnis—Tendenzen—Fragen" [Feminist theology: Self-understanding—directions—questions]. ThLZ 109 (1984): 561–92. ("Feministische Theologie", 1984)

——. "Feministische Theologie". In Schöpsdau (1985), 103–41. ("Feministische Theologie" 1985)

——. *Die feministische Eroberung der Theologie* [The feminist conquest of theology]. Munich, 1987. (*Evoberung*)

Gerhard, Ute. "Feminismus". In FLex, 301–7.

Gerhards, Albert. "'. . . Der uns zu seinen Söhnen zählt'? Zum Stand der Bemühungen um eine frauengerechte Liturgie" ["... Who counts us among his sons"? The current state of attempts to achieve a liturgy accept-able to women]. StZ 117 (1992): 115–24. ("Frauenger-echte Liturgie")

——. "'Einschließende Sprache' im Gottesdienst—eine übertriebene Forderung oder Gebot der Stunde?" ["Inclusive language" in divine service—an exagger-ated demand or the need of the moment?], LJ 42 (1992): 239–48.

Gerl, Hanna-Barbara. *Die bekannte Unbekannte: Frauen-Bilder in der Kultur- und Geistesgeschichte* [The fa-miliar unfamiliar: Images of women in cultural and intellectual history]. Mainz, 1988.

——. "Ganzheitlichkeit" [Wholeness]. In FLex, 399–404.

——. *Wider das Geistlose im Zeitgeist. 20 Essays zu Reli-gion und Kultur* [Against the spiritless in the Age of the Spirit: 20 essays on religion and culture]. Munich, 1992.

Giese, Cornelia. *Gleichheit und Differenz. Vom dualis-tischen Denken zur polaren Weltsicht* [Similarity and difference: From dualistic thinking to a polar world-view]. Munich, 1990.

Goldenberg, Naomi. *Changing of the Gods: Feminism and the End of Traditional Religions.* Boston, 1979.

Goldstein, Horst. *Kleines Lexikon zur Theologie der Befrei-ung* [Concise lexicon on liberation theology]. Düssel-dorf, 1991.

Gordan, Paulus, ed. *Gott schuf den Menschen als Mann und Frau* [God created mankind as male and female]. Salzburger Hochschulwochen 1988. Graz, Vienna, and Cologne, 1989.

Görres, Albert. "Erneuerung durch Tiefenpsychologie?" [Renewal through psychoanalysis?]. *Tiefenpsychologische Deutung des Glaubens? Anfragen an Eugen Drewermann,* edited by A. Görres and Walter Kasper, 133–74. QD 113. Freiburg, 1988.

Gössmann, Elisabeth. *Die streitbaren Schwestern. Was will Feministische Theologie?* [The quarrelsome sisters: What does feminist theology want?]. Freiburg, 1981. (*Schwestern*)

——. "Maria und die Frauen" [Mary and women]. *Lebendiges Zeugnis* 43 (1988): 54–63. ("Maria und die Frauen")

——. *Die Zeit der Frau* [The era of woman]: *Apostolisches Schreiben "Mulieris dignitatem"* of John Paul II. Commentary by Elisabeth Gössmann. 123–50. Freiburg, 1988.

——. "Mariologische Thesen in der Feministischen Theologie. Darstellungen und Kritik" [Mariological theses in feminist theology: Outline and critique]. In Gössmann and Bauer (1989), 168–79. ("Mariologische Thesen")

——. "Anthropologie". In Wb, 16–22.

——. "Mariologie". In Wb, 279–83.

——. "Zukunft" [Future]. In Wb, 440f.

Gössmann, Elisabeth, and D. R. Bauer, eds. *Maria—für alle Frauen oder über allen Frauen?* [Mary—for all women or above all women?]. Freiburg, 1989.

Greeley, Andrew. *The Mary Myth—On the Femininity of God.* New York, 1977.

Greshake, Gisbert. Priestersein (To be a priest). 5th ed. Freiburg, 1991.

Greule, Albrecht. "Frauengottesdienste, feministische Liturgien und integrative Sprache" [Women's religious services, feminist liturgies, and integrative language]. In Berger and Gerhards (1990), 621–34.

Grochtmann, Harald. *Unerklärliche Ereignisse, überprüfte Wunder und juristische Tatsachenfestellung* [Inexplicable happenings, researched miracles, and juristic establishment of facts]. Langen, 1989.

Gutting, Ernst. *Offensive gegen den Patriarchalismus. Für eine menschlichere Welt* [Offensive against patriarchalism: For a more human world]. 4th ed. Freiburg, 1988. (*Offensive*)

———. "Kinder, Küche, Kirche?—Und was dann?" [Children, cooking, Church—and what then?], *Neue Stadt* 30 (10/1987): 4–7.

Haber, Barbara. *Women in America. A Guide to Books, 1963–1975.* Boston, 1978.

Habermann, Ruth, and Dorothee Sölle. "Phantasie" [Imagination]. In Wb, 326f.

Habermas, Jürgen. *Erkenntnis und Interesse* [Knowledge and interest]. 3d ed. Frankfurt, 1975.

Halkes, Catharina. "Eine 'andere' Maria" [A "different" Mary]. *Una sancta* 32 (1977): 323–37.

———. "Feministische Theologie. Eine Zwischenbilanz" [Feminist theology: An interim assessment]. *Concilium* 16 (1980): 293–300. ("Zwischenbilanz")

———. "Motive für den Protest in der feministischen Theologie gegen Gott den Vater" [Motives for the protest in feminist theology against God the Father]. *Concilium* 17 (1981): 256–62. ("Protest")

——. *Gott hat nicht nur starke Söhne. Grundzüge einer feministischen Theologie* [God has not only strong sons: Basic elements of a feminist theology]. 4th ed. Gütersloh, 1985. (*Söhne*)

——. *Suchen, was verlorenging. Beiträge zur feministischen Theologie* [Seeking what was lost: Contributions to feminist theology]. Gütersloh, 1985. (*Suchen*)

——. "Frau und Mann als Ebenbild Gottes. Aus der Sicht der feministischen Theologie" [Woman and man as God's likeness: From the viewpoint of feminist theology]. In *Frau — Partnerin in der Kirche. Perspektiven einer zeitgemäßen Frauen-Seelsorge,* edited by H. Erharter and R. Schwarzenberg, 89–105. Vienna, 1985. ("Ebenbild Gottes")

——. "Maria, die Frau. Mariologie und Feminismus" [Mary, the woman: Mariology and feminism]. In Schöpsdau (1985), 42–70. ("Mariologie und Feminismus")

——. "Theologie, feministische". In FLex, 1100–10. ("Theologie, feministische")

——. "Maria — inspirierendes oder abschreckendes Vorbild für Frauen?" [Mary — an inspiring or intimidating model for women?]. In Moltmann-Wendel, Küng, and Moltmann (1988), 113–30.

——. *Das Antlitz der Erde erneuern: Mensch — Kultur — Schöpfung* [Renewing the face of the earth: Man — culture — creation]. Gütersloh, 1990. (*Antlitz*)

——. "Frau/Mann. B. Aus feministisch-theologischer Sicht" [Woman/man. B. From a feminist-theological viewpoint]. In *Neues Handbuch Theologischer Grundbegriffe* 2, edited by Peter Eicher, 59–65. 2d ed. Munich, 1991. ("Frau/Mann")

——. "Maria/Mariologie. B. Aus der Sicht feministischer Theologie" [Mary/Mariology. B. From the viewpoint of feminist theology]. In *Neues Handbuch Theologischer Grundbegriffe* 3, edited by Peter Eicher, 315-23. 2d ed. Munich, 1991. ("Maria/Mariologie")

——. "Maria" [Mary]. In Wb, 268-75.

Halkes, Catharina, and Hedwig Meyer-Wilmes. "Feministische Theologie/Feminismus/Frauenbewegung. I. Im westlichen Kontext" [Feminist theology/feminism/women's movement. I. In the Western context]. In Wb, 102-5.

Hamerton Kelly, Robert G. "Gott als Vater in der Bibel und in der Erfahrung Jesu. Eine Bestandsaufnahme" [God as Father in the Bible and in the experience of Jesus: A summary review]. *Concilium* 17 (1981): 247-56.

Haneke, B., and K. Huttner, eds. *Spirituelle Aufbrüche: New Age und "Neue Religiosität" als Herausforderung an Kirche und Gesellschaft* [Spiritual departures: New Age and "New Religiosity" as challenge to Church and society]. Regensburg, 1991.

Hauch, Regine. "Neue Nonnen. Es gärt in Amerikas Frauenorden" [New nuns: It is seething in America's convents]. *Die neue Ordnung* 41 (1987): 374-81.

Hauke, Manfred. *Women in the Priesthood? A Systematic Analysis in the Light of the Order of Creation and Redemption.* San Francisco, 1988. German ed.: *Die Problematik um das Frauenpriestertum vor dem Hintergrund der Schöpfungs- und Erlösungsordnung.* 3d ed. Paderborn, 1991.

——. "Das Weihesakrament für Frauen—eine Forderung der Zeit?" [Ordination of women—a demand of our times?]. FKTh 3 (1987): 119-34. ("Weihesakrament")

——. "Überlegungen zum Weihediakonat der Frau" [Reflections on ordaining women as deacons]. *ThGl* 77 (1987): 108-27.

——. "Gott als Androgyn—Zum Gottesbild der Feministischen Theologie" [God as androgyne: On the image of God in feminist theology]. *Kath. Bildung* 89 (1988): 65-75.

——. "Zielbild: Androgyn. Anliegen und Hintergründe feministischer Theologie" [Ideal goal: Androgyne. The concern and background of feminist theology]. FKTh 5 (1989): 1-24.

——. "Die Auflösung der Ganzheit. Zum Menschenbild der Feministischen Theologie" [The dissolution of wholeness: On the image of man in feminist theology]. *Kath. Bildung* 90 (1989): 392-403.

——. "Frau" [Woman]. ML 2 (1989): 520-24.

——. " 'Mutter unsere', 'Heilige Geistin' und 'Jesa Christa'. Bemerkungen zum feministischen Gottes- und Christusbild" ["Our Mother", "Holy Spiritess", and "Jesa Christa": Observations on the feminist images of God and Christ]. FKTh 6 (1990): 22-37.

——. Review of Ahl. *Kath. Bildung* 91 (1990): 382f.

——. Review of Meyer-Wilmes (1990). *Kath. Bildung* 91 (1990): 381f.

——. "Maria als Vorbild der Jungfrauen" [Mary as a model for virgins]. ML 3 (1991): 484-87.

——. "Feministische Theologie—Hilfe zum Glauben?" [Feminist theology—an aid to faith?]. *Der Dom,* no. 32 (August 9, 1992): 18.

——. " 'Die Kirche is doch echt frauenfeindlich!' Emanzipation und kirchliches Frauenbild" ["But the Church is genuinely hostile to women!" Emancipation and the Church's image of woman]. In *Plädoyer für die Kirche,* edited by Michael Müller, 199–215. 4th ed. Aachen, 1992. ("Frauenbild")

——. "Für ein neues Selbstbewußtsein der katholischen Frau" [For a new self-confidence in the Catholic woman]. *Deutsche Tagespost,* June 15, 1993, 5f.

——. "Die Diskussion um die weibliche Symbolik in der Pneumatologie" [The debate about feminine symbolism in pneumatology]. In *Der dreifaltige Gott und das Leben der Christen,* edited by Johannes Stöhr, 130–50. St. Ottilien, 1993. ("Pneumatologie")

——. *Heilsverlust in Adam. Stationen griechischer Erbsündenlehre: Irenäus—Origenes—Kappadozier* [The loss of salvation in Adam: Stages in the Greek doctrine of original sin: Irenaeus—Origen—the Cappadocians]. Paderborn, 1993. (*Heilsverlust*)

Hauschildt, Ingeborg. "Feministische Theologie. Eine fragwürdige neue Welle" [Feminist theology: A questionable new trend]. *idea-Dokumentation,* no. 40. Wetzlar, 1981.

——. " 'Feministische Theologie'—eine neue Irrlehre" [Feminist theology—a new heresy]. In *Informationsbrief No. 94 der Bekenntnisbewegung "Kein anderes Evangelium" (Gal 1:6),* 5–13. Lüdenscheid, 1982.

——. "Die Verunsicherung der Gemeinden durch die Feministische Theologie" [The creation of uncertainty in the churches by feminist theology]. In Beyerhaus (1983), 11–22. ("Feministische Theologie")

——. *Gott eine Frau? Weg und Irrweg der feministischen Theologie* [God a woman? The direction and aberration of feminist theology]. Wuppertal, 1983. (*Gott eine Frau*)

——. *Die feministische Versuchung und die Antwort der*

christlichen Frau [The feminist temptation and the response of the Christian woman]. Wuppertal and Zurich, 1989.

——. "Feministische Theologie". ELTG 1 (1992): 604f.

Heine, Susanne. *Frauen der frühen Christenheit. Zur historischen Kritik einer feministischen Theologie* [Women of early Christianity: Toward a historical critique of feminist theology]. Göttingen, 1986. (*Frauen*)

——. *Wiederbelebung der Göttinnen? Zur systematischen Kritik einer feministischen Theologie* [Revival of the goddesses? Toward a systematic critique of feminist theology]. Göttingen, 1987. (*Göttinnen*)

——. "Feministische Theologie—Zur Unterscheidung der Geister" [Feminist theology—toward a differentiation of positions]. In Gordan (1989), 155–84.

——. "Maria, die Mutter Jesu, in der feministischen Theologie" [Mary, the Mother of Jesus, in feminist theology]. In *Maria, die Mutter unseres Herrn. Eine evangelische Handreichung,* edited by Manfred Kießig, 121–35. Lahr, 1991.

——. "Feministische Theologie—Theologischer Feminismus. Über die Bedeuting des Austauschs der Adjektiva" [Feminine theology—theological feminism: On the significance of the exchange of adjectives]. In *Mann und Frau—Frau und Mann. Hintergründe, Ursachen und Problematik der Geschlechterrotten* [Man and woman—woman and man: Background, motives, and problems of gender-based roles], edited by Winfried Böhm and Martin Lindauer, 171–86. Stuttgart, 1992.

Heinzelmann, Gertrud. *Die geheiligte Diskriminierung. Beiträge zum kirchlichen Feminismus* [Sanctified discrimination: Contributions to Church-oriented feminism]. Bonstetten, 1986.

Hermisson, H.-J. "Der Rückschritt oder: Wie Jahwe mit Astarte versöhnt werden soll" [The regress, or how Yahweh is to be reconciled with Astarte]. EvTh 42 (1982): 290–94. ("Rückschritt")

———. "Zur 'feministischen' Exegese des Alten Testaments" [On the "feminist" exegesis of the Old Testament]. Theol. Beiträge 22 (1991): 120–26.

Herzig, Anneliese. "Maria—hoffnungslos entferntes Ideal oder Schwester im Glauben?" [Mary—a hopelessly distant ideal or a sister in faith?]. Ordenskorrespondenz 33 (1992): 65–76.

Heyward, Carter. Und sie rührte sein Kleid an. Eine feministische Theologie der Beziehung [And she touched his robe: A feminist theology of relationship]. With an introduction by Dorothee Sölle. Stuttgart, 1986.

Hoffmann, Gottfried. Der Ökumenismus heute. Geschichte—Kritik—Wegweisung [Ecumenism today: History—criticism—future directions]. Stein am Rhein, 1978.

Hojenski, Christine, et al., eds. Meine Seele sieht das Land der Freiheit. Feministische Liturgien—Modelle für die Praxis [My soul sees the land of freedom: Feminist liturgies—practical models]. Münster, 1990.

Hopkins, Julie. "Sind Christologie und Feminismus unvereinbar?" [Are Christology and feminism incompatible?]. In Strahm and Strobel (1991), 194–207.

Hörmann, Karl. "Sünde" [Sin], in Lexikon der christlichen Moral [Lexicon of Christian morality], edited by K. Hörmann, 1529–47. Innsbruck, 1976.

Huntemann, Georg. Die Zerstörung der Person—Umsturz der Werte—Gotteshaß der Vaterlosen—Feminismus

[Destruction of the person—overthrow of values—hatred of God by the fatherless—feminism]. Bad Liebenzell, 1981.

Jacobi, Jolande. *Die Psychologie von C. G. Jung. Eine Einführung in das Gesamtwerk* [The psychology of C. G. Jung: An introduction to his work as a whole]. 4th ed. Zurich, 1959.

Janssen-Jurreit, Marielouise. *Sexismus. Über die Abtreibung der Frauenfrage* [Sexism: On the miscarriage of the women's question]. 2d ed. Munich and Vienna, 1977.

[Jepsen, Maria.] *". . . Das Weib rede in der Gemeinde." Maria Jepsen: Erste lutherische Bischöfin. Dokumente und Stellungnahmen* [". . . Women should speak in the churches." Maria Jepsen: The first Lutheran bishop. Documents and critical standpoints]. Gütersloh, 1992.

Jeremias, Joachim. *Abba. Studien zur neutestamentlichen Theologie und Zeitgeschichte* [Abba: Studies in New Testament theology and cultural history]. Göttingen, 1966.

John Paul II. *Apostolic Letter Mulieris dignitatem concerning the Dignity and Calling of Woman on the Occasion of the Marian Year.* Boston, 1988.

Johnson, E. A. "Mary and the Female Face of God". *Theological Studies* 50 (1989): 500–526.

——. "Jesus der Mann" [Jesus the man]. *Concilium* 27 (1991): 521–26.

Johnston, Francis. *So hat Er keinem Volk getan. Das Wunder von Guadalupe* [He has done nothing like this for any people. The miracle of Guadalupe]. Stein am Rhein, 1986.

Jonas, Hans. *Gnosis und spätantiker Geist 1* [Gnosticism

and the spirit of late antiquity 1]. In FRLANT 51. 2d ed. Göttingen, 1957.

Kall, Alfred. *Katholische Frauenbewegung in Deutschland. Eine Untersuchung zur Gründung katholischer Frauenvereine im 19. Jahrhundert* [The Catholic women's movement in Germany: A study of the founding of Catholic women's groups in the 19th century]. Paderborn, 1983.

Kassel, Maria, ed. *Feministische Theologie.* Stuttgart, 1988.

——. "Tod und Auferstehung" [Death and resurrection]. In her *Feministische Theologie,* 191-226.

——. "Maria—Urbild des Weiblichen im Christentum?" [Mary—a prototype of the feminine in Christianity?]. In Moltmann-Wendel, Küng, and Moltmann (1988), 142-60.

Katappo, Marianne. *mitleiden—mithandeln. Theologie einer asiatischen Frau* [Suffering with—acting with: Theology of an Asian woman]. Erlangen, 1981.

Keintzel, Raimar. *C. G. Jung: Retter der Religion? Auseinandersetzung mit Werk und Wirkung* [C. G. Jung: Savior of religion? An analysis of his work and influence]. Mainz and Stuttgart, 1991.

Kimel, A. F. "The Holy Trinity Meets Ashtoreth: A Critique of the Episcopal 'Inclusive' Liturgies". *Anglican Theological Review* 71 (1989): 25-47.

King, Ursula. "Feminismus". In *Evangelisches Kirchenlexikon* 1, 1280-89. 3d ed. Göttingen, 1986.

——. "Frauen in Weltreligionen I. Hinduismus" [Women in world religions I. Hinduism]. In Wb, 111-14.

Kleinau, Elke. *Die freie Frau. Soziale Utopien des frühen 19. Jahrhunderts* [The free women: Social utopias in the early 19th century]. Düsseldorf, 1987.

Kleindienst, Eugen. *Partnerschaft als Prinzip der the pastoral* [Partnership as the principle of the pastoral letter on marriage]. Würzburg, 1982.

Knie, Ute. "Der Einfluß auf das Verständnis vom Pfarramt" [The influence of women pastors on the understanding of ministry]. In *Aufbruch der Frauen. Herausforderungen und Perspektiven feministischer Theologie* [The journey of women: Challenges and perspectives of feminist theology], edited by Birgit Janetzky, 177–83. Münster, 1989.

Knoch, Otto B. " 'Nennt uns nicht Brüder! Überlegungen zu einer 'Entmännlichung' liturgischer Texte" ["Don't call us brethren!" Reflections on a "demasculinizing" of liturgical texts]. *Klerusblatt* 67 (1987): 134f.

Knußmann, Rainer. *Der Mann—ein Fehlgriff der Natur* [The male—a blunder of nature]. Hamburg, 1984.

Kocher, Richard. *Herausgeforderter Vorsehungsglaube. Die Lehre von der Vorsehung im Horizont der gegenwärtigen Theologie* [Challenged faith in providence: The doctrine of providence in the context of present-day theology]. St. Ottilien, 1993.

Koepcke, Cordula. *Geschichte der deutschen Frauenbewegung. Von den Anfängen bis 1945* [History of the German women's movement: From the beginnings to 1945]. Freiburg, 1981.

———. "Frauenbewegung" [Women's movement]. In FLex, 322–30.

König, René. *Die Familie der Gegenwart. Ein interkultureller Vergleich* [The family today: An inter-cultural comparison]. 3d ed. Munich, 1978.

Köpf, Ulrich. "Bemerkungen zur feministischen Auffassung der Kirchengeschichte" [Remarks on the feminist view of the history of the Church]. *Theol. Beiträge* 22 (1991): 139–41.

Koslowski, Peter. "Hegel—der Philosoph der Trinität? Zur Kontroverse um seine Trinitätslehre" [Hegel—the philosopher of the Trinity? On the controversy surrounding his doctrine of the Trinity]. *Theol. Quartalschrift* 162 (1982): 105–31.

Köster, Heinrich. *Urstand, Fall und Erbsünde. Von der Reformation bis zur Gegenwart* [Primal state, fall, and original sin: From the Reformation to the present]. HDG II, 3c. Freiburg, 1982.

Krattiger, Ursa. *Die perlmutterne Mönchin. Reise in eine weibliche Spiritualität* [The mother-of-pearl female monk: Journey to a feminine spirituality]. Hamburg, 1987 (orig. Zurich, 1983).

Krebsbach-Gnath, Camilla. "Diskriminierung" [Discrimination]. In FLex, 160–63.

Kreuzer, Siegfried. "Gott als Mutter in Hosea 11?" [God as mother in Hosea 11?]. *Theol. Quartalschrift* 169 (1989): 123–32.

Krobath, Evi. "Sünde/Schuld III. Feministisch-theologische Diskussion" [Sin/guilt III. Feminist-theological debate]. In Wb, 387–90.

Krüger, Hanfried. "Werden und Wachsen des Ökumenischen Rates der Kirchen" [Development and growth of the Ecumenical Council of Churches]. In *Handbuch der Ökumenik,* edited by H. J. Urban and H. Wagner, 2:53–63. Paderborn, 1986.

Kuhn, Annette. "Frauengeschichte" [History of women]. In FLex, 338–46.

Lanczkowski, Günter, et al. "Makrokosmos/Mikrokosmos" [Macrocosm/microcosm]. TRE 21 (1991): 745–54.

Laurentin, René. "Marie dans la perspective du féminisme américain" [Mary in the perspective of American feminism]. *Études mariales* 44/45 (1989): 81–111.

Le Fort, Gertrud von. *Die ewige Frau* [Eternal woman]. 1934. Munich, 1963.

Lehmann, Karl. "Das Bild der Frau. Versuch einer anthropologisch-theologischen Standortbestimmung" [The image of woman: An attempt at anthropologico-theological assessment of the current situation]. *Herder Korrespondenz* 41 (1987): 479–87.

——. "Mann und Frau als Problem der theologischen Anthropologie" [Man and woman as a problem of theological anthropology]. In Schneider (1989), 53–72.

Lersch, Philipp. *Vom Wesen der Geschlechter* [On the nature of the sexes]. 4th ed. Munich and Basel, 1968.

Lewis, C. S. *Undeceptions. Essays on Theology and Ethics.* London, 1971.

——. *The Screwtape Letters.* New York, 1946.

Lissner, Anneliese. *Erneuert euch in eurem Denken. Eine Auswahl von Referaten, Ansprachen, geistlichen Worten* [Renew yourselves in your thinking: A selection of scholarly papers, addresses, spiritual sayings]. 143–95. Düsseldorf, 1989.

——. *Seid nicht so geduldig! Warum der Kirche widersprochen werden muß* [Don't be so patient! Why the Church must be contradicted]. Zurich, 1993.

Little, J. A. "Sexual Equality in the Church: A Theological Resolution to the Anthropological Dilemma". *The Heythrop Journal* 28 (1987): 165–78.

——. "Mary and Feminist Theology". *Thought* 62 (1987): 343–57.

Lorenzer, Alfred. *Das Konzil der Buchhalter. Die Zerstörung der Sinnlichkeit, eine Religionskritik* [The council of book-keepers. The destruction of sensuality: A critique of religion]. Frankfurt, 1981.

Lucchetti Bingemer, Maria Clara. "Frau: Zeitlichkeit und Ewigkeit. Das ewige Weib und das weibliche Antlitz Gottes" [Woman: Temporality and eternity. Eternal woman and the feminine face of God]. *Concilium* 27 (1991): 514–20.

Lueg, Claudia. " 'Vater unser'—ein Gott für Frauen?" ["Our Father"—a God for women?]. *Katechetische Blätter* 112 (1987): 588–96.

Luyten, N. A., ed. *Wesen und Sinn der Geschlechtlichkeit* [Essence and meaning of sexuality]. Grenzfragen 13. Freiburg and Munich, 1985.

Maas-Ewerd, Theodor. "Frauen sprachlich nicht ausgrenzen. Zu einer Empfehlung der Liturgiekommission der Diözese Aachen" [No linguistic exclusion of women: Comments on a recommendation by the liturgical commission of the diocese of Aachen]. *Klerusblatt* 72 (1992): 233f.

Maassen, Monika. "Macht/Bemächtigung" [Power/empowerment]. In Wb, 262–65.

Macca, Valentino. "Sorella". *Nuovo dizionario di Mariologia,* edited by Stefano de Fiores and Salvatore Meo, 1323–27. 2d ed. Milan, 1986.

Maeckelberghe, Els. *Desperately Seeking Mary: A Feminist Appropriation of a Traditional Religious Symbol.* Kampen (Netherlands), 1991.

Marcus, Wolfgang. *Der Subordinationismus als historiologisches Problem* [Subordinationism as a historiological problem]. Munich, 1963.

——. "Subordinationismus" [Subordinationism]. LThK, 2d series, 9 (1964): 1138f.

Marcuse, Herbert. "Marxismus und Feminismus". In *Jahrbuch Politik* 6 (Berlin 1974): 86–95.

Marrs, Wanda. *New Age Lies to Women*. Austin, Tex., 1989.

Marti, Kurt. *Zärtlichkeit und Schmerz* [Tenderness and pain]. 4th ed. Neuwied, 1980.

Marx, Karl. "Thesen über Feuerbach" [Theses on Feuerbach]. In his *Frühe Schriften* 2. Stuttgart, 1971.

May, W. E. "Marriage and the Complementarity of Male and Female". *Anthropotes* 8 (1992): 41–60.

Menschik, Jutta. *Feminismus. Geschichte, Theorie, Praxis* [Feminism: History, theory, practice]. Cologne, 1977.

Mertin, Andreas. "Der Griff zur Freiheit. Die 'andere Eva' im Blick der Kunst" [Reaching for freedom: The "other Eve" in the view of art]. *forum religion,* no. 3 (1987): 13–26.

Metz-Göckel, Sigrid. "Sexismus" [Sexism]. In FLex, 989–93.

Meves, Christa. "Verführerisch erklingt das alte Lied der Schlange" [The serpent's old song makes itself temptingly heard]. *Deutsche Tagespost,* August 14, 1987, 3.

——. *Ein neues Vaterbild. Zwei Frauen unserer Zeit entdecken Josef von Nazaret* [A new father-image: Two women of our time discover Joseph of Nazareth]. Stein am Rhein, 1989.

——. "Gemeinsam am Reich Gottes wirken. Warum es in der Kirche unterschiedliche Dienst von Frauen und Männern gibt" [Working together for God's Kingdom: Why there are differing roles for women and men in the Church]. *Deutsche Tagespost,* April 9, 1991, 5.

——. "Die Krise der Katholischen Kirche in Deutschland"
[The crisis in the Catholic Church in Germany].
Theologisches 22 (3/1992): 106–14.

——. "Feministische Theologie ante portas" [Feminist theology ante portas]. *Theologisches* 22 (9/1992): 370f.

Meyer-Abich, K. M. *Wege zum Frieden mit der Natur.
Praktische Naturphilosophie für die Umweltpolitik*
[Ways toward peace with nature: A practical philosophy of nature for politics of the environment]. Munich,
1984.

Meyer-Wilmes, Hedwig. *Rebellion auf der Grenze. Ortsbestimmung feministischer Theologie* [Rebellion on the
borders: The present situation in feminist theology].
Freiburg, 1990.

Millett, Kate. *Sexual Politics.* Garden City, N.Y., 1969.
German ed.: *Sexus und Herrschaft. Die Tyrannei des
Mannes in unserer Gesellschaft.* Munich, 1971.

Moir, Anne, and David Jessel. *Brainsex.* Düsseldorf, 1990.

Moll, Helmut. " 'Feministische Theologie'—eine Herausforderung" ["Feminist theology"—a challenge]. MThZ
34 (1983): 118–28.

Mollenkott, Virginia. *Gott eine Frau? Vergessene Gottesbilder der Bibel* [God a woman? Forgotten images of
God in the Bible]. Munich, 1985.

Moltmann, Jürgen. *Trinität und Reich Gottes* [Trinity and
Kingdom of God]. Munich, 1980.

——. "Der mütterliche Vater. Überwindet trinitarischer
Patripassianismus den theologischen Patriarchalismus?" [The motherly Father: Does trinitarian patripassianism overcome theological patriarchalism?].
Concilium 17 (1981): 209–13. ("Vater")

——. "Die Gemeinschaft des heiligen Geistes. Zur trinitarischen Pneumatologie" [The community of the Holy Spirit: On trinitarian pneumatology]. ThLZ 107 (1982): 705–15. ("Gemeinschaft")

———. *Gott in der Schöpfung* [God in creation]. Munich, 1985. (*Gott*)

———. *Der Geist des Lebens* [The spirit of life]. Munich, 1991.

———. "Theologie in den Erfahrungen des gelebten Lebens" [Theology in the experiences of lived life]. In Pissarek-Hudelist and Schottroff (1991), 151–61.

Moltmann-Wendel, Elisabeth. "Sexismus in den siebziger Jahren. Ökumenischer Frauenkongreß in Berlin" [Sexism in the seventies: The Ecumenical Women's Congress in Berlin]. EK 7 (1974): 484f.

———, ed. *Frauenbefreiung. Biblische und theologische Argumente* [Women's liberation: Biblical and theological arguments]. 2d ed. Munich and Mainz, 1978.

———. "Ein ganzer Mensch werden. Reflexionen zu einer feministischen Theologie" [Becoming a whole person: Thoughts for a feminist theology]. EK 12 (1979): 340–42, 347.

——— et al., eds. *Feministische Theologie—Praxis. Ein Werkstattbuch* [Feminist theology—practice: A workshop book]. Arbeitshilfen 3. Bad Boll, 1981. (*Werkstattbuch*)

———, ed. *Frau und Religion: Gotteserfahrungen im Patriarchat* [Woman and religion: Experiences of God in the patriarchy]. Frankfurt, 1983. (*Frau und Religion*).

———. *Ein eigener Mensch werden. Frauen um Jesus* [Becoming one's own person: Women around Jesus]. 4th ed. Gütersloh, 1984. (*Eigener Mensch*)

——— et al., eds. *Seid fruchtbar und wehrt Euch. Frauentexte zum Kirchentag* [Be fruitful and defend yourselves: Women's texts for Church congresses]. Munich, 1986. (*Frauentexte*)

——. *Das Land, wo Milch und Honig fließt. Perspektiven einer feministischen Theologie* [The land flowing with milk and honey: Prospects for a feminist theology]. 2d ed. Gütersloh, 1987. (*Milch*)

——. "Werkstatt ohne Angst. Zur 'Feministischen Theologie' " [Workshop without fear: On "feminist theology"]. *forum religion* 3/1987, 34. ("Werkstatt")

——. "Maria oder Magdalena—Mutterschaft oder Freundschaft?" [Mary or Magdalen—motherhood or friendship?]. In Moltmann-Wendel, Küng, and Moltmann (1988): 51–59.

——. *Wenn Gott und körper sich begegnen. Feministische Perspectiven zur Zeiblichkeit* [When God and body meet: Feminist perspectives on corporeality]. 2d ed. Gütersloh, 1991.

——. "Ganzheit" [Wholeness]. In Wb, 136–42.

——. "Gegenseitigkeit II. Feministische Diskussion" [Reciprocity II. Feminist discussion]. In Wb, 144f. ("Gegenseitigkeit")

Moltmann-Wendel, Elisabeth, and Günter Kegel, eds. *Feministische Theologie im Kreuzfeuer. Der Streit um das "Tübinger Gutachten". Dokumente—Analysen—Kritiken* [Feminist theology under fire: The controversy over the "Tübingen Report". Documents—analyses—critiques]. Gütersloh, 1992.

Moltmann-Wendel, Elisabeth, Hans Küng, and Jürgen Moltmann, eds. *Was geht uns Maria an?* [What does Mary have to do with us?]. Gütersloh, 1988.

Moltmann-Wendel, Elisabeth, and Ina Praetorius. "Körper

der Frau/Leiblichkeit" [Woman's body/corporality]. In Wb, 219–24.

Montagu, Ashley. *The Natural Superiority of Women*. 2d ed. New York and London, 1968.

Mörsdorf, Josef. *Gestaltwandel des Frauenbildes und Frauenberufs in der Neuzeit* [Changes in women's image and women's work in modern times]. Munich, 1958.

Motschmann, Elisabeth. "Religiöse Selbstversorgerinnen. Die Feministische Theologie" [Religious self-providers: Feminist theology]. *Die neue Ordnung* 39 (1985): 289–96.

Motschmann, Jens. *So nicht, Herr Pfarrer! Was wird aus der evangelischen Kirche* [Not like that, Mr. Pastor! What is happening to the Protestant Church]. Berlin and Frankfurt, 1991.

Mulack, Christa. *Die Weiblichkeit Gottes. Matriarchale Voraussetzungen des Gottesbildes* [The womanliness of God: Matriarchal suppositions in the image of God]. Stuttgart, 1983. (*Weiblichkeit*)

——. "Maria und die Weiblichkeit Gottes—Ein Beitrag feministischer Theologie" [Mary and the womanliness of God—an essay in feministic theology]. In *Maria—eine ökumenische Herausforderung,* edited by Wolfgang Beinert et al., 143–70. Regensburg, 1984.

——. *Maria—die geheime Göttin im Christentum* [Mary—the secret goddess in Christianity]. Stuttgart, 1985. (*Göttin*)

——. *Jesus—der Gesalbte der Frauen. Weiblichkeit als Grundlage christlicher Ethik* [Jesus—anointed by women: Womanliness as the foundation of Christian ethics]. Stuttgart, 1987. (*Jesus*)

——. "Gnosis (Verdrängte christliche Erkenntnis)" [Gnosis

(suppressed Christian knowledge)]. In Kassel (1988), 227–56. ("Gnosis")

———. *Natürlich weiblich. Die Heimatlosigkeit der Frau im Patriarchat* [Naturally feminine: The homelessness of woman in the patriarchate]. Stuttgart, 1990. (*Natürlich weiblich*)

———. "Ritual/Magie" [Ritual/magic]. In Wb, 351–54.

Müller, G. L. "Gottesmutter" [Mother of God]. ML 2 (1989): 684–92.

Müller, H.-M. "Feministische Theologie und kirchliche Praxis" [Feminist theology and Church practice]. *Theol. Beiträge* 22 (1991): 146–49.

Müller, Iris. "Frauen in Weltreligionen. IV. Islam" [Women in world religions. IV. Islam]. In Wb, 121–26.

Müller, St. E. *Personal-soziale Entfaltung des Gewissens im Jugendalter. Eine moralanthropologische Studie* [The personal-social development of conscience in adolescence: A moral-anthropological study]. Mainz, 1984.

Nagl-Docekal, Herta. "Dualismus" [Dualism]. In Wb, 64–67.

Nebel, Richard, and Horst Rzepkowski. "Guadalupe". ML 3 (1991): 38–42.

Nellessen, Ernst. "Die Einsetzung von Presbytern durch Barnabas und Paulus (Apg 14,23)" [The appointment of presbyters by Barnabas and Paul (Acts 14:23)]. In *Begegnung mit dem Wort. FS H. Zimmermann,* edited by J. Zmijewski and E. Nellessen, 175–93. Bonn, 1980.

Neuer, Werner. *Mann und Frau in christlicher Sicht* [Man and woman from the Christian viewpoint]. 5th ed. Gießen, 1993.

———. "Frau (c) systematisch-theologisch" [Woman (c) systematic-theologically]. ELTG 1 (1992): 632–34.

Neumann, Erich. *Zur Psychologie des Weiblichen* [On the psychology of the feminine]. 2d ed. Munich, 1975.

Niggemeyer, Margarete. "Feministische Theologie—Hilfe zum Glauben und Leben" [Feminist theology—an aid to faith and life]. *Der Dom,* no. 24 (June 14, 1992): 5, 18.

Nikolajczyk, Paul. "Das Geschwistererleben im Lebensraum der Familie" [Experiencing brothers and sisters in the life-context of the family]. In *Erziehung und Seelsorge im Dienste des Menschen,* edited by Manfred Balkenohl and Hermann Wesseln, 181–97. Paderborn, 1991.

Noelle-Neumann, Elisabeth. *Die Schweigespirale* [The spiral of silence]. Frankfurt, 1982. English ed.: *The Spiral of Silence: Public Opinion, Our Social Skin.* 2d ed. Chicago, 1993.

Oddie, William. *What Will Happen to God? Feminism and the Reconstruction of Christian Belief.* London, 1984; San Francisco, 1988.

Oduyoye, Mercy. "Frauendekade 1988–1998" [Women's decade 1988–1998]. *Ökumenische Rundschau* 37 (1988): 257–70.

Oeing-Hanhoff, Ludger. "Hegels Trinitätslehre. Zur Aufgabe ihrer Kritik und Rezeption" [Hegel's doctrine of the Trinity: On the task of criticizing and appropriating it]. *Theologie und Philosophie* 52 (1977): 378–407.

Ott, Ludwig. *Das Weihesakrament* [Priestly ordination]. Handbuch der Dogmengeschichte, vol. 4, no. 5. Freiburg, 1969.

Padberg, Lutz von. *Feminismus—eine ideologische und theologische Herausforderung* [Feminism—an ideological and theological challenge]. Evangelium und Gesellschaft 5. Wuppertal, 1985.

———. *New Age und Feminismus* [New Age and Feminism]. Asslar, 1987.

———. "Feminismus" [Feminism]. ELTG 1 (1992): 602–4.

Pagels, Elaine. *Versuchung durch Erkenntnis. Die gnostischen Evangelien* [Temptation through knowledge: The Gnostic gospels]. Frankfurt, 1987 (orig.: New York, 1979).

Pahnke, Donate. *Ethik und Geschlecht. Menschenbild und Religion in Patriarchat und Feminismus* [Ethics and sex: Image of man and religion in patriarchy and feminism]. Marburg, 1991.

Pannenberg, Wolfhart. *Systematische Theologie* 1 [Systematic theology 1]. Göttingen, 1988.

Parvey, C. F., ed. *Die Gemeinschaft von Frauen und Männern in der Kirche* [The community of women and men in the Church]. Neukirchen and Vluyn, 1985.

Petersdorff, Egon von. *Dämonologie* 2 [Demonology 2]. 2d ed. Aschaffenburg, 1982.

Piepke, J. G. "Befreiungstheologie" [Liberation theology]. ML 1 (1988): 400f.

Piper, John, and Wayne Grudem, eds. *Recovering Biblical Manhood and Womanhood: A Response to Evangelical Feminism.* Wheaton, Ill., 1991.

Pissarek-Hudelist, Herlinde. "Feministische Theologie—eine Herausforderung?" [Feminist theology—a challenge?]. ZKTh 103 (1981): 289–308, 400–425.

———. "Feministische Theologie—eine Herausforderung an Kirche und Theologie?" [Feminist theology—a challenge for the Church and theology?]. In *Frauenbe-*

freiung und Kirche. Darstellung—Analyse—Doku-mentation [Women's liberation and the Church: Survey—analysis—documentation], edited by W. Beinert, 15–50. Regensburg, 1987.

——. "Maria—Schwester oder Mutter im Glauben?" [Mary —sister or mother in faith?]. In Gössmann and Bauer (1989), 146–67.

——. "Gott/Göttin I. Praktische Theologie" [God/goddess I. Practical theology]. In Wb, 158–63.

——. "Offenbarung" [Revelation]. In Wb, 307–10.

——. "Trinität" [Trinity]. In Wb, 421–28.

Pissarek-Hudelist, Herlinde, and Luise Schottroff, eds. *Mit allen Sinnen glauben: feministische Theologie unterwegs. FS E. Moltmann-Wendel* [Believing with all one's senses: Feminist theology under way. Essays in honor of E. Moltmann-Wendel]. Gütersloh, 1991.

Ploeg, J. P. M. van der. "Die theologische Fakultät der katholischen Universität Nijmegen" [The theological faculty of the Catholic University of Nijmegen]. *Theologisches* 22 (1992): 502–6.

Podles, L. J. "The Alienation of Men from Christianity". HPR 89 (1988): 56–63.

Pohlenz, Max. *Die Stoa* 1/2 [The Stoics 1/2]. 5th ed. Göttingen, 1978–1980.

Praetorius, Ina. "Androzentrismus" [Androcentrism]. In Wb, 14f.

——. "Autonomie/Emanzipation". In Wb, 36–38.

——. "Gen- und Reproduktionstechnologien" [Genetic and reproductive technologies]. In Wb, 151–53.

Praetorius, Ina, Luise Schottroff, and Helen Schüngel-

Straumann. "Schöpfung/Ökologie" [Creation/ecology]. In Wb, 354–60.

Prüller, Veronika. *Wir Frauen sind Kirche — worauf warten wir noch? Feministische Kirchenträume. Anregungen für das Leben in christlichen Gemeinden* [We women are the Church — what are we waiting for? Feminist dreams of the Church: Suggestions for life in Christian communions]. Freiburg, 1992.

Pusch, L. F. *Das Deutsche als Männersprache* [German as a men's language]. Frankfurt, 1984.

——. *Alle Menschen werden Schwestern. Feministische Sprachkritik* [All men will be sisters: Feminist critique of language]. Frankfurt, 1990. (*Schwestern*)

Quispel, Gilles. *Gnosis als Weltreligion* [Gnosticism as a world religion]. Zurich, 1951.

Rad, Gerhard von. *Theologie des Alten Testaments* 1 [Theology of the Old Testament 1]. 7th ed. Munich, 1978.

Rahner, Karl. "Maria und das christliche Bild der Frau" [Mary and the Christian image of woman]. In his *Schriften zur Theologie* 13:353–67. 1978.

Raming, Ida. *Frauenbewegung und Kirche. Bilanz eines 25jährigen Kampfes für Gleichberechtigung und Befreiung der Frau seit dem 2. Vatikanischen Konzil* [The women's movement and the Church. Assessing the 25-year struggle for equal rights and the liberation of women since the Second Vatican Council]. Weinheim, 1989.

Ramshaw-Smith, Gail. "Lutheran Liturgical Prayer and God as Mother". *Worship* 52 (1978): 517–42.

Ratzinger, Joseph. *The Ratzinger Report.* San Francisco, 1985. (*Report*)

——. "Die Frau, Hüterin des Menschen. Versuch einer

Hinführung zum Apostolischen Screiben 'Mulieris Dignitatem' " [Woman: The protector of man: Attempt at an introduction to the apostolic letter *Mulieris dignitatem*]. In *Die Zeit der Frau* [The era of woman]: *Apostolisches Schreiben "Mulieris dignitatem"* of Pope John Paul II, 109–20. Freiburg, 1988.

Rauscher, Anton. *Kirche in der Welt. Beiträge zur christlichen Gesellschafts verantwortung* 1/2 [Church in the world: Essays on Christian social responsibility 1/2]. Würzburg, 1988.

Reichle, Erika. *Die Theologin in Würtemberg. Geschichte—Bild—Wirklichkeit eines neuen Frauenberufes* [The female theologian in Würtemberg: History—image—reality of a new calling for women]. Bern and Frankfurt, 1975.

——. "Reformation". In FLex, 927–34.

Riedel, Ingrid. "Leben/Tod" [Life/death]. In Wb, 237–41.

Riedel-Spangenberger, Ilona. "Christentum" [Christianity]. In FLex, 141–51.

Rieger, Renate. "Befreiungstheologie" [Liberation theology]. In Wb, 39–44.

Rieplhuber, Rita. "Islam". In FLex, 515–24.

Rinser, Luise. "Ich möchte den weiblichen Geist einbringen" [I would like to bring in the feminine spirit]. In Sommer (1985), 32–39.

Rogalla von Bieberstein, Johannes. "Frauen-Quotierung als feministisch-soziale Politik" [Quotas for women as feminist-social politics]. *Criticón* 118 (March/April 1990): 81–84.

Röper, Anita. *Ist Gott ein Mann? Ein Gespräch mit Karl Rahner* [Is God a man? A conversation with Karl Rahner]. Düsseldorf, 1979.

Rösler, Augustin. *Die Frauenfrage vom Standpunkt der Natur, der Geschichte und der Offenbarung* [The women's question from the standpoint of nature, history, and revelation]. 2d ed. Freiburg, 1907.

Roy, Louis. "Inclusive Language Regarding God". *Worship* 65 (1991): 207–15.

Rudolph, Kurt. *Die Gnosis* [Gnosticism]. 3d ed., Göttingen, 1990.

Ruether, Rosemary Radford. *New Woman—New Earth: Sexist Ideologies and Human Liberation.* New York, 1975. (*New Woman*)

———. *Mary—The Feminine Face of the Church.* Philadelphia, 1978. (*Mary*)

———. *Disputed Questions: On Being a Christian.* Abingdon, 1982.

———. *Sexism and God-talk: Toward a Feminist Theology.* Boston, 1983, 1993. German ed.: *Sexismus und die Rede von Gott. Schritte zu einer anderen Theologie.* Gütersloh, 1985.

———. *Women-Church: Theology and Practice of Feminist Liturgical Communities.* San Francisco, 1985. (*Women-Church*)

———. "Frauenkirche. Neuentstehende feministische liturgische Gemeinschaften" [Women-church: Recently arising feminist liturgical associations]. *Concilium* 22 (1986): 275–80. ("Frauenkirche")

———. "Weibliche Symbole und ihr gesellschaftlicher Kontext" [Feminine symbols and their social context]. *Reformatio* 36 (1987): 178–86. ("Symbole")

Ruppert, H.-J. *New Age. Endzeit oder Wendezeit?* [New Age: Concluding phase or transitional period?]. Wiesbaden, 1985. (*New Age*)

———. *Die Hexen kommen: Magie und Hexenglauben heute* [The witches are coming: Magic and belief in witches today]. Wiesbaden, 1987. (*Hexen*)

Rupprecht, Friederike. "Frauen im Pfarramt" [Women in ministry]. *Theologia practica* 22 (1987): 113–21.

Salomon-Delatour, Gottfried, ed. *Die Lehre Saint-Simons* [The teaching of Saint-Simon]. Neuwied, 1962.

Sartre, Jean-Paul. *Ist der Existentialismus ein Humanismus?* [Is existentialism a humanism?]. Zurich, 1947.

———. *Das Sein und das Nichts* [Being and nothingness]. Hamburg, 1962.

Schaumberger, Christine. "Erfahrung" [Experience]. In Wb, 73–78.

Schaumberger, Christine, and Monika Maassen, eds. *Handbuch Feministische Theologie* [Handbook of feminist theology]. Münster, 1986.

Schaup, Susanne. *Wandel des Weiblichen. Der Aufbruch der Frau ins New Age* [Evolving of the feminine: Women's journey into the New Age]. Freiburg, 1988.

Scheffczyk, Leo. *Gott-loser Gottesglaube?* [God-less belief in God?]. Regensburg, 1974.

———. *Neue Impulse zur Marienverehrung* [New stimuli to veneration of Mary]. St. Ottilien, 1974.

———. *Einführung in die Schöpfungslehre* [Introduction to the doctrine of creation]. 3d ed. Darmstadt, 1987.

———. *Aspekte der Kirche in der krise. Um die Entscheidung für das authentische Konzil* [Aspects of the Church in crisis: About the decision for the authentic Council]. Sieburg, 1993.

Schenk, Herrad. *Die feministische Herausforderung. 150 Jahre Frauenbewegung in Deutschland* [The feminist challenge: 150th anniversary of the women's movement in Germany]. 3d ed. Munich, 1983.

Scherzberg, Lucia. *Sünde und Gnade in der Feministischen Theologie* [Sin and mercy in feminist theology]. Mainz, 1991.

Schillebeeckx, Edward. *Christus und die Christen. Die Geschichte einer neuen Lebenspraxis* [Christ and Christians: The history of a new life experience]. Freiburg, 1977.

Schilling, Hans. "Frauen im Kirchen- und Gemeindedienst: Hilfskräfte oder Partnerinnen der Männer?" [Women in church and community service: Auxiliary workers or partners of the men?]. MThZ 39 (1988): 93–107.

Schirmer, Eva. *Eva—Maria. Rollenbilder von Männern für Frauen* [Eve—Mary: Role images by men for women]. Offenbach, 1988.

Schlichting, Wolfhart. *Maria. Die Mutter Jesu in Bibel, Tradition und Feminismus* [Mary: The Mother of Jesus in the Bible, tradition, and feminism]. Wuppertal and Zurich, 1989.

Schmetterer, Eva. *"Was ist die Frau, daß du ihrer gedenkst". Eine systematisch-dogmatische Untersuchung zum hermeneutischen Ansatz Feministischer Theologie* ["What is woman that you are mindful of her": A systematic-dogmatic inquiry into the hermeneutic approach of feminist theology]. Frankfurt, 1989. (*Frau*)

———. "Trägt Feministische Theologie zur Befreiung von Frauen bei? Einige kritische Gedanken zu fragwürdigen Tendenzen in der feministischen Theologie" [Does feminist theology contribute to the liberation of women? Some critical thoughts on questionable tendencies in feminist theology]. *Wissenschaft und Glaube* 2 (1989): 137–49.

Schmidhäuser, Ulrich. *Soll "Gott" nicht mehr "Herr" genannt werden? Zum gegenwärtigen Feminismus in Gesellschaft und Kirche* [Should "God" no longer be called "Lord"? On present-day feminism in society and the Church]. Stuttgart, 1991.

Schmoll, Heide. "Ist Gott-Vater für Frauen unerträglich? Feministische Theologie und christlicher Glaube" [Is God as Father unbearable to women? Feminist theology and Christian belief]. *FAZ,* March 12, 1992, 14.

Schneider, Oda. *Vom Priestertum der Frau* [On women in the priesthood]. Edited by D. J. Hilla. Abensberg, 1992 (orig. 1934).

——. *Die Macht der Frau* [The power of women]. Salzburg, 1938.

Schneider, Theodor, ed. *Mann und Frau—Grundproblem theologischer Anthropologie* [Man and woman—fundamental problem of theological anthropology]. QD 121. Freiburg, 1989.

Schneider-Böcklen, Elisabeth. *Feminismus.* EZW-Arbeitstexte 28. Stuttgart, 1990.

Schneider-Böcklen, Elisabeth, and Dorothea Vorländer. *Feminismus und Glaube* [Feminism and belief]. Mainz and Stuttgart, 1991.

Schoenthal, Gisela. "Geschlecht und Sprache" [Sex and language]. In Deutsche Akademie für Sprache und Dichtung, *Jahrbuch 1991,* 90–105. Darmstadt, 1992.

Schöpp-Schilling, H. B. "Women's Studies in den USA". In *Weiblichkeit oder Feminismus?,* edited by Claudia Opitz, 23–42. Weingarten, 1984.

——. "Frauenforschung" [Women's studies]. In FLex, 334–38.

Schöpsdau, Walter, ed. *Mariologie und Feminismus* [Mariology and feminism]. Göttingen, 1985.

Schormann, Gerhard. "Hexen" [Witches]. TRE 15 (1986): 297–304.

Schottroff, Luise. "Die Crux mit dem Kreuz. Feministische Kritik und Re-Vision der Kreuzestheologie" [The crux of the Cross: The feminist critique and re-vision of the theology of the Cross]. EK 25 (1992): 216–18.

———. "Gnosis". In Wb, 156–58.

———. "Kreuz I./II." [Cross I./II.]. In Wb, 226–31.

Schottroff, Luise, and Dorothee Sölle. "Auferstehung" [Resurrection]. In Wb, 34–36.

Schröder, Hannelore, ed. *Die Frau ist frei geboren. Texte zur Frauenemanzipation I: 1789–1870* [Woman is born free: Texts on the emancipation of women I: 1789–1870]. Munich, 1979.

Schroer, Silvia. "Der Geist, die Weisheit und die Taube . . . " [The Spirit, wisdom, and the dove . . .]. *Freiburger Zeitschrift für Philosophie und Theologie* 33 (1986): 197–225.

———. "Gott/Göttin III. Neues Testament" [God/goddess III. New Testament]. In Wb, 165–67.

Schuhmacher, Joseph. "Mariologische Verkündigung vor dem Hintergrund gegenwärtiger Zeitströmungen" [The mariological message in the context of present-day socio-cultural currents]. In *Maria in der Evangelisierung,* edited by Anton Ziegenaus, 9–31. Mariol. Studien 9. Regensburg, 1993.

Schulze, W. *Das androgyne Ideal und der christliche Glaube* [The androgynous ideal and the Christian faith]. Lahr-Dinglingen, 1940 (extract from a dissertation, Heidelberg, 1939).

Schüngel-Straumann, Helen. "Gottebenbildlichkeit I. In der biblischen Überlieferung" [Being in the likeness of God I. In biblical tradition]. In Wb, 173-77.

Schürmann, Heinrich. *Jesu ureigener Tod* [Jesus' uniquely own death]. Freiburg, 1974.

———. *Gottes Reich—Jesu Geschick* [God's Kingdom—Jesus' destiny]. Freiburg, 1983.

Schüssler Fiorenza, Elisabeth. "Die Rolle der Frau in der urchristlichen Bewegung" [The role of women in the original Christian movement]. *Concilium* 12 (1976): 3-9. ("Rolle")

———. "Für eine befreite und befreiende Theologie: Frauen in der Theologie und feministische Theologie in den USA" [For a liberated and liberating theology: Women in theology and feminist theology in the USA"]. *Concilium* 14 (1978): 287-94.

———. "Der Beitrag der Frau zur urchristlichen Bewegung. Kritische Überlegungen zur Rekonstruktion urchristlicher Geschichte" [The contribution of women to the original Christian movement: Critical thoughts on reconstructing original Christian history]. In *Traditionen der Befreiung, Bd 2. Frauen in der Bibel,* edited by W. Schottroff and W. Stegemann, 60-90. Munich, 1980.

———. *In Memory of Her: A Feminist Theological Reconstruction of Christian Origins.* New York, 1983.

———. "Für Frauen in Männerwelten. Eine kritische feministische Befreiungstheologie" [For women in men's worlds: A critical feminist theology of liberation]. *Concilium* 20 (1984): 31-38.

———. "Biblische Grundlegung" [Biblical foundations]. In Kassel (1988), 13-44. ("Grundlegung")

——. *Brott statt Steine. Die Herausforderung einer feministischen Interpretation der Bibel* [Bread instead of stones: The challenge of a feminist interpretation of the Bible]. 2d ed. Freiburg, Switzerland, 1991.

Schweizer, Eduard. "Soma...". *Theol. Wörterbuch zum NT* 7 (1964): 1024–91.

Seifert, Josef. "Zur Verteidigung der Würde der Frau. Feminismus und die Stellung der Frau in Kirche und Gesellschaft: Philosophische und Christliche Aspekte" [In defense of the dignity of women. Feminism and the position of women in Church and society: Philosophical and Christian aspects]. *Wissenschaft und Glaube* 2 (1989): 65–98.

Sexism in the 1970s: Discrimination against women: A Report of a World Council of Churches Consultation, West Berlin, 1974. Geneva, 1975.

Sichtermann, Barbara. *Wer ist wie? Über den Unterschied der Geschlechter* [Who is what? On the difference between the sexes]. Berlin, 1987.

Siebel, Wigand, ed. *Herrschaft und Liebe. Zur Soziologie der Familie* [Governance and love: On the sociology of the family]. Soziologische Schriften 40. Berlin, 1984.

Siegele-Wenschkewitz, Leonore, ed. *Verdrängte Vergangenheit, die uns bedrängt* [The repressed past that troubles us]. Munich, 1988.

——. "Antijudaismus" [Anti-judaism]. In Wb, 22–24.

Sill, Bernhard. *Androgynie und Geschlechtsdifferenz nach Franz von Baader. Eine anthropologisch-ethisch Studie* [Androgyny and sexual difference according to Franz von Baader: An anthropologico-ethical study]. Regensburg, 1986.

Simonis, Adrian J. "Einige beschouwingen rond de feministische theologie". *Communio* (Flemish) 11 (6/1986) 464–84.

———. "Maria und der Feminismus. Zur Wirkung der Gottesmutter in der Freiheitsgeschichte der Menschheit" [Mary and feminism: On the influence of the Mother of God in the history of human freedom], *L'Osservatore Romano* (German ed.) 17, no. 27 (July 3, 1987): 8.

Simpfendörfer, Karl. *Verlust der Liebe. Mit Simone de Beauvoir in die Abtreibungsgesellschaft* [Loss of love: Toward the abortion society with Simone de Beauvoir]. Stein am Rhein, 1990.

Solanas, Valerie. *Manifest der Gesellschaft zur Vernichtung der Männer* [Manifesto of the Society for Cutting Up Men (SCUM), 1968]. 5th ed. Berlin, 1982.

Söll, Georg. "Eva-Maria-Parallele" [Eve-Mary parallels]. ML 2 (1989): 420f.

Sölle, Dorothee. "Vater, Macht und Barberei. Feministische Anfragen an autoritäre Religion" [Father, power, and barbarism: Feminist questions for authoritarian religion]. *Concilium* 17 (1981): 223–27. ("Vater")

———. "Kreuz IV. Kreuz und Auferstehung" [The Cross IV. Cross and Resurrection]. In Wb, 233–36.

———. "Gegenseitigkeit I. Theologisch" [Reciprocity I. Theological]. In Wb, 142–45. ("Gegenseitigkeit")

Sommer, Norbert, ed. *Nennt uns nicht Brüder! Frauen in der Kirche durchbrechen das Schweigen* [Don't call us brethren! Women in the Church break the silence]. Stuttgart, 1985.

Sorge, Elga. *Religion und Frau. Weibliche Spiritualität im*

Christentum [Religion and woman: Feminine spirituality in Christianity]. 2d ed. Stuttgart, 1987.

Splett, Jörg. *Die Trinitätslehre G. W. F. Hegels* [G. W. F. Hegel's doctrine of the Trinity]. 3d ed. Freiburg, 1984.

Stapenhorst, Lucie. *Als Tochter der Göttin von Zwängen befreit* [As a daughter of the goddess, freed of constraints]. Olten, 1992.

Stein, Edith. "The Ethos of Women's Professions". (1930). In her *Essays on Woman,* 41–56. Collected Works, vol. 2. Washington, D.C., 1987. Werke 5. Louvain, 1959.

Stellung der Frau in Kirche und Gesellschaft, zu Fragen der [On the question of the position of women in Church and society]. Die Deutschen Bischöfe 30. Bonn, 1981.

Stickel, Gerhard. "Beantragte staatliche Regelungen zur 'sprachlichen Gleichbehandlung'. Darstellung und Kritik" [Proposed state regulations for "equal linguistic treatment": Summary and critique]. *Zeitschrift für germanistische Linguistik* 16 (1988): 330–55.

Strahm, Doris. *Aufbruch zu neuen Räumen. Eine Einführung in feministische Theologie* [Departure for new regions: An introduction to feminist theology]. Freiburg, Switzerland, 1987. (*Aufbruch*)

———. "Jesus Christus". In Wb, 200–207.

Strahm, Doris, and Regula Strobel, eds. *Vom Verlangen nach Heilwerden. Christologie in feministisch-theologischer Sicht* [On the longing to be saved: Christology in feminist-theological perspective]. Fribourg and Lucerne, 1991.

Strobel, Regula. "Feministische Kritik an traditionellen

Kreuzestheologien" [Feminist criticism of traditional theologies of the Cross]. In Strahm and Strobel (1991), 52–64.

——. "Das Kreuz im Kontext feministischer Theologie. Versuch einer Standortbestimmung" [The Cross in the context of feminist theology: An attempt to assess the current situation]. In Strahm and Strobel (1991), 182–93.

Stuhlmacher, Peter. "Feministische Theologie und Auslegung des Neuen Testaments" [Feminist theology and interpretation of the New Testament]. *Theol. Beiträge* 22 (1991): 127–38.

Sudbrack, Josef. *Neue Religiosität—Herausforderung für Christen* [The new religiosity—a challenge for Christians]. Mainz, 1987. (*Neue Religiosität*)

——. "Feministische Theologie. Fragen um ein aktuelles Thema" [Feminist theology: Questions about a current topic]. *Geist und Leben* 59 (1986): 301–16.

Sullerot, Evelyne, ed. *Die Wirklichkeit der Frau* [The reality of woman]. Munich, 1979.

Süssmuth, Rita. "Partnerschaft" [Partnership]. In FLex, 883–90.

——. "Frauenpolitik" [Politics of woman]. In FLex, 367–74.

Sutter Rehmann, Luzia. "Eschatologie". In Wb, 86–89.

Teilhard de Chardin, Pierre. *Hymne an das Ewig Weibliche* [Hymn to the Eternal Feminine]. With a commentary by H. de Lubac. Einsiedeln, 1968.

Trömel-Plötz, Senta. "Sprachkritik, feministische" [Language critique, feminist]. In FLex, 1067–74.

"Tübinger Stellungnahme zu Fragen der Feministischen Theologie" [The Tübingen position on questions of feminist theology]. *Theol. Beiträge* 22 (3/1991): 118–53.

Tukker, C. A. "Der Prozess gegen Kardinal Simonis" [The case against Cardinal Simonis]. In *Luther und die Folgen für die Geistesgeschichte,* FS Theobald Beer, edited by Remigius Bäumer and Alma von Stockhausen, 195–203. Weilheim and Bierbronnen, 1992.

Ulrich, Miorita. " 'Neutrale' Männer—'markierte' Frauen. Feminismus und Sprachwissenschaft" ["Neutral" men—"indicated" women: Feminism and linguistics]. *Sprachwissenschaft* 13 (1988): 383–99.

Unterste, Herbert. *Theologische Aspekte der Tiefenpsychologie von C. G. Jung* [Theological aspects of C. G. Jung's psychoanalysis]. Düsseldorf, 1977.

U.S. Bishops' Meeting. "Inclusive Language in Liturgy: Scriptural Texts". *Origins* 20 (1990): 405–8.

Vock, Ursula, et al. *Bibliographie zur Feministischen Theologie* [Bibliography on feminist theology]. Zurich, 1988.

Voss, Jutta. *Das Schwarzmondtabu. Die kultische Bedeutung des weiblichen Zyklus* [The black-moon taboo: The cultic significance of the female cycle]. Stuttgart, 1988.

Vries, Josef de. "Erfahrung" [Experience]. In *Philosophisches Wörterbuch,* edited by Walter Brugger, 88–90. 14th ed. Freiburg, 1976.

Wacker, Marie-Theres, ed. *Der Gott der Männer und die Frauen* [Men's God and women]. Düsseldorf, 1987.

Wagner-Hasel, Beate, ed. *Matriarchatstheorien der Altertumswissenschaft* [Theories of a matriarchate in archaeological scholarship]. WdF 651. Darmstadt, 1992.

Wainwright, Geoffrey. "An Inclusive Language Lectionary. Systematic Liturgical Observations". BTB 14 (1984): 28–30.

Walter, Meinrad. "Die andere Maria. Das Marienbild in der feministischen Theologie" [The other Mary: The image of Mary in feminist theology]. In *"Dein leuchtend Angesicht, Maria . . . " Das Bild der Mutter Jesu in der Glaubensgeschichte,* edited by Wolfgang Beinert and Jürgen Hoeren, 76–88. Freiburg, 1988.

Warner, Marina. *Alone of All Her Sex: The Myth and Cult of the Virgin Mary.* New York, 1976.

Warrior, Betsy. *"Man as an Obsolete Life Form": Women's Liberation: Blueprint for the Future.* New York, 1970.

Weber, L. M. "Feminismus". LThK, 2d series, 4 (1960): 74f.

Wegener, Hildburg. "Von Kindergärtnern, Amtsfrauen und Ratsdamen. Sprachkritik und Sprachpolitik in feministischem Interesse" [On male kindergarten-teachers, female officials, council ladies: Linguistic criticism and linguistic politics in the feminist interest]. In Wegener, Köhler, and Kopsch (1990), 9–24. ("Sprachkritik")

———. " 'Siehe, das ist meine Beauftragte'. Frauengerechte Sprache in der Übersetzung der Bibel" ["Behold, that is my (female) delegate" (German: *meine Beaufragte,* which is the feminine form): language that does justice to women in the translation of the Bible]. In Wegener, Köhler, and Kopsch (1990): 84–101. ("Bibel")

Wegener, Hildburg, Hanne Köhler, and Cordelia Kopsch, eds. *Frauen fordern eine gerechte Sprache* [Women demand a just language]. Gütersloh, 1990.

Wehr, D. S. *Jung and Feminism.* Boston, 1987.

Weiler, Gerda. *Das Matriarchat im Alten Testament* [The matriarchate in the Old Testament]. Berlin, 1989.

Weismayer, Josef. "Hochmut" [Haughtiness]. In *Lexikon*

der christlichen Moral, edited by Karl Hörmann, 795–98. Innsbruck, 1976.

Wenck, Inge. *Gott ist im Mann zu kurz gekommen. Eine Frau über Jesus von Nazareth* [God has not been well-served in maleness: A woman on Jesus of Nazareth]. Gütersloh, 1982.

Wesel, Uwe. *Der Mythos vom Matriarchat. Über Bachofens Mutterrecht und die Stellung von Frauen in frühen Gesellschaften* [The myth of the matriarchate: On Bachofen's maternal law and the position of women in early societies]. Frankfurt, 1980.

Wesseln, Hermann. "Der Vater in der Erziehung" [The father's role in child-raising]. In *Erziehung in Verantwortung,* edited by Manfred Balkenohl and Hermann Wesseln, 142–52. Hamm, 1982.

Wiederkehr, Dietrich. "Entwurf einer systematischen Christologie" [Outline of a systematic Christology]. *Mysterium Salutis* 3, no. 1 (1970): 477–648.

Wiethaus, Ulrike. "Gott/Göttin IV. Theologiegeschichte/Mittelalter" [God/goddess IV. History of theology/Middle Ages]. In Wb, 167–69.

Winter, Urs. *Frau und Göttin. Exegetische und ikonographische Studien zum weiblichen Gottesbild im Alten Israel und in dessen Umwelt* [Woman and goddess: Exegetical and iconographic studies on the female image of God in ancient Israel and its surrounding cultures]. 2d ed. Fribourg and Göttingen, 1987.

Wissmann, Hans, et al. "Erfahrung" [Experience]. TRE 10 (1982): 83–141.

Witherington, Ben. *Women in the Earliest Churches.* Cambridge, 1988.

Wolff, Hanna. *Jesus der Mann. Die Gestalt Jesu in tiefenpsychologischer Sicht* [Jesus the man: The figure of Jesus from the psychoanalytic viewpoint]. 2d ed. Stuttgart, 1976.

Wöller, Hildegunde. "Glaube an den dreieinigen Gott. Versuch einer Neuinterpretation" [Belief in the triune God: Attempt at a new interpretation]. *Frauen. Anstöße* 28 (3/1981): 101-7.

Wollrad, Eske, et al. "Lesbische Existenz" [Lesbian existence]. In Wb, 243-45.

Wörterbuch der Feministischen Theologie. Ed. Elisabeth Gössmann et al. Gütersloh, 1991. (Wb)

Zauner, "Brüderlichkeit und Geschwisterlichkeit" [Brotherliness and brother-sisterliness]. ThPQ 137 (1989): 228-37.

Ziegenaus, Anton. " 'Als Mann und Frau erschuf er sie' (Gen 1,27). Zum sakramentalen Verständnis der geschlechtlichen Differenzierung des Menschen" ["Male and female he created them" (Gen 1:27): On the sacramental understanding of man's sexual differentiatedness"]. MThZ 31 (1980): 210-22.

——. "Maria als Abbild der Person des Hl. Geistes nach M. J. Scheeben" [Mary as a figuration of the Person of the Holy Spirit according to M. J. Scheeben]. In *Maria und der Heilige Geist,* edited by A. Ziegenaus, 25-38. Mariol. Studien 8. Regensburg, 1991.

——. "Häresie" [Heresy]. ML 3 (1991): 67-69.

——. "Die Umweltproblematik in schöpfungstheologischer Sicht" [The environmental problem from the creation-theological perspective]. FKTh 8 (1992): 81-98.

Zimmer, D. E. *Redens Arten. Über Trends und Tollheiten im neudeutschen Sprachgebrauch* [Speaking's ways:

On trends and follies in recent German use of language]. Zurich, 1988.

Zimmerling, Peter. *Gott in Gemeinschaft. Zinzendorfs Trinitätslehre* [God in community: Zinzendorf's doctrine of the Trinity]. Gießen, 1991.

Zöller, Ursula, et al. *Deine Dich liebende . . . Briefe an Mutter Kirche* [Your loving . . . Letter to Mother Church]. Aschaffenburg, 1993.

Zollitsch, Robert. *Amt und Funktion des Priesters. Eine Untersuchung zum Ursprung und zur Gestalt des Presbyterats in den ersten zwei Jahrhunderten* [Office and function of the priest: An inquiry into the origin and structure of the presbyterate in the first two centuries]. FThSt 96. Freiburg, 1974.

Zulehner, P. M. *Pastorale Futurologie* [Pastoral futurology]. Düsseldorf, 1990.

——. "Mann" [The male]. In *Neues Lexikon der christlichen Moral,* edited by Hans Rotter and Günter Virt, 461f. Innsbruck, 1990.

INDEX OF PERSONS

INDEX OF SUBJECTS